The Presidency of
WARREN G.
HARDING

AMERICAN PRESIDENCY SERIES

Donald R. McCoy, Clifford S. Griffin, Homer E. Socolofsky
General Editors

The Presidency of
WARREN G.
HARDING

by
Eugene P. Trani
and David L. Wilson

UNIVERSITY PRESS OF KANSAS

Published by the University Press of Kansas (Lawrence, Kansas 66045),
which was organized by the Kansas Board of Regents and is
operated and funded by Emporia State University, Fort Hays State
University, Kansas State University, Pittsburg State University,
the University of Kansas, and Wichita State University

Library of Congress Cataloging in Publication Data

Trani, Eugene P.
The Presidency of Warren G. Harding.

(American Presidency series)
Bibliography: p.
Includes index.
1. United States—Politics and government—1921-1923.
2 Harding, Warren Gamaliel, Pres. U. S., 1865-1923.
1. Wilson, David L., 1943-   joint author.
II. Title   III. Series.
E785.T7   973.91′4′0924 [B]   76-26110
ISBN 0-7006-0152-X

Printed in the United States of America

To
Lois E. Trani
and Nanci K. Wilson

Editors' Preface

The aim of the American Presidency Series is to present historians and the general reading public with interesting, scholarly assessments of the various presidential administrations. These interpretive surveys are intended to cover the broad ground between biographies, specialized monographs, and journalistic accounts. As such, each will be a comprehensive, synthetic work which will draw upon the best in pertinent secondary literature, yet leave room for the author's own analysis and interpretation.

Each volume in the series will deal with a separate presidential administration and will present the data essential to understanding the administration under consideration. Particularly, each book will treat the then current problems facing the United States and its people and how the president and his associates felt about, thought about, and worked to cope with these problems. Attention will be given to how the office developed and operated during the president's tenure. Equally important will be consideration of the vital relationships between the president, his staff, the executive officers, Congress, foreign representatives, the judiciary, state officials, the public, political parties, the press, and influential private citizens. The series will also be concerned with how this unique American institution—the presidency—was viewed by the presidents, and with what results.

All this will be set, insofar as possible, in the context not only of contemporary politics but also of economics, international relations, law, morals, public administration, religion, and thought. Such a broad approach is necessary to understanding, for a presidential administration is more than the elected and appointed officers composing it, since its work so often reflects the major problems, anxieties, and glories of the nation. In short, the authors in the series will strive to recount and evaluate the record of each administration and to identify its distinctiveness and relationships to the past, its own time, and the future.

Donald R. McCoy
Clifford S. Griffin
Homer E. Socolofsky

Preface

The purpose of this work is to review the presidency of Warren G. Harding. Harding and his administration have long fascinated students of American history. With the opening in recent years of vast amounts of primary materials on the Harding administration, there has been an outpouring of interpretations of the events in Washington between 1921 and 1923. This work is an attempt to evaluate the Harding administration by synthesizing published secondary accounts on this topic.

Our first and greatest obligation is to the many authors whose works are listed in the Bibliographical Essay. While only a portion of the books and articles mentioned in the essay are cited in the notes to the different chapters of this volume, that is only because we limited citations in the notes to direct quotes, unique points made by authors, or widely differing interpretations of events. But many of the works listed in the essay proved invaluable in the writing of this volume.

We also wish to thank the people who helped us in the writing of this work. The secretaries of the history department at Southern Illinois University, Beth Haas, Jennie Calonne, and Lorie Zaleskas, took time from their many other duties to type a draft of the book, and did it with good cheer. Nancy Nelson typed the final draft and provided much editorial assistance in the process. The Office of Research and Projects of Southern Illinois University supplied financial support for typing of the final draft. Two of our colleagues at Southern Illinois University, Professors John Y. Simon and Howard Allen, read the whole manuscript, subjecting it to their keen knowledge of history. And Professor Robert H. Ferrell of Indiana University gave the manuscript the benefit of his amazing abilities, improving it both in terms of style and content.

Finally, our wives, Lois E. Trani and Nanci K. Wilson, and our children, Anne and Frank Trani and Christopher and newly born Sarah Wilson, cooperated more than we deserved, as we made Warren G. Harding's presidency the major focus of our energies.

Carbondale, Illinois
August 1975

Contents

1

★★★★★

THE UNITED STATES IN 1920

I

The American people in the year 1920 were preening themselves upon the quality of their lives and livelihoods, and surely a visitor from foreign shores would have found much to admire, even if he encountered much to deplore. The nation had just finished participating in the greatest war in recorded history, and most Americans were certain that the victors, the Allies, would have lost without the help of the United States. The government of the United States had sent two million soldiers to France. It had also lent the Europeans more than ten billion dollars. The American economy was utterly untouched by the hand of war—there were no devastated, pocked landscapes like those in the northern regions of France, which looked almost like moonscapes. All the while, the country's population had been growing and had reached around a hundred million during the great conflict itself. By 1920 the census was showing a population of 106 million, with every indication that the "American multiplication table" so well noted during the nineteenth century would continue to send the population ever higher. The excess of births over deaths alone would increase the population even if immigration were to halt, as in truth there was some sign that it might. All the while, too, the quality of American life was keeping up with the growth in population. Books, colleges and universities, symphony orchestras—sure signs of the life of the mind—were appearing across the land. The cities of America, growing by leaps and bounds, were reaching maturity, showing that they, too, like the cities of ancient Greece and Rome, could be veritable fireplaces of civilization, to use a phrase from the writings of the nineteenth-century theologian Theodore Parker, from whence could radiate the best of the American intellect to all Americans across the country and even to peoples and countries across the seas.

The United States that elected Warren G. Harding president on November 2, 1920, was a country that had changed dramatically from the one that had reelected Harding's fellow Ohioan William McKinley just twenty years earlier. By 1920 the United States was coming of age.[1] The differences were staggering. The population stood at 106,466,000, up from 76,094,000 in 1900, an increase of almost 30 percent. The huge expanse of the continental United States amounted to more than three million square miles and possessed a population density of 35.6 people per square mile. If the population of America's overseas possessions was added, the figure went up to 118,107,855; most of the additional twelve million were in the Philippine Islands. The United States also controlled Puerto Rico, Hawaii, Alaska, Guam, the Canal Zone, the Virgin Islands, American Samoa, Midway, and miscellaneous small islands in the Pacific.

The most important finding of the fourteenth decennial census, taken in 1920, was that for the first time more Americans lived in urban areas (towns of 2,500 or more), 54,158,000, than in rural areas, 51,552,000. This was a considerable change from 1900 when there were 30,160,000 urban Americans and 45,835,000 were living in the countryside. By 1920 there were three cities with more than a million residents, nine between 500,000 and a million, thirteen between 250,000 and 500,000, forty-three between 100,000 and 250,000, and seventy-six between 50,000 and 100,000.

The urban population was heavily concentrated in the East and Upper Midwest, with Maine, New Hampshire, Vermont, Massachusetts, Rhode Island, Connecticut, New York, New Jersey, Pennsylvania, Ohio, Indiana, Illinois, Michigan, and Wisconsin having almost half the population of the country, more than fifty million people. New York and Mississippi stood at opposite ends of the urban-rural population ratios in the 1920 census. New York counted nearly 8,600,000 urban and 1,800,000 rural residents, while Mississippi, the most rural state (86.6 percent), had 240,000 urban and 1,500,000 rural dwellers. The comparison between New York and Mississippi served as a mirror for the political, social, and economic differences in the United States in 1920.[2] The greatest

2

population growth between 1900 and 1920 took place in California, destined to become the most populous state by the 1970 census. In 1900 California had 1,485,053 residents, while Massachusetts had nearly twice as many, 2,805,346. By 1920 California, with 3,426,861 people, had almost caught up with Massachusetts, with 3,852,356, and the greatest growth had been in cities. So the urbanization of the United States was rapidly advancing by 1920, and that trend was to continue in the years ahead.

The census taken in 1920 showed that there were more males than females, 54,295,000 to 52,171,000, a fact that was not to change until 1947. The median age of the population had increased from 22.9 years in 1900 to 25.3. Of the more than 106 million people in the United States in 1920, 95,511,000 were white, 10,463,000 black, 240,000 Indian, 110,000 Japanese, and 61,000 Chinese.[3]

The 1920 census revealed some interesting facts about the vast white population. Of the 95 million whites, more than 13.9 million had been born outside the United States, and another 22.7 million were what the census referred to as white natives of "foreign or mixed parentage." These huge figures resulted, of course, from the increasing number of immigrants entering the United States between 1900 and 1920. While the year 1920 saw only 430,000 immigrants (246,295 from Europe, 17,505 from Asia, and 162,666 from other parts of the Americas), there had been six years in the previous twenty in which more than a million came (1905, 1906, 1907, 1910, 1913, and 1914). In four of those years, 1906, 1907, 1913, and 1914, more than a million immigrants had journeyed to the United State from Europe alone. The source of European immigration had also changed after 1900. Italy had seen 100,000 citizens emigrate to the United States for the first time in 1900, but that figure was exceeded every year from 1900 to 1914, with 1907 the peak year, when 285,731 crossed the Atlantic. The two decades between 1900 and 1920 had seen larger percentages of Russian, Polish, Austrian, and Hungarian immigrants enter from Europe. And these immigrants and their offspring had contributed to the increasing urbanization between 1900 and 1920, for 11.3 million of the 13.9 million foreign-born Americans lived in the northeastern or north central portions of the United States, with just under a fourth of the residents of the Northeast being born outside of America.

All these figures show that the percentage of the population of "native whites of native parentage" (the Census Bureau's phrase) had decreased between 1900 and 1920. In fact, in 1920 only a little more than half the Americans (58 million out of 106 million) could

3

claim to be "native whites of native parentage." This change had a good deal of significance in the years when Warren G. Harding served as president.

Another important shift that the 1920 census revealed had to do with black Americans. The number of blacks had grown from 8.7 million in 1900 to 10.4 million in 1920. Even more significant was the change in where they lived. The vast majority of blacks in 1920 (8.9 million) still lived in the South. But in the twenty years after 1900, and especially during World War I, there was a large black migration to the northern industrial cities. The percentage of blacks living outside the South more than doubled between 1900 and 1920, with much of that change taking place in the years of World War I. During an eighteen-month period in 1917–1918, more than 50,000 blacks moved to Chicago, and Detroit's black population grew from 5,700 in 1910 to 41,500 in 1920. The black migration to the North continued during the 1920s. While 680,000 blacks lived in the Northeast and 793,000 in the north central part of the country in 1920, by 1930 these figures increased to 1,146,000 and 1,262,000, respectively.

These facts make the point that the population of the United States had changed in many ways between 1900 and 1920, and other changes were occurring too. Americans were healthier in 1920 than they were in 1900, with the life expectation rising from 47.3 years at the turn of the century to 54.1 in 1920. There were still great differences among the races, as the life expectancy for whites was 54.9 years and 45.3 for blacks. But even that latter figure was a dramatic change from the 33.0 year life expectation for blacks in 1900. Americans were healthier, in part, because of the increase in the number of medical personnel and facilities. In 1900 there were 119,749 physicians and surgeons in the United States. By 1920 the number was up to 144,977. In 1900 the United States had thirty-three dentists per 100,000 people, while in 1920 that number had risen to fifty-three per 100,000. The number of hospital beds had more than doubled between 1900 and 1920. The standards for training medical doctors and dentists were going up all the time, as knowledge in the field of medicine increased. The twenty years after the turn of the century had seen significant advances against certain kinds of diseases, with the death rate per 100,000 people for tuberculosis going from 194.4 in 1900 down to 113.1 in 1920, for typhoid from 31.3 to 7.6, for diphtheria from 40.3 to 15.3, and for gastritis from 142.7 to 53.7. The suicide rate per 100,000 was the same in both years, 10.2, but for 1920 that figure was a sharp drop from 16.8 in 1908. The rate was to go up again, reaching 17.4 in 1932. There were still many diseases that remained unconquered, with the figure for cardiovascular deaths per 100,000 people being 364.9 in 1920 and for influenza, 207.3. There was another cause of death in 1920 that was almost unknown in 1900. Motor vehicle accidents claimed 10.3 Americans per 100,000 population in the year of Harding's election, a figure that was to increase sharply after that.

Another factor contributing to longer life spans, besides better health care, was an improvement of the diet of the average American. By 1920 the diet showed greater variety, with more per capita annual consumption of fresh fruits (145.4 pounds in 1920) and fresh vegetables (95.0 pounds), and less consumption of meats (down from 150.7 pounds in 1900 to 136.0 pounds in 1920) and potatoes (down to 140 pounds in 1920).

Statistics also showed that Americans were better educated in 1920 than in 1900. The number of students attending elementary and secondary schools in 1920 was 23,277,797, up from 16,854,832 in 1900. And the number and percentage of high school graduates were both up significantly, from 94,883 or 6.4 percent of students who attended school to 311,266, almost 17 percent of the students. Blacks showed the greatest increase in school attendance, from 31.1 percent of the 5- to 19-year-olds attending school in 1900 to 53.5 percent in 1920. Overall, the figures went from 50.5 percent of the 5- to 19-year-olds attending school in 1900 to 64.3 percent in 1920. There were many more teachers in 1920 than 1900, and their annual compensation had more than doubled, from $325 in 1900 to $871 in 1920. One interesting change the census showed was that 583,648 of the 679,533 teachers in public elementary and secondary schools in 1920 were female, a much higher percentage than in 1900. While there had been much improvement in public education, there were still more than 190,000 one-teacher public schools. Nonetheless, all of this increased attention to public education brought results in the most important category of all, for the percentage of illiterate Americans dropped from 10.7 percent in 1900 to 6.0 percent in 1920, with nonwhite Americans making the greatest strides, going from 44.5 percent in 1900 down to 23.0 percent in 1920.

Higher education showed a comparable explosion in the first twenty years of the century. While the number of institutions of higher education increased only slightly in this period, the number of faculty members more than doubled, with male professors outnumbering females almost three to one, and the number of students

5

went from 238,000 (4.01 percent of the 18- to 21-year-old population) to 598,000 (8.9 percent of the 18- to 21-year-olds). Those twenty years also saw the offering of a much greater variety of courses in higher education and the establishment and improvement of graduate schools, which produced better-trained specialists. There were nearly twice as many graduates of higher education in 1920 (48,622) than 1900 and many more recipients of master's (4,279) and doctor's (615) degrees in 1920.

In addition to being healthier and better educated in 1920, more Americans than ever before were members of the labor force —over 40 million. All told, 54.3 percent of Americans 14 years and older were part of the labor force. The number of female workers rose from 4.9 million in 1900 to 8.2 million in 1920. While only 20.7 percent of white females worked in 1920, more than four in every ten nonwhite female Americans sought employment. Unemployment changed from year to year but had risen markedly as World War I came to a close, going from 1.4 percent in 1918 to 2.3 percent in 1919 and up to 4.0 percent in 1920. The worst was yet to come, for that figure was to climb to 11.9 percent, with more than 5 million unemployed in 1921.

The increasing urbanization of America was also displayed in the sorts of jobs Americans held. In 1900, 10,710,000 out of a total of 29,070,000 workers were employed in agricultural occupations. There were slightly more agricultural workers in 1920, 11,120,000, but they constituted a much smaller percentage of the total work force of 41,610,000. The greatest number of the 30 million nonfarm workers in 1920 were employed in manufacturing, 10.5 million, with 1.2 million in mining; 850,000 in construction; 4 million in transportation and public utilities; 4.6 million in wholesale and retail trade; 1.1 million in finance, insurance, and real estate; 2.1 million in service occupations; and 2.6 million in government employment. Work weeks had decreased between 1900 and 1920, going, for example, from 59 hours in 1900 down to 51 hours in 1920 in manufacturing industries, and from 52.6 to 48.2 hours in bituminous coal mining. And compensation had increased in the same period, rising from an annual average for all nonfarm labor of $490 in 1900 to $1,489 in 1920, with the best-paying jobs in 1920 in construction, mining, and transportation. Perhaps the most dramatic change in the labor field between 1900 and 1920 occurred in union membership, which rose from 791,000 in the former year to 5,034,000 in the latter, the highest until that time and in fact the highest figure until 1937. There were large numbers of union members in mining, construction, machinery, clothing manufacturing, and transportation and communication.

These changes that occurred in the twenty years after 1900 in the labor force were only one part of the major economic transformation that had accompanied urbanization. The United States showed a significant increase in wealth in the years after the turn of the century, as industrialization accompanied the change from a rural to an urban nation. The accumulation of wealth and increased concentration of industrialization were obvious in every statistical index. The total national wealth of the United States, in 1929 prices, stood at $179.5 billion in 1900, and would rise to $336.6 billion by 1922. The gross national product (GNP), also in 1929 prices, went from $37.1 billion in 1900 to $73.3 billion in 1920, with the average per capita income increasing from $496 to $688. Almost all of that increase in the GNP was in the nonfarm sector. Farm products amounted to $8.4 billion of the $37 billion GNP in 1900, but those products amounted to only $9.5 billion of the $73 billion GNP in 1920. Increased wealth was also obvious in the growth of the assets of banks and savings and loan institutions. There were 13,053 banks with assets of $11,388 million and 5,356 savings and loan institutions with assets of $571 million in 1900. By 1920 there were 30,905 banks, whose assets had reached $53,094 million, and 8,633 savings and loan institutions, with assets of $2,500 million. And Americans, who had only $7,573,000,000 worth of life insurance in 1900, had $40,540,000,000 worth in 1920.

Most of the increased wealth came as a result of industrialization, which brought a sizeable growth in the amount of manufactured products for domestic and foreign markets. American exports totaled $1,499,000,000 and imports $930,000,000 in 1900, with a trade surplus of $570,000,000. By 1920 exports had skyrocketed to $8,664,000,000 and imports to $5,784,000,000, bringing a huge surplus of $2,880,000,000. American exports to Europe went way up in those years but also increased more than tenfold to the rest of the Americas and almost fifteenfold to Asia. Imports showed similar regional gains. But industrialization was not just in the factories. It also took place on the farms, which saw the value of agricultural implements and machinery go from $750,000,000 in 1900 to $3,595,000,000 in 1920. While there were only about 1,000 tractors on farms in 1910, there were 246,000 ten years later. During that same decade the number of cars owned by farmers went from 50,000 to 2,146,000. In rural areas the machine had taken over, and in the country at large the increase in automobiles was even greater. In 1900 there were about 8,000 cars, but the number was over 8,000,000 in 1920. The industrialization also brought increases in both railroad mileage and usage. Railroad mileage rose from 258,784 in 1900 to 406,580 in 1920. And passengers increased from 576,831,000 in 1900 to 1,269,913,000 in 1920, a good year for the railroads, which also shipped 1,255,421,000 tons of freight that year. But the industry, which employed 3,754,281 Americans in 1920, had its problems, and a major one was safety. A total of 168,309 Americans were injured and 6,958 died as a result of accidents involving railroads in the year Harding was elected president. These facts reflect the increased wealth and the rapid industrialization in America by 1920.

Other statistics, involving technology, communication, and conveniences, also indicate how the United States changed between 1900 and 1920. The telephone had taken over the country by 1920. There were only 1,356,000 in 1900, 17.6 per 1,000 population. Twenty years later there were 13,329,000, 123.9 per 1,000 people, with over 50,000,000 daily local calls in the latter year. Americans purchased more than three times the number of stamps in 1920 as they did in 1900, while the postal rates remained two cents per ounce for letters and one cent for post cards. There were more people reading newspapers, with more than 27,000,000 daily newspapers, 17,000,000 Sunday papers, and 20,000,000 weekly papers sold. And those first twenty years of the twentieth century saw the emergence of chain stores, with over 800 merchandise chains, 180 grocery chains, and more than 100 drug chains, while in 1900 there were less than 100 chain complexes altogether. America, viewed through statistics, had clearly come of age between 1900 and 1920.

II

Given all the progress that had taken place in those twenty years, it might be concluded that the United States in 1920 was far more contented than in 1900, for more Americans had more—much, much more—material things. But such was not the case. The United States in the year 1920 was not a particularly happy country. There is an old sports saying that statistics do not tell the whole story of the game, and that saying might well be transferred to America in 1920. Two major events occurring between 1900 and 1920 had had profound effects upon the United States that elected Harding president in 1920, but the statistics accumulated in that year's census did not tell the whole story, about either one. Those events were the Progressive movement and World War I, and each played a part in shaping American society in 1920.

The first, the Progressive movement, was largely spent by 1920.[4] The Progressives had burst upon the national scene with the ascendancy of Theodore Roosevelt to the presidency, following the assassination of McKinley in 1901. From that time until at least the entrance of the United States into World War I in 1917, Progressives changed the role of government at local, state, and federal levels in American society. Believing that governmental regulation was necessary to bring order, efficiency, and justice to American life, Progressives engineered the passage of much legislation to reorder the United States in the early twentieth century. On the national level, Roosevelt, during his presidency, significantly increased the power of the presidency and the federal government as a whole through the institution of a vigorous trust-busting policy, which was reflected in the Northern Securities case in 1902, and in such legislation as the Newlands Reclamation Act, the Elkins Act, the Hepburn Act, the Pure Food and Drug Act, and the Meat Inspection Act. Even under conservative William Howard Taft, the power and size of the federal government continued to expand as he continued Roosevelt's policy on trusts. In the 1912 election the strength of the Progressives was obvious in the combined vote of Woodrow Wilson and Roosevelt, about 70 percent of the vote. Dominating the Wilson years until 1917, progressivism brought the establishment of the Federal Reserve system and the Federal Trade Commission and passage of the Clayton Antitrust Act and the Federal Farm Loan Act. All this legislation and the style and goals of Roosevelt and Wilson meant that the role of government, especially at the national level, had changed considerably in the first two decades of the twentieth century.

Progressives themselves were divided over the future course for American society. By 1920 the participants in the Progressive movement had different views as to the direction America should take. But there was little doubt about where America had been. After 1900 the power and size of the federal government had increased significantly. To cite just a few examples: the number of federal employees had grown from 239,476 in 1901 to 655,265 in 1920, while federal expenditures had gone from $520,861,000 in 1900 to $6,403,344,000 in 1920, and the gross federal debt had grown from $1,263,417,000 in 1900 to $24,299,321,000 twenty years later. Whether alive or dead as a movement in 1920, the influence of progressivism in that year was great.

9

The other event, not so obvious in census statistics, that made America in 1920 profoundly different from what it was in 1900 was World War I. With the outbreak of the war in 1914, the United States under Wilson's leadership attempted to pursue a course of neutrality toward the struggle that engulfed Europe. Neutrality proved impossible, and almost three years later, in April, 1917, the United States declared war upon Germany. Though the war for America was relatively short, it nonetheless brought many changes. The American armed services, numbering only 125,923 persons in 1900, had grown to 2,897,167 in 1918. While active servicemen had decreased to 343,302 in 1920, the United States had more than 5,000,000 veterans in that year. More than 117,000 Americans had lost their lives in the war, and estimates of the monetary costs of the war ranged between $13 and $37 billion.[5]

Whatever the direct costs of the war in men and money, it was the war's aftereffects that had great impact on the United States. The demobilization of American armed forces; the reconversion of American society, especially the economy, from wartime to peacetime footing; the wartime emotionalism that brought the Red Scare in 1919 and 1920; the movement for women's rights; the black protest movement; the success of the prohibitionists in gaining passage of the Eighteenth Amendment; Wilson's preoccupation with the League of Nations; and the president's stroke and paralysis, which halted leadership in the nation's capital—all affected the country as a whole. Americans looked for direction; but the Progressive movement and the war had consolidated leadership in the presidency, and in 1920 none came from that office. John V. A. MacMurray, chief of the Far Eastern Division of the State Department, wrote that Wilson had been so "exclusively responsible for policies," with the administration so "much of a one man show," that "his disability has paralyzed the whole executive. One has that queer feeling of a ship at sea with engines stopped."[6]

Indeed, the United States in 1920 did resemble a ship stopped at sea because of engine trouble, with passengers shouting directions to those trying to repair the machinery. To understand the American ship in 1920, it is necessary to examine the shocks that affected the United States in the two years between the armistice and Harding's election.

The first shock, and one that helped produce many of the others, was the rapid, unplanned demobilization of the American army and navy that began soon after the armistice, which went into effect at 11:00 A.M. (Paris time), Thursday, November 11, 1918.

Word of the armistice, of course, had brought jubilation to the United States. It also brought demands for the immediate return of American miltary personnel. This was no easy task, for there were more than 2,000,000 serving in the American Expeditionary Force at that time in Europe—81,800 officers, 1,892,600 men, and 47,700 civilian workers. In addition, the American Expeditionary Force had shipped thousands of tons of equipment to Europe.[7] Further, there was a vast military establishment and supply network in the United States and on the seas—the navy had almost half a million men on its rolls. Demobilization was made even more difficult by the lack of planning. Secretary of War Newton D. Baker admitted on November 12, the day after the armistice, that "no plans had been finally formulated." In fact, at that very time Baker and his chief of staff, General Peyton C. March, were disagreeing over how demobilization should be carried out. Baker favored demobilizing the armed forces "largely on a basis of the ability of trades and occupations to absorb" the returning men, while March thought the men should be mustered out by military units. On November 16, 1918, March gave orders to discharge the first 200,000 men according to their units, which he thought was "the promptest, fairest and most efficient manner" of demobilization.

Demobilization had massive effects upon American society in 1918–1919. Home the men came, as fast as transportation became available. In November the first 26,000 returned from Europe, and by August 1919, nine months later, only 40,000 men were left in Europe. By the end of June 1919 a total of 2,600,000 men and 128,436 officers had been mustered out, and surplus military goods amounting to $1,330,000,000 in Europe and an estimated $2,000,000,000 in the United States had been disposed of. The soldiers came home sick of war in general and of army life in particular, expecting to return to their former lives and jobs and believing they had "made the world safe for democracy." Many veterans became disillusioned and disappointed, and by 1920 their disappointment was obvious.

Further dislocation resulted from the Wilson administration's failure to plan for the reconversion of the economy from wartime to peacetime. As little thought had been given to reconversion as to demobilization. The president told a joint session of Congress several weeks after the armistice that Americans did not need to be "coached and led" to economic and industrial readjustment. Wilson noted that Americans "know their own business, are quick and resourceful at every readjustment . . . and self-reliant in action. Any leading strings we might seek to put them in would speedily become hopelessly tangled because they would pay no attention to them and go their own way."[8] He made his position clear on many subsequent occasions. Well before the war ended he had received advice from such government officials as War Industries Board Chairman Bernard M. Baruch that he should hold reconstruction meetings and possibly appoint a separate Reconstruction Commission, or at least that he should determine how agencies such as the War Industries Board, the Food Administration, and the Fuel Administration would be used in the reconstruction process. But Wilson showed little interest. Part of the problem was his concentration on foreign affairs, as he prepared for and then participated in the peace conference. Also important was his belief that no government plan would satisfy all segments of American society.

Congress did no better than the president on the reconversion. Divided because of the November 1918 elections, Democrats and Republicans in Congress showed little interest in the reconstruction problem. Some plans were put forward, notably by Republican Senator John W. Weeks of Massachusetts and Democratic Senator Lee S. Overman of North Carolina, but nothing resulted. During both of its sessions (May 19–November 19, 1919, and December 1, 1919–June 1920), the Sixty-sixth Congress was dominated by obstructionist Republican majorities and uncompromising Democratic minorities. Rather than trying to deal with the country's problems, Congress debated Wilson's treaty and then the president's illness, and investigated the origins of the radicalism that many people believed threatened the country in 1919 and 1920.

Between Wilson and Congress, problems worrying Americans in 1920 received little attention. The presidential decision not to establish a reconstruction agency was accompanied by his determination to dismantle the wartime agencies as quickly as possible; and soon the War Industries Board, the Food and Fuel Administration, and other such agencies had disappeared. All this meant that the American economy had to make its own way from 1918 on.

By late 1920 the results of presidential and congressional inaction were all too obvious. Local and state authorities, unions, industrial combines, individual businessmen, and farmer organizations, all put forward ideas to ease economic reconversion. Without guidance, chaos reigned. Unions wanted continued government control of railroads and municipal control of utilities, a forty-hour week, and continuation of the many benefits promised by the wartime economy; while businessmen demanded that wartime controls be eliminated, the railroads be returned to private ownership, war-

time taxes on business be rescinded. Farmers wanted price maintenance, increased farm credit, and more government concern for
agrarian America. These demands tended to be self-serving, ig-
noring the economy in general.

The economy suffered immediately after the armistice, with
unemployment reaching three million in February 1919. It recovered in the last half of 1919, possibly because of consumer demand
unfilled during the war, continued high government spending, and
reconstruction loans to Europe. But even during the recovery, inflation continued. The wholesale price index (with 1926 prices
equaling 100) had risen from 69.5 in 1915 to 85.5 in 1916, to 117.5
in 1917, 131.3 in 1918, 138.6 in 1919, and finally to 154.4 in 1920.
Inflation brought enormous increases in the cost of food, clothing,
fuels, and building materials. Bread, which cost 7 cents per pound
in 1915, rose to 11.5 cents in 1920; bacon went from 26.9 cents per
pound in 1915 to 52.3 cents in 1920; butter from 35.8 cents per
pound in 1915 to 70.1 cents in 1920; and 10 pounds of potatoes,
which sold for 15.0 cents in 1915, cost 63 cents in 1920. If throughout the last part of 1919 the economy continued to grow, in the
spring of 1920 a collapse occurred. Agricultural prices started to
slide, and by 1921 the wholesale price index that had reached 154.4
had dipped to 97.6, one of the sharpest declines in a short period
in American history. The depression that hit the United States in
late 1920 and early 1921 was most serious on the countryside, where
the farmer saw prosperity disappear. Agricultural prices, which
had risen since 1914 (83 percent by 1919 for livestock and meats
and even higher for crop prices), fell by more than half between
July and December 1920 and by May 1921 were about a third what
they had been eleven months earlier. Corn brought $1.88 a bushel
in August 1919 but only 42 cents in the autumn of 1921. Using 1914
as 100, net farm income fell from 219 in 1919 to 185 in 1920, and
all the way to 84 in 1921. This dramatic collapse brought much
dissatisfaction to rural America, but labor and industry also suffered. Unemployment in nonfarm jobs grew from 2.3 percent in
1919 to 4.0 percent in 1920, and up to 11.9 percent in 1921, with
more than five million unable to find work. For those persons who
remained employed, wages declined 20 percent. And businesses
closed as capital dried up, with 100,000 bankruptcies in 1921.

What had caused this collapse? Some Americans, especially
farmers, charged a conspiracy by banking leaders, aided by the
Federal Reserve Board. While such charges were popular, they
were not accurate. The decline was part of a worldwide economic

dislocation that followed the war. In the United States the economic downturn reflected a basic reallocation of economic resources. The decline of wartime and reconstruction loans to the European countries was also significant, for this decline soon brought a reduction in American exports to Europe, from $4,466,000,000 in 1920 to $2,364,000,000 in 1921.[9] Whatever the causes, the Wilson administration did little to cure the problems and in fact appeared unable, because of the incapacitated president, to do anything.

Economic difficulties and the lack of government action led to unhappiness among the American people. Strikes became commonplace in 1919 and 1920, with more than 3,600 in 1919 alone. The best known were the steel strike, the Boston police strike, and the Seattle general strike.[10] Strikes, unemployment, high prices, high cost of living, and agricultural surpluses were all on the minds of the voters in November 1920.

Also contributing to the outlook of the Americans who elected Harding president that fall was the overflow of emotionalism known as the Great American Red Scare, another of the shocks resulting from the war. The close of the war did not mean an end to the emotionalism that had been stirred up as America fought the Central Powers. Even after the armistice, Americans felt the need for an enemy, especially since 1919 and 1920 brought a number of threats to traditional American society. The arrival before the war of millions of immigrants, and inflation, labor strife, racial unrest, unemployment, business depression, bomb explosions, an outpouring of radical literature, all added social stress and confirmed the hostility of many Americans to minority groups. These forces also added new converts to nativism from those ordinarily not hostile toward radicals or immigrants.[11]

While the Red Scare was only one outburst of the periodic appearance of nativism in American history, the Bolshevik revolution of 1917 in Russia, which had a worldwide effect, made it different. The United States, thousands of miles from the newly created Soviet state, reacted with alarm. The reaction expressed itself in foreign affairs, with American troops finding themselves in Russia, and the United States refusing to recognize the Soviet government. It also expressed itself in domestic affairs as hostile emotions, which the war had stirred in some Americans, were directed against other Americans who expressed sympathy with the Soviet experiment. Such reactions occurred partly because of the antidemocratic and anticapitalist views of the Bolsheviks and also because the Bolsheviks had withdrawn Russia from the war in 1917 and signed a separate peace with Germany. In 1919 and 1920 Soviet sympathizers in the United States and those people who called for fundamental reform of American society were attacked as Bolsheviks.

The Red Scare wore many faces. Elected officials who were members of radical parties were harassed, and five Socialist members of the New York State Assembly were expelled from that body in April 1920 because of the party to which they belonged. Striking workers were made to appear as Bolshevik sympathizers. The mayor of Seattle, Ole Hanson, said that his city's general strike of 1919 was the first step in a nationwide workers' revolt, which he blamed on the Bolsheviks and the Industrial Workers of the World (IWW). Many Americans believed him. All violent demonstrations and acts of sabotage were thought to be part of a concerted effort to overthrow the government. Letter bombs, sent to government and other officials in 1919, were proof that such a conspiracy existed. A clash between members of the IWW and the American Legion in Centralia, Washington, on Armistice Day, 1919, with deaths resulting on both sides, showed how high emotions had risen. The Bolshevik danger was never great, for the combined membership of the IWW, the Socialist party, which was non-revolutionary, the Communist-Labor party (left-wing Socialists), and the Communist party was fewer than 200,000. But Americans felt threatened in 1919 and 1920.

The peak of the Red Scare came on January 2, 1920, when Justice Department agents, aided by local police, conducted simultaneous raids in thirty-three cities in twenty-three states. More than 5,000 people were taken into custody. The purpose of the raids, according to their coordinator, Attorney General A. Mitchell Palmer, was to "drive from our midst the agents of Bolshevism." When fewer than 600 of those persons arrested that January day were deported for membership in the Communist party and when May Day passed without the gigantic terrorist demonstrations Palmer said the radicals planned, Americans began to relax. Even the explosion of a large bomb in front of the offices of J. P. Morgan and Company on Wall Street, just before the lunch hour on September 16, which resulted in the deaths of 38 people and injuries to more than 200, as well as property damage of over $2,000,000, did not rekindle the fear that existed in late 1919 and early 1920. Still, the Red Scare had an important impact on America and its voters, for it promoted intolerance and encouraged conformity.[12]

Two groups of Americans, women and blacks, emerged from

the war with new attitudes toward their places in society, and their efforts to better themselves produced further shocks in 1920. While the movement for women's rights had gathered momentum in the first fifteen years of the twentieth century, the war had a marked effect upon it. As Carrie Chapman Catt wrote, "the greatest thing that came out of the war was the emancipation of women, for which no man fought." The war acted as a catalyst to the feminist movement. Women did much for the war. They spoke across the country for Liberty loans, canvassed for food conservation, worked for the Red Cross, took over jobs in industry vacated when men went off to fight, used the Woman's Committee of the United States Council of National Defense to organize and coordinate women and the war effort, and served in the army and navy, with more than 11,000 nurses assigned to military duty. The war proved that women could handle many kinds of jobs, from trainmen to lathe operators, blacksmiths, and mechanics.[13] While postwar depression, reconversion, and union pressure forced some women out of their jobs, many held on, and the number of female factory workers in 1920 was notably up from 1910. As a result of the war, women demanded equal opportunity and equal pay.

All the while, the feminist movement kept up the struggle for full citizenship for women. President Wilson had endorsed the suffrage amendment in January 1918. Despite great pressure it was not approved by Congress until June 1919. Within fourteen months, twenty-nine states had ratified the amendment, and women were eligible to vote in the election of November 1920. The war effort and the passage of national suffrage proved to be only the beginning of the drive for equality of the sexes, but even these two experiences made 1920 very different from 1900.

Much the same process happened to black Americans as a result of the war. Both in Europe and on the home front, black Americans made substantial contributions to the war effort. Between 350,000 and 400,000 black troops served in the armed services. While only about 50,000 were combat troops, with the rest in support, Europe proved a liberating experience for black soldiers, even if they did serve in segregated units. They went to Europe to fight for democracy and returned home to segregation, and they objected. Meanwhile, the domestic need for labor had brought migration of many blacks to the North. During the war about 500,000 blacks left the South. They hoped for a better life in the North but found the same discrimination they had left. Whites objected to blacks in defense plants, with a race riot in East St. Louis in 1917 resulting in deaths of about 50 blacks and whites.

The combination of black soldiers returning from the fight for democracy and the building resentment that the southern blacks found in their new northern homes led to militancy. Blacks demanded equal treatment before the law, with the National Association for the Advancement of Colored People working in 1919 for federal antilynching laws, equal job opportunities, and equal pay. New militancy, plus other shocks of the aftermath of war, led to virtual race warfare in many sections of the United States in the last half of 1919, with more than a hundred deaths. While the turmoil of 1919 was only part of America's long history of racial difficulties, blacks now refused to submit meekly to white violence. Racial conflict thus contributed to the uneasiness that dominated America in 1920.[14]

Another attempt at social change that the war speeded up was prohibition. Using the emergency created by the war and arguments that prohibition would bring a new morality, prohibitionists had gotten the Eighteenth Amendment (to prohibit the manufacture, transportation, and sale of liquor in the United States) approved by Congress on December 22, 1918. In less than a month thirty-six states adopted the amendment. The amendment reflected, at least to some extent, the growing rural-urban tension resulting from the increasing urbanization and industrialization of the country.[15] Prohibition and the Volstead Act, its enforcement statute, went into effect on January 16, 1920. While many, such as William Jennings Bryan, the three-time Democratic presidential aspirant, thought this reform good for the United States, others were opposed, especially in the cities.

Whether the ensuing conflict over prohibition during the 1920s was an urban-rural division, it created division and further trouble on top of demobilization, reconversion, the Red Scare, the feminist movement, and racial conflict—all shocks resulting from participation in the war. With all these difficulties, Americans in 1919 and 1920 looked to the federal government and especially to the president for leadership to help solve the problems and guide the country. But from Wilson, and the federal government as a whole, they received little or no direction. The president was too engaged in the battle over the League of Nations, which further divided the United States in 1920.

President Wilson had left the United States for Europe in December 1918 to participate in negotiations to end the war. Except

17

for a brief visit home in late February, he remained in Europe until the end of negotiations with Germany. During those difficult months one issue took precedence in his mind—an international organization to preserve the peace. The president had been willing to compromise on other issues, such as the Shantung Peninsula in China and reparations, but not on the League of Nations. He opposed the French idea of a league of victors, holding for a concert of nations. From the outset he insisted that the constitution, or covenant, of the League be embodied in the Treaty of Versailles and that execution of the treaty be the League's responsibility. In the end he had his way. Consent to the treaty by the Senate meant participation in the League.

Wilson hoped his return to the United States on July 8, 1919, would mean speedy ratification of the treaty and a new experiment in world government. He soon found opposition. Many Americans were concerned with domestic problems, and they had little interest in the League. One journal discovered that some Americans thought the League of Nations was a baseball league. Many groups opposed the treaty; liberals, hyphenate-Americans, especially the German-, Italian-, and Irish-Americans; British haters; and the majority of Republicans—all fought ratification, though for different reasons. Wilson then refused to compromise with the Senate leadership, especially Senator Henry Cabot Lodge, and chances for ratification of the treaty dimmed.

Seeing that he was making little progress, the president decided to go to the people. He announced in early September 1919 that he would make a "swing around the circle." His health was not good, and advisers urged him not to make the trip. Wilson responded: "Even though, in my condition, it might mean the giving up of my life, I will gladly make the sacrifice to save the Treaty."[16] It was a long trip—over 8,000 miles—and took him through the Middle and Far West. In the three weeks of the trip he delivered thirty-seven addresses, general and idealistic, which did not stress the benefits America would gain from League membership. Nonetheless, the reception became more and more enthusiastic as he moved to the West Coast. The strain increased, and after his September 25 speech at Pueblo, Colorado, on his way back to Washington, the president was near collapse. The rest of the stops were canceled. Wilson returned to Washington, where on October 2 he suffered a stroke that paralyzed the left side of his face and body and brought him to the edge of death.

The treaty thereupon failed. By early September the Foreign

Relations Committee had reported the treaty out of committee with forty-five amendments and four reservations. The Senate defeated the amendments, and Lodge boiled these points into fourteen reservations providing mainly that the United States could undertake no important action in conjunction with the League without the approval of Congress. No compromise proved possible, and on November 19, 1919, the Senate voted against the Lodge reservations and also against the treaty without reservations, by almost identical margins. In the next months much pressure was exerted to get the Senate to reconsider the treaty, and it finally did in March 1920. By that time some of the Democrats decided to abandon Wilson's no-amendment stand, but there were not enough of them and the treaty again went down.

All the while, as mentioned, domestic affairs were not getting presidential attention. Even before his stroke in October 1919, the president's interest in domestic affairs had been limited. From 1917 onward he was concerned with the war, and from the time of the armistice until his stroke, almost a year later, he was preoccupied with foreign affairs, especially the League. After the stroke, the problem became even more serious. In fact, from that moment until Harding was inaugurated in March 1921, the country was without a functioning chief executive. At first, there was a news blackout on the seriousness of the president's illness, and even members of his cabinet did not know how ill he was. Some cabinet members guessed the seriousness of the illness, and Secretary of State Robert Lansing wondered if Vice-President Thomas R. Marshall should take over presidential duties. Marshall refused. Lansing began to convene cabinet meetings in late 1919 to keep the government running.

Wilson meanwhile was kept in virtual isolation by his wife, Edith Bolling Wilson, and his personal physician, Rear Admiral Cary T. Grayson. Mrs. Wilson refused to allow most visitors to see the president and screened information that went to the president's bedroom. Wilson was able to give only momentary attention to problems engulfing the country, for no more than five to ten minutes at a time. For the rest of her husband's term Mrs. Wilson, a woman with little interest in affairs of state, was to a considerable degree the country's president. No one could see the president without her approval, and she kept members of the cabinet away. In fact, two men were appointed to the cabinet during this period without seeing Wilson. When the president did see visitors they were generally friends and supporters, and the topic of conversation was the League. Domestic problems went unattended, correspondence from heads of agencies unanswered. Gossip questioning the capacities of the president spread. It was not until mid-April 1920 that the president could attend a cabinet meeting, and meetings were infrequent and unproductive. Wilson's collapse signaled a paralysis in government itself, made all the more tragic by the turbulent conditions of the immediate postwar era.[17] Without national leadership Americans were left to deal with the effects of the war, and those conditions made the country unhappy as the election of 1920 approached.

There were diversions from the gloom in American life in 1920. Noteworthy was the rise of hero worship. The chaos of 1919 and 1920 introduced uneasiness as Americans saw industrialization, urbanization, immigration, and the war alter the United States. The changes, welcomed as progress, also raised fears about the passing of the frontier and the eclipse of the individual in society. While the country had changed in the first two decades of the twentieth century, many American values were still those of the frontier, which stressed individualism. During the 1920s the cult of the hero emerged, stressing individual strength, courage, honor, and self-reliance.

Many personages benefited from the hero cult. Sports figures were the most notable, as the nation went sports crazy in the postwar period. There were, of course, nonsports heroes. Billy Sunday, a preacher with a fundamentalist message, was important to Americans in 1920. Henry Ford became a symbol of the age after the World War. Between May and December 1920 nearly 700,000 Model-T Fords rolled off the assembly lines, a figure that went up to a million in 1921. Some of the heroes Americans loved in 1920 did not exist, living only in the writings of Gene (Geneva) Stratton-Porter, Harold Bell Wright, Zane Grey, and Edgar Rice Burroughs. The latter's best-known hero had been created in 1914 with publication of *Tarzan of the Apes*, a book about an English orphan boy brought up by apes in the jungles of Africa. Thirty more Tarzan stories followed the first, and by 1920 the fictional character had nationwide admiration. Burroughs reached millions through newspaper syndication and motion pictures. Tarzan's prowess captured the popular imagination to a staggering degree. For people restricted by the dictates of civilization, Tarzan became a symbol for freedom and individuality, which were traditional American values.[18]

III

Whatever diversions Americans sought, the problems of 1920 would not go away. While some, such as the Red Scare, had receded somewhat by late 1920, many other problems had increased in intensity. A presidential election was on the horizon in November of that year, and all the factors thus far described helped Americans decide how to vote. With the Wilsonian legacy of "a disintegrating presidency, a confused and rebellious Congress, a foreign policy in chaos, a domestic economy in shambles, a society sundered with hatreds and turmoil," it was a testimony to ambition that anybody would want to become president.[19] Yet each of the major parties had several candidates seeking nomination for the election.

The Republican convention was held first, beginning on June 8 in the Chicago Coliseum. Before that day a good deal of campaigning had taken place. By 1916 the Republican split of 1912 had been generally healed, but the Republican candidate, Charles Evans Hughes, went down to defeat. Following the decisive victory the Republicans had scored in the 1918 congressional elections, the party looked forward to the 1920 presidential race. It was widely presumed that Theodore Roosevelt would be the party's nominee, but the former president died in January 1919.

The four principal Republican contenders in 1920 were General Leonard Wood, Governor Frank O. Lowden of Illinois, Senator Hiram Johnson of California, and Warren G. Harding, then at the end of his first term as senator from Ohio. There were other candidates—among them Herbert Hoover, Governor Coolidge of Massachusetts, and General John J. Pershing, but the four major candidates, especially Wood and Lowden, dominated the preconvention publicity. Wood campaigned for delegate strength as the candidate representing the Roosevelt bloc of the party. His campaign emphasized preparedness, attacked radicalism, and dwelt on patriotism, and it alarmed many liberal and moderate Republicans. His lavish expenditures, totaling $1,773,000, offended other Republicans. Lowden, Wood's main opponent, was backed by many moderates who were appalled by Wood. Lowden also received support from Old Guard Republicans. He had much personal attraction and a reputation as an efficient governor. His campaign was also well financed and he spent more than $400,000 in the prenomination fight. Johnson, Roosevelt's vice-presidential running mate in 1912 on the Progressive ticket, was outspoken against the League of Nations. His support came from Progressive Republicans as well as those individuals opposed to participation in the League.

Harding was apparently not interested, at least initially, in running for the presidency. Pushed by friends and his adviser Harry M. Daugherty, he had begun as a favorite son from Ohio, largely to keep state Republicans in line and guarantee his re-election to the Senate. He entered only two of the twenty state primary elections and did not do well in either. He finished a poor fourth in the Indiana primary, and while he won in Ohio he lost 9 of the state's 48 delegates to Wood. Nonetheless, he became convinced that Wood, Lowden, and Johnson could not be nominated, and sought delegate support, especially second- or third-choice commitments. He received encouragement, though not much financial support, as his campaign expenditures up to the nomination were only $113,109. Harding had the smallest number of committed first-ballot delegates (Wood 124, Johnson 112, Lowden 72, and Harding 39). Harding's apparent weakness, however, was deceiving. An enormous reservoir of good will among the delegates had been accumulated by the Harding forces in the preceding months.[20]

With the opening of the convention, the delegates elected Senator Lodge as chairman and spent two days debating and finally approving the most conservative platform "written by a Republican convention in two decades," a testimony to the strength of the conservatives within the party.[21] The platform, as expected, attacked President Wilson and his programs. On June 11 the delegates began to choose their nominee. The first ballot showed Wood with 287½ votes, Lowden 211½, Johnson 133½, Governor William C. Sproul of Pennsylvania 84, and Harding 65½. The remaining candidates shared 201 votes. Wood's strength was in the Northeast, Lowden's in the South, Johnson's in the West, Sproul's from the Pennsylvania delegation, Harding's mainly from Ohio. The predicted deadlock between Wood and Lowden had begun. Three ballots later, with adjournment closing the day, Wood had 314½, Lowden 289, Johnson 140½, and Harding 61½, with no one close to the 493 votes needed.

The night of Friday, June 11, 1920, is one of the best known in American political history. During that night, or rather early on the morning of June 12, delegates at meetings in a "smoke-filled room" in the Blackstone Hotel supposedly settled upon Harding as the candidate of the Senate Old Guard. But this is more myth than reality. There was much activity as Wood and Johnson forces tried to put together enough votes for the nomination, and Lowden and Harding supporters tried to preserve their delegates. A good deal of the activity centered in the rooms in the Blackstone occupied by Republican National Chairman Will Hays and the publicist George Harvey. Many people visited the Hays-Harvey suite and discussed the convention, but no decision seemed to have been reached, at least to support Harding. Next morning, amidst a rumor that the Senate cabal had decided for Harding, balloting resumed. By the end of the eighth ballot the deadlock remained: Lowden 307, Wood 299, Harding 133½, and Johnson 87. Only Harding showed a sizeable increase. A three-hour recess followed, during which a stop-Harding movement was attempted, and then the tired delegates began to ballot for a ninth time. Results showed a change: Harding 374½, Wood 249, Lowden 121½, and Johnson 82. Bandwagon psychology took over, and on the next ballot Harding won. And the myth of the "smoke-filled room" was born, giving little credit to Harding's adroit campaign. Indeed, the key to Harding's nomination was the inability of the "bosses" to control the convention.[22] With many delegates tired and confused on the convention's last day, they turned to the congenial Harding, the most available, acceptable candidate.

The delegates completed their work by again overriding the bosses on the vice-presidential nomination. Leaders suggested Senator Irvine L. Lenroot of Wisconsin but the delegates went for Coolidge, the Massachusetts governor who had earned admiration by speaking up during the Boston police strike. Coolidge was more acceptable because he had no connection with those individuals who appeared to be controlling the convention. And the delegates were in a hurry, wanting to leave sweltering Chicago that Saturday night. The ticket became Harding-Coolidge.

Little more than two weeks after the Republicans had concluded their business in Chicago, the Democratic delegates convened in San Francisco on June 28. As with the Chicago convention, the Democratic nomination seemed wide open. Only a quarter of the delegates were committed, and many were tied to favorite sons. Preconvention activity among the Democrats was less than among Republicans. The reason was President Wilson. Democrats wondered about a third term, because even after his collapse the president refused to withdraw his name. Whether he declined to withdraw because of desire for reelection or to make the 1920 election a referendum on the League is unclear. "It is certain,

23

however, that he supported no one else for the nomination, and thereby dampened any open campaign by possible competitors."[23]

William G. McAdoo, Wilson's son-in-law and former secretary of the treasury, was perhaps the best known of the other candidates. Because of the president's refusal to withdraw, McAdoo remained a passive candidate, going so far as to announce ten days before the Democrats convened that he would not allow his name to be placed in nomination. No such reticence was shown by Attorney General A. Mitchell Palmer, famous for the Red Scare raids, who entered some primaries and conducted a campaign based on exposing the radical threat. The other major candidate was the reform governor of Ohio, James M. Cox, a mild "wet" and supporter of the League. He had announced in January 1920 but had not been active, counting on delegates from the Midwest as well as from northern states to keep him in the running. Other candidates were John W. Davis, then ambassador to Great Britain, Governor Al Smith of New York, and Congressman Champ Clark of Missouri. And, of course, William Jennings Bryan was always ready.

If Wilson was not to emerge as the candidate from the convention, the president and his two administrations were central to the gathering. His supporters were in control of the meeting, with National Committee Chairman Homer Cummings delivering the keynote address, an attack on anti-League adherents. Senator Joseph T. Robinson of Arkansas was named permanent convention chairman, and Senator Carter Glass of Virginia, a Wilson favorite, was named chairman of the Resolutions Committee. The delegates spent five days debating the platform. The adopted document was silent on prohibition but not on the League—the first plank called for the "immediate ratification" of the Treaty of Versailles "without reservations." From the outset, the Democratic party ran on the League.

Nominations took place on June 30, and the first ballot, July 2, showed McAdoo with 226 votes, Palmer with 256, Cox 134, and Smith 109. Deadlock ensued, with McAdoo blocked because he was a "dry," a liberal, and a known intimate of Wilson. McAdoo and Governor Cox traded the lead and loomed as the favorites. Ballot after ballot went by, with Cox picking up strength when Palmer withdrew after the thirty-eighth ballot. Six ballots later Cox became the nominee. The convention had chosen him out of exhaustion and because his identification with the president was slight. The business of the convention was finished in quick fashion with the selection of Assistant Secretary of the Navy Franklin D. Roosevelt as vice-presidential nominee.

Other parties nominated candidates in 1920, the most important being Eugene V. Debs on the Socialist ticket. Debs was then serving a ten-year sentence in the federal prison in Atlanta, as Convict Number 9653, for opposing the war. The chances for election of any of the candidates of minor parties were, of course, slight.

So the United States was to choose between Harding and Cox. The Republicans began their campaign first, with Harding formally accepting the nomination on July 22 in his home town of Marion. Cox accepted several weeks later, on August 7, at the fairgrounds near his home in Dayton, just eighty-five miles southwest of Marion. The two Ohio newspaper editors were off and running.

From the outset, a Republican victory seemed inevitable. The Harding campaign was well financed (the Republicans spent about $8 million, more than three times what the Democrats spent), well organized, and generally well run. The Republican campaign had two centers. Will Hays, whom Harding asked to stay on as chairman of the Republican National Committee, conducted the party campaign. Hays concentrated on party matters, finances, and publicity, and worked out of New York. The other center of the campaign, in Marion, dealt with strategy and the candidate and was headed by Harding's political adviser, Daugherty.

Even before his acceptance speech in late July, Harding had decided to follow the advice of friends to spend much of the campaign in Marion running a "front-porch" campaign similar to McKinley's in 1896. Harding determined that Americans in the troubled year of 1920 did not want further contention. He decided to base his campaign on generalities, stressing that he planned to return the United States to stability. His slogans—"Back to normalcy" and "Let's be done with wiggle and wobble"—emphasized that theme. The candidate concentrated on projecting an image to the electorate—he would provide decent, economical government in a dignified manner—rather than discussing the issues. Harding stuck to his campaign strategy. He generally remained in Marion until late September, when he began the first of several trips. Instead of Harding going out to meet America, Americans came to Marion. Days were set for special groups to meet Harding, with blacks, farmers, workers, veterans, businessmen, and many others having their day in Marion. Between July 31, when the front-porch campaign began, and late September when it ended, approximately 600,000 people visited Marion. An effective press operation and the scores of sympathetic reporters who camped in Marion made sure that the United States read about Harding. He continued to talk generally. While his speeches set out some specific programs—for agriculture and business, for example—more often than not Harding talked of good government, arresting the high cost of living, and increasing production. Much of his campaign was set in the speech that opened his front-porch effort in which he stressed the need for cultivating friends and neighbors. "Out of such relations grow mutual respect, mutual sympathy and mutual interest, without which life holds little of real enjoyment," Harding advised his listeners.[24]

Two other decisions were made by Harding and his staff on strategy. One stressed party unity, and from the beginning Harding went out of his way to encourage good relations with all segments of the party. His competitors for the nomination came to Marion, and people as divergent as William E. Borah, Hiram Johnson, William H. Taft, Robert La Follette, and Lodge all campaigned for Harding. The other aspect of strategy involved the vice-presidential candidate, Coolidge, who stayed in New England until October, when he made an eight-day swing through the South. In Massachusetts he conducted his own front-porch campaign, and this was the way Harding's strategists wanted it.

The Democrats conducted a very different sort of campaign. Almost from the time of their nomination, Cox and Roosevelt were on the go. They visited President Wilson at the White House on July 18, where Cox told Wilson "we are going to be a million per cent with you, and your Administration, and that means the League of Nations."[25] The League was a central issue in Cox's campaign; another issue was the size and nature of contributions to the Republicans. After the Wilson meeting both Cox and Roosevelt were on the road. Cox traveled 22,000 miles in thirty-six states, making almost 400 speeches, and Roosevelt 18,000 miles from coast to coast with an equally vigorous schedule.

Cox faced many problems. The Democrats were not united following the 1918 elections and events of 1919 and 1920. Many officials concentrated on state and local campaigns. Palmer and Bryan did not want to campaign for Cox, and because of illness Wilson could not. Like Harding, Cox was not well known; but unlike Harding he was divorced, a wet, and a supporter of the League, and all these factors worked against him. He spoke frequently on campaign expenditures, charging that the Republicans were attempting to purchase the presidency. Harding exploited

Cox's exaggerations to dilute the Democrat's charges. Cox also tried to portray Harding as the candidate of big business and himself as the more progressive candidate. Since Harding's supporters included Borah, La Follette, William Allen White, and Raymond Robins, this issue did not prove effective. Cox did not get much more specific about his program to solve America's problems than Harding did, and this worked against him. Meanwhile, Franklin Roosevelt moved across the country, criticizing the Republicans. His speeches were the most interesting of the campaign, but his influence on the election was not large.

Potentially, two issues could have caused Harding difficulty. The first involved Harding's ancestry. A professor from Wooster College in Ohio, William E. Chancellor, published circulars stating that Harding possessed Negro blood. This charge was not new, as the allegation was well known in Ohio and had appeared at the Chicago nominating convention. Three weeks before the election the charge came to the fore again, but newspapers refused to print it and the Democrats decided to ignore the issue. Harding was angered, but concluded that silence and inaction were the best response. He was right and the charge apparently did not affect the election.[26]

The other issue was the League, far more complicated and much more dangerous to Harding than any other. Harding's difficulty was that the Republicans were divided. His problem was staking out a position acceptable to Borah and Johnson, opponents of the League, and to Hoover, Taft, and Elihu Root, supporters of some sort of a league. Generally, Harding successfully balanced both sides. Unable to avoid discussing the issue because of increasing pressure from all sides, he came out in support of an association of nations, legal in nature, based on The Hague Tribunal. This stand irritated the irreconcilables of his party and allowed Cox to accuse him of wobbling. Harding's answer was silence, and then clarification of his association of nations idea, at the same time welcoming irreconcilable support. He said that his position was flexible enough for all Republicans. He was right. While a few Republicans bolted, most worked for Harding right up to election day, whether they were for or against the League. On October 14, thirty-one well-known pro-League Republicans, including Taft, Root, and Hughes, publicly endorsed him while Borah and Johnson continued to campaign for him. In the end it was Cox who had to temper his position. Sensing public opposition to Article X of the Covenant of the League of Nations, Cox in the closing weeks of the campaign indicated that some reservations on the League might be helpful. Cox's change took pressure off Harding and allowed him to lapse into silence on the issue.[27]

On November 2, 1920, Harding's fifty-fifth birthday, Americans went to the polls and gave a smashing victory to the Republicans. The result was not unanticipated, because of Harding's large victory in the September election in Maine. But the margin did surprise some. Harding won 37 states, including Democratic Tennessee, and 16,181,289 votes. Cox carried 11 states, with 9,141,750 votes. Debs, who had criticized both candidates as being similar, received 941,827 votes. Harding's total, 60.2 percent, was the largest popular majority in the nation's history, a record unbroken until 1936, and brought a victory in the electoral college of 404 votes to Cox's 127. The election also was a great victory for the Republicans in Congress, where their membership reached 303 in the House, a gain of 63 seats, and 59 in the Senate, an increase of 10, the margin in the House being the largest in the party's history. The turnout (49.3 percent) was not large, but because of woman suffrage the electorate was the largest in history. All in all, it was a great victory.

Why had Harding won? The election was much more than a referendum on the League of Nations. If it was any kind of a referendum, it was on Wilson and the problems that had plagued the United States between the armistice and the election, which contrasted with the rosy image of "normalcy" conjured up by Harding. Equally important in the size of the margin of victory was Harding's skillful campaign, which avoided contention; however, almost any Republican would have beaten Cox in 1920.[28] Americans were tired of turmoil and in need of a hero who would bring tranquility back to the country. In the final analysis Harding was the more believable candidate.

And so in 1920 the nation in a sense had turned over a leaf, albeit perhaps not a new leaf. The people had asked to go back —if political leaders indeed could take the country back—to the simple life exemplified by Marion, Ohio, rather than face up to the worldwide contention the nation had been involved in under the leadership of the Democratic party and Wilson. They yearned to escape from the host of problems that had beset the country as a result, in large part, of participation in the World War and to return to more simple times. This fascinating yearning—fascinating because it was being indulged in by a people who possessed more material wealth and cultural wealth than any other people on earth—might have been described as retrogression or regression by a later generation. The country had changed enormously since the era of William McKinley, and yet the banalities and comfortableness of rural or small-town Ohio could still exert more attraction for the people than life as it really was.

2

★★★★★

PEOPLING THE GOVERNMENT

I

Warren Gamaliel Harding, born in Blooming Grove, Ohio, shortly after the conclusion of the Civil War, grew up largely untouched by the profound social and political realities of his time. America was undergoing rapid social and economic change during the last decades of the nineteenth century. Industrialization and urbanization, with all their attendant problems, transformed the United States. Harding's upbringing was typical of small-town and rural America, and his formal educational achievements were modest, leaving him with little knowledge of the broader world. Yet, this man became the twenty-ninth president of the United States, holding perhaps the most powerful position in the world.

There is little question that Harding was deeply influenced by his surroundings during his youth, with his conservatism a direct reflection of his environment. He preferred the status quo to a society in flux, a trait often found in people from rural societies. Because of its intimacy, rural life in nineteenth-century America emphasized the static and noncontroversial. The nonconformist who broke local folkways was ignored, even ostracized from polite society. People who could get along with others were extolled; people who were uncompromising, unbending, or outwardly immoral were shunned. Harding understood these all-important aspects of small-town life and was a superb practitioner of getting along with his fellow-men. His congeniality was legendary. His

31

ability to compromise, to soothe hurt feelings, was highly developed. These characteristics served him well when he acquired a local newspaper and later went into local and state politics. He understood the workings of rural America and translated this understanding into a political base.

Harding was not an intellectual, although from all accounts he was not unintelligent either. At the age of fourteen he had enrolled in Ohio Central College in Iberia, a school with a limited curriculum and even more limited faculty. While his intellect did not undergo an awakening during his two years at this college, he sustained an interest in newspapers by publishing the school paper, the *Iberia Spectator*. Harding was awarded a bachelor of science degree in the spring of 1882, and thus ended his formal education. He then tried his hand at being a teacher, with discouraging results. In February 1883 he wrote to his aunt: "Next Friday, one week, *i.e.*, the 23rd inst., forever my career as a pedagogue will close and oh, the joy! I believe my calling to be in some other sphere and will follow out the belief. . . . I will never teach again without better (a good deal better too) wages, and an advanced school."[1] He tried his hand at reading law; but this did not suit him, and he was pleased when funds for the endeavor ran out. He tried working as an insurance agent. This new career ended within the year when he sold an insurance policy for a newly constructed hotel by giving lower rates than the company permitted. All the while, he found time to play in the local band, manage a baseball team, and widen his circle of friends and admirers.[2]

After several false starts he turned to editing a newspaper. Marion, Ohio, the sizeable town near which Harding grew up, had two substantial weekly papers and one anemic daily. The *Marion Star*, in existence since 1877, was on the verge of financial collapse in 1884. With two partners, John Warwick and John O. Sickle, Harding acquired the paper for a few hundred dollars. His partners lasted a few months, but Harding exhibited unaccustomed determination to make the paper a success. Often only a jump ahead of his creditors, the nineteen-year-old editor set type, gathered news stories, and wrote editorials. He became skilled at soliciting advertising, the lifeblood of any newspaper. With his congeniality beginning to pay, he had created a six-page daily by 1890 and was on his way to becoming Marion's most influential citizen and booster.

Harding was blessed with a handsome face as well as an imposing physical stature. He used both of these features to good advantage in business, politics, and social life. Years later, his physical appearance enhanced his credibility as a presidential candidate. Yet this apparent robustness concealed some severe emotional problems in early life as well as incapacitating illnesses later. On five different occasions between 1890 and 1902 Harding spent prolonged periods in a sanitarium in Battle Creek, Michigan, run by Dr. J. P. Kellogg, for nervous breakdowns. The cause of these emotional disturbances probably were at first business-related and then his uneasy relationship with his wife. In any case, there was no public record of further problems of this nature later.

Harding on July 8, 1891, married Florence Mabel Kling, daughter of Marion's wealthiest citizen, Amos Kling. She was a divorcée, as well as several years Harding's senior. Her father approved of neither of her marriages and refused to speak to her for more than seven years after the marriage to Harding. But it was a helpful match indeed. Harding's wife, the "Duchess" as she came to be called, provided order to his existence. She became involved in the work of the *Star*, managing its circulation. Incorrectly, she later was to receive credit for making the paper a financial success. There may have been some truth in this, but not a great deal. Her principal role was to help stabilize her husband's previously drifting life. And then, of course, there were the difficult aspects of her personality, perhaps stemming from her earlier difficult life as the wife of the ne'er-do-well Henry A. (Pete) DeWolf. She was shrewish and sharp and had pronounced likes and dislikes. Her personality soon began to jar upon the easy habits of her husband. Gradually there was a drifting apart, though it was not often apparent to outsiders. Her harsh and unforgiving character was probably ever present in Harding's mind, and she perhaps gave definition to Harding's own growing social and political ambitions.

Life went on, and Harding became a rock-ribbed Republican devoted to the GOP.[3] He had been a devoted supporter of James G. Blaine in the latter's unsuccessful bid for the presidency in 1884. Thereafter Harding challenged the county Republican leadership in the pages of his paper. He joined the Young Men's Republican Club, a direct outgrowth of the split in the local party organization. Then time eroded his difficulties with local political enemies. In July 1899 he announced his candidacy for the state senate. Although he failed to carry Marion, he received enough votes in the remainder of the district to win. Harding now controlled the Marion Republican party and was achieving statewide recognition.

In the course of his rise in the state GOP, ability to get along with diverse factions served him well. Ohio politics was a welter of groups working at cross purposes. While the Republicans generally controlled the state, they were constantly engaged in a civil war of their own making. He brought the local groups together. He was the first person to receive renomination for the state senate from his district in fifty-seven years. By 1902 Harding had decided he wanted to run for governor. He was elected lieutenant governor in 1903. In 1905 he was passed over for his party's gubernatorial nomination and spent the next few years tending to the *Star*. He received the Republican nomination for governor in 1910 but was defeated at the polls by Judson Harmon, a conservative Democrat who was able to point to corruption in Ohio's Republican party. Nineteen ten was also an election year dominated by Democrats. Ironically, had Harding been elected governor he probably would have considered the honor the capstone of his political career.

Harding kept in good stead with Republican party regulars during the awkward years of progressivism. In 1912 he earned the contempt of Theodore Roosevelt's supporters by nominating William Howard Taft for a second term at the national convention. He disliked the treatment Taft was receiving at the hands of the Progressives, and viewed Progressive party activities as next to treason. He believed in loyalty to one's party, and the Progressives had fractured the Republican party, allowing the Democrats to triumph throughout the nation. His yeoman service was not forgotten, and in 1914 he was elected to the United States Senate, one of the first senators elected in popular elections.

Harding truly enjoyed his years in the Senate. Unaccustomed to national attention, he basked in the publicity he received as a member of the United States Senate. By 1914 Harding was well off financially, with an income of at least $20,000 a year from the *Star* to supplement his senatorial salary and expense account. He purchased a large Neo-Georgian brick duplex at 2314 Wyoming Avenue for $50,000. The Hardings were soon heavily involved in the social whirl of the nation's capital and became close friends of the rich and erratic Ned and Evalyn McLean. He also played poker three or four evenings a week with Nicholas Longworth, a member of the House of Representatives from Ohio, and another new senator, Albert B. Fall, and others. Harding used his position as senator to satisfy his wanderlust, traveling frequently to places that captured his interest. At the same time, Harding was content to be an undistinguished member of a Senate that was not then noted for greatness.

Harding's service in the upper house in Washington was no more than mediocre. In his first years in that body he served on various committees—Commerce, Claims, Coastal Defenses, Investigations of Trespasses on Indian Lands, and Sale of Meat Products —but gained no distinction. In 1916 he delivered a ringing anti-Wilson keynote address at the national convention, raising his stock within his party. During his tenure in the Senate, he supported wartime measures, woman suffrage, and prohibition. He voted for the Eighteenth Amendment, not out of conviction but to pass the buck to the state legislatures. He was a wet and believed prohibition would be impossible, but the dry forces in Ohio were powerful and had to be recognized. He ducked the issue by apparent support, hoping the amendment would die in the state legislatures.[4] It of course did not. In the Sixty-sixth Congress he was appointed to the Committee on Foreign Relations. He belonged to the group of Republicans known as "strong reservationists" and voted against the League of Nations.

While in the Senate, Harding introduced 134 bills, with 122 of them pertaining to local matters such as securing back pension for veterans. His twelve national bills were of little significance, encouraging the teaching of Spanish, celebrating the pilgrims' landing, lending surplus government tents to the public to alleviate the housing shortage of 1920, investigating influenza, changing the McKinley Memorial Association Act, and giving obsolete rifles to the Sons of Veterans Reserves. He demonstrated his aversion to controversy by being conspicuously absent on roll-call votes on controversial matters. Partially for this reason, and because he was somewhat lazy, he failed to vote on more than 46 percent of the roll calls during his years in the Senate. This was an extremely high absence rate, even for a senator. On matters pertaining to labor, he voted seven times in favor, eleven times against, and was absent on ten votes. When he managed to vote, Harding demonstrated party loyalty by voting approximately 95 percent of the time with the GOP. With this undistinguished background, Harding announced in December 1919 his candidacy for the presidency, primarily to maintain his political position in Ohio and to lay the groundwork for reelection to the Senate.

To his surprise, Harding was nominated. He then was elected by an overwhelming vote. After victory the president-elect indulged in his passion for travel by taking a vacation in Texas and the Panama Canal Zone. He returned to Washington, where he gave his last formal speech to the Senate, and spent the remainder

35

of his time as president-elect in Marion and sunning in Florida. During this period his thoughts turned to the presidency and his conceptions of it. He engaged in long consultations with the leaders of the Republican party to select a cabinet as well as to set priorities during his administration.

Harding has long had a reputation as a lazy president, unable or unwilling to keep his own house in order, yet evidence indicates the contrary. He worked long hours, usually reaching his desk by 8:00 A.M. and rarely retiring before midnight. Judson Welliver and Charles Hard served as political secretaries, while George Christian, Jr., son of his next-door neighbor and long-time friend, took care of more personal matters. The typical Harding day would consist of breakfast before 8:00, then appointments followed by a cabinet meeting at 10:00. Afternoon and evening would be cluttered with appointments, ceremonials, social engagements. He met with the public almost every day at noon, shaking hands while beaming all the time. These sessions seemed to reassure him and give him added vigor. He paid close attention to public opinion, often answering correspondence from well-wishers late into the night. He limited his outside reading to a bound volume of press clippings prepared daily by the White House staff. He had little patience with, or interest in, long government documents and reports. Such was the daily life of the president.[5]

Harding also worked hard at relaxation. He had a passion for golf and played at least twice a week. While criticized for this activity, he certainly spent no more time on the links than Woodrow Wilson had before his stroke. The president also found relaxation in card playing. He particularly enjoyed poker and played twice a week, usually once in the White House and once at a friend's. These sessions were often attended by Harding's "cronies" and included an occasional drink. These "vices" must have seemed a helpful break in the day-to-day pressures of the White House routine.

The Duchess made the most of her years in the White House. She had not adjusted well to Washington society in Harding's years in the Senate. Snubbed by many, she kept a "little red book" which she used to good purpose after her husband gained the presidency. Despite this vengeful nature, she was a real asset to Harding. Some form of entertainment, social or official, occurred almost every evening; and, in contrast to the Wilson years, the White House was thrown open to the public. The Duchess became renowned for her willingness to meet people. Often she would go downstairs to meet

White House tourists, much to their delight. The White House was the people's house, and she did all in her power to make visitors feel at ease. At the same time, she spent many hours touring veterans hospitals. A severe illness in 1922 brought much of this rigorous schedule to an end, but her activities were a real political benefit to Harding.

The new president's newspaper background and congenial nature paid handsome dividends in his relationship with the press. Many correspondents assumed that upon elevation to the presidency he would revamp his informal relations with journalists, developed during the campaign. To the journalists' pleasant surprise Harding revived the practice of biweekly press conferences. These conferences were informal, and Harding often took the press into his confidence. The press rarely took advantage of this trust. Much of the traditional advocacy relationship between executive and press was thus tempered for Harding's presidency. He enjoyed his conferences with the press on a "give-and-take" basis, and the few reporters in attendance (the White House press corps then numbered only six or eight individuals) often laid aside their critical faculties. Harding enjoyed an almost unprecedented relationship with the press. The attitude of the national press toward Harding was generally favorable and changed only after his death in 1923.[6]

Harding developed a view of the presidency that was decidedly conservative. While in the Senate he had abhorred Wilson's arrogant handling of Congress in general, the Senate in particular. Harding believed in separation of powers and deeply respected congressional prerogatives. He was suspicious of strong presidential power, believing that such power could be used only within narrow limits. He never viewed the president as a legislative leader and was appalled at the thought of forcing his views on Congress, although this did not prevent him from presenting legislation to Congress. His ideal president was McKinley, not Theodore Roosevelt or Wilson. A strong presidency could only lead to misuse of power and troubled relations with Congress.

In Harding's view the president's role was largely ceremonial. In fact, the part of the presidency he most enjoyed was its pomp and ceremony. Although a humble man, he was impressed by the deference given the president and basked in the social activities connected with the post. This enjoyment was rooted in belief that the president could not gain national respect if "the chief executive entered the political arena like an armed gladiator. Only a president who was loved could properly retain the public faith and be a symbol of national pride and confidence."[7] Hence Harding's emphasis on the symbolic functions of his office. He believed that his other main function was to act as a conciliator. It was part of his nature to avoid conflict. The president's duty was to bring together the "best minds," yet remain above them. This would ensure the broadest possible support.

Taken together, Harding's outstanding trait was his ability to get along with others and serve as a conciliator of interests. This compulsion to arbitrate diverse views often led him to avoid troublesome questions or to ignore facts that might shatter the unity he sought. He wanted a cabinet which would serve his conception of the presidency. He would arbitrate between the best opinions on an issue. He thus placed a high premium on loyalty.

II

It was Harding's misfortune that one of his selections for the cabinet was the first individual to serve a jail sentence as a result of activities engaged in while a cabinet member. That a second member of his cabinet came close to conviction conspired to cast doubt on Harding's judgment of human nature. Rumor long persisted that a weak president had allowed outside interests to dictate cabinet selections which led to tragic consequences.

The facts do not support the myths. Harding selected his cabinet on the basis of wide consultation with the leadership of his party. He wanted men who were knowledgeable, and this dictated the candidates under consideration. It is true that he relied upon friends in the Senate for advice. It is equally true that he often discounted the advice of his senatorial colleagues, to their dismay and discomfort. The decision on the cabinet was Harding's and reflected his views both of human nature and as a politician. He wanted to satisfy elements within the Republican party, yet maintain quality appointments. Harding owed few political debts, and this allowed him more freedom of choice than most presidents-elect. He informed reporters, "Three things are to be considered in the selection of a Cabinet. First, there is the man's qualification for public service. That is the most important consideration of all. Second, there is the attitude of the public concerning the man under consideration. Third, there is the political consideration. As to that—well. This is going to be a Republican Cabinet!"[8]

Much has been written about Harding's inclinations concerning the first position of the cabinet—secretary of state. There is evidence that Harding may have briefly considered awarding the post to a friend, Senator Albert Fall, because of Fall's supposed knowledge of Mexican affairs and the fact that Fall spoke Spanish, albeit a bastardized version.[9] In any event, Harding did not consider Fall for long, because he offered the position to Charles Evans Hughes early in December 1920.

Hughes was an ideal choice for secretary of state. He was not the choice of the more conservative wing of the Republican party. Elihu Root and Senator Philander Knox were advanced as alternatives by the Republican senators, although they were mild internationalists. Hughes was anathema to them because he had supported an active internationalist position. But the man from New York was respected across the country, and contrary to detractors in the Senate he would be able to work well with members of Congress. He had been his party's standard-bearer in 1916, and —given Harding's views on party loyalty—was the natural choice. Hughes was an able lawyer and experienced negotiator. Despite protests from the conservative wing of his party, Harding stood by his decision, demonstrating in his first appointment that no one would dictate the membership of his cabinet.[10]

Appointment of Henry C. Wallace as secretary of agriculture was another indication of Harding's priorities. Wallace was the outspoken editor of an Iowa farm journal, *Wallace's Farmer*; his politics were moderately progressive. Wallace had been a great help on farm issues during the campaign, in a region disturbed by price dislocations in an election year. Shortly before the election, Harding wrote Wallace, "If the verdict of Tuesday is what we are expecting it to be I shall very much want your assistance in making good the promises which we have made to the American people."[11] Wallace's qualifications as a "dirt farmer" and agricultural expert made him attractive.

Outspoken views on the packing and food-processing industries had earned Wallace the enmity of interest groups within the Republican party. His liberal tendencies were obnoxious to the conservative wing. Progressive Republicans rallied to his support; and, since Harding wanted a dirt farmer, he stood by his decision to nominate the Iowan.

In terms of infighting there was more opposition among the Republican leadership to Harding's interest in Herbert Hoover for a cabinet post than to any other appointment. Most of the leadership waged a relentless campaign to keep Hoover out. But "Hoover, even more than Hughes, had a 'good press,' and there was wide support in the country at large for his appointment."[12] Harding wanted men of reputation, and the pugnacious Hoover appealed to him.

Hoover was opposed because he was "too liberal in his social philosophy, too internationally-minded, too popular, and too ambitious for the old guard." This combination of traits made him somewhat unappealing to some progressive elements of the Republican party as well. Progressives like George W. Norris and Gifford Pinchot failed to evince enthusiasm for Hoover.[13] But Hoover's qualifications for a cabinet position were unassailable, and he had supporters. Moreover, the intense pressure to avoid Hoover enhanced him in Harding's mind. The more he considered Hoover, the better Hoover appeared. "Of course," he wrote, "I have no quarrel with those who do not think as I do, but inasmuch as I have the responsibility to assume, I think my judgment must be trusted in the matter. The main thing to consider at present is whether Mr. Hoover will accept the post which I am prepared to offer to him."[14] Harding offered a choice of the Department of the Interior or the Department of Commerce. Although Hoover professed reluctance to accept appointment as secretary of commerce, Harding's wishes prevailed and the appointment was announced in February 1921.

Harding was able to quiet criticism of Hoover by tying his appointment to the selection of Andrew W. Mellon as secretary of the treasury. At the outset, Harding had not considered Mellon for the position. Indeed, his first choice was Charles G. Dawes, a Chicago banker. He had served in the McKinley administration as comptroller of the currency and during World War I reached the rank of brigadier general. Serving on General John J. Pershing's staff, he earned a solid reputation as a procurer and expediter of supplies and matériel. Dawes was offered the post in December but would not commit himself.[15] Hesitation provided Harding with an opportunity for a trade-off. Easterners were suspicious of Dawes, viewing him as unreliable. Harding did not want to appoint a secretary of treasury from New England or New York, in order to avoid the charge of "Wall Street" dominance. Senator Knox first had mentioned Mellon, a heavy contributor to the Republican party. When eastern interests united behind the Pittsburgh multimillionaire, Harding realized the advantages of a Mellon appointment. He asked Dawes not to make known the fact that he had refused the post. He tied Mellon's appointment to Hoover's. He would make Mellon secretary of the treasury but, in exchange, the conservatives had to cease their attacks on Hoover. Harding was able to play the role of compromiser and, at the same time, silence criticism of his preference as commerce secretary. In the selection of Mellon, Harding also had maintained independence.

The president-elect turned to the position of secretary of war and ultimately settled on his friend John W. Weeks, a graduate of the Naval Academy who had served in the Spanish-American War. Weeks had returned to Boston and rapidly expanded his banking business. From 1905 to 1913 he was in the House of Representatives and in 1912 was elected to the Senate, where he had met Harding. To the surprise of all, he was defeated for reelection in 1918. After defeat he continued to serve the party, providing substantial financial contributions during the election campaign of 1920. Weeks had all the credentials for a cabinet post and was considered for both postmaster general and secretary of the navy. He declined the latter position on the sensible grounds that he did not want to pass on qualifications for promotion of individuals he either had served with or who were classmates. Harding wanted him in the cabinet, so offered him the position of secretary of war. Weeks's appointment proved popular with both Congress and the military. Harding was satisfied because Weeks was a known quantity.

Another troublesome position was secretary of labor. The postwar years were rife with labor disturbances, and the party wanted to placate the labor rank and file if possible. Since Samuel Gompers, the president of the American Federation of Labor, had opposed Harding's election, the president-elect wanted someone with labor credentials who was anti-Gompers.

The search narrowed to James Davis, a former iron-worker who still maintained his union credentials. He was better known for work as director-general of the Loyal Order of Moose. Lodges across the country endorsed him, along with labor organizations. Davis was anti-Gompers and a Republican of long-standing and had supported Harding during the campaign. Gompers sealed Davis's nomination when he telegraphed the president-elect to protest Davis's appointment, saying that "no man is fully capable to fill the position of secretary of labor who lacks the sympathy, respect and confidence of the wage workers of our country."[16] Davis was appointed.

Harding's search for a secretary of the navy lacked the intensity devoted to the other positions. He wanted to reward Governor Frank Lowden for support during the campaign and offered

41

the post on three separate occasions. Edwin L. Denby was first mentioned by Weeks and later by Lowden. Denby had served in the House from 1905 to 1911, on the Committee on Naval Affairs. He had been in the Spanish-American War as a gunner's mate and enlisted in the Marine Corps in 1917 at the age of 47. Discharged as a major, he had proceeded to make a fortune manufacturing automobiles in Detroit. A conservative Republican, he was appointed to the navy post after a haphazard search made as the March inauguration closed in on Harding.

Will Hays's appointment as postmaster general came as no surprise, for as chairman of the Republican National Committee he had done yeoman service. An appointment to some position was a natural outcome of his activity. Appointment of the committee chairman as postmaster general was almost traditional, and it placed him where he could reward party stalwarts. Ironically, he believed in advancement through merit. Hays had hoped to be secretary of commerce but, once Hoover had expressed a preference, that was out of the question, and he had to settle for what he received. Harding would have been harshly criticized if he had not placed Hays in the cabinet.

The two positions which eventually brought great trouble—after, of course, the president's death—were posts he had reserved for friends. Harding believed it was the president's right to have one or two friends in the cabinet. Both Albert Fall and Harry Daugherty fell into this category. Daugherty was the president's closest political adviser, and Harding was deeply in debt for years of loyal service. Given Harding's views on loyalty, he had to include these men. He owed it to them, as well as to himself.

Fall was a likeable character who had ridden with the Rough Riders during the Spanish-American War and returned to New Mexico from where, in 1912, he was elected to the Senate. There he had become one of Harding's intimate friends. There was much to commend him to Harding for the Department of the Interior. Although anticonservationist, he was from the West, an important consideration. Personally, Fall's credentials were thought impeccable. On receiving his nomination as secretary of the interior, the Senate confirmed him by acclamation without referring his case to committee, the first such instance in American history. Some conservationists were opposed, but Fall's selection was a logical choice.

Daugherty's appointment as attorney general was by far Harding's most criticized act. A long-standing adviser and friend, he had laid much of the groundwork for Harding's nomination and therefore was the president-elect's largest political creditor. Daugherty did not run Harding, contrary to myth. If anything, the reverse was true, with Daugherty extremely deferential to Harding. The president-elect nonetheless wanted to award Daugherty with a cabinet appointment. That Harding stood by Daugherty in the face of criticism was a measure of the emphasis he placed on loyalty.

Because of Daugherty's past as a manipulator in the backrooms of Ohio politics, rumor that he would be made attorney general brought immediate protests. The president-elect was determined to appoint his friend and faced down all opposition. While there was no evidence that Daugherty pressed Harding for the job, there was little doubt that the campaign manager–political manipulator wanted the appointment, if for no other reason than to impress friends and show up enemies. That there was some merit in the appointment, then, was lost in Daugherty's performance. A competent lawyer well-acquainted with the seamy side of politics, he was a first-rate political troubleshooter and someone Harding could trust. Given these circumstances, it was easy to see why Harding insisted on Daugherty.

In looking at Harding's performance as a cabinet-maker, the results were mixed. He certainly appointed some of the strongest cabinet-level officers in history. For quality it would be hard to surpass men such as Hoover, Hughes, and Wallace. Mellon and Weeks were competent, if conservative, while Hays and Davis met political needs. The remaining three men—Fall, Daugherty, and Denby—were, of course, not good appointments. Taken together, Harding constructed an above-average cabinet in talent and political ability. He alone was responsible for the selection. A senatorial cabal was not able to dictate a list of names. Often he went against the advice of sages, and in most cases to his own credit. Indeed, he came close to meeting the criteria he had established. Yet strength did not cancel weakness, and therein was the cabinet tragedy.

Harding lost his first cabinet member in 1922 when Hays resigned to become president of the Motion Picture Producers and Distributors of America. Not a wealthy man, the Indiana politico felt he had to accept the offer of $150,000 a year to become the first "czar" of the movie industry. His duty was to clean up the movies, which some people felt were getting too smutty. His appointment was reckoned to be a device, admittedly expensive to the movie industry, to get reformers off the industry's back.

As postmaster general, Hays performed adequately. Later, in his *Memoirs*, he noted that one of his gravest problems was mail robberies. During 1920 and early 1921, more than $6,000,000 had been lost in thirty-six major mail robberies. Angered by a $750,000 robbery in Chicago, Hays ordered the arming of postal employees. The War Department issued sixteen thousand .45 caliber pistols and numerous riot guns to the Postal Department. Widely publicized, this drastic action caused an apparent decline in mail predators. But nonetheless the New York Post Office suffered a $1,000,000 robbery in October 1921. Further humiliation occurred when postal employees reenacting the crime were arrested by passing police who believed another robbery in progress. A cabinet meeting devoted solely to mail robberies soon followed, and Hays secured approval to use one thousand marines to protect the mails. The marines rode shotgun on the mails until early in 1922, when the Postal Department introduced its own security force. These drastic measures cut the losses in mail theft to a mere $300,000, bringing some minor reduction to the annual postal deficit.

The new postmaster general, Hubert Work, was a physician who had been active in the 1920 campaign. Work did not believe in the merit system, which Hays had emphasized. He was shifted to the Department of the Interior in 1923 when Fall resigned, and in this office Work performed well, especially as the department's image had become tarnished because of Fall's involvement in Teapot Dome. The third postmaster general under Harding was Harry S. New from Indiana, a friend from Senate days. New was also opposed to the merit system in the postal service.[17] Harding's additions to his cabinet perhaps failed to measure up to some original appointments, but they were men he could rely on and work with. They thus met the test of office. Perhaps Harding had discovered that dealing with so many "best minds" in a cabinet could be a trying experience.

Harding relied on his cabinet appointees more than most presidents, depending upon them for the operation of the government. In his mind, they were men of quality and integrity and deserved his support. Cabinet discussions played an important role in determining governmental policy, and Harding allowed each cabinet officer relative autonomy in his particular sphere, seldom interfering with the day-to-day operations of government. Hence these men became the key to the operation of the government during the Harding administration. They often determined the direction of the country. When they were men of quality, the government operated in an efficient, even enlightened manner. When they were bad, they governed accordingly, and Harding's reputation as president suffered. When they disagreed, Harding was often slow to intervene, because such disputes made him intensely uncomfortable. Even so, Harding viewed himself as the conciliator of diverse opinion, the keeper of the peace. This was his prime job, and he tried to adhere to his conception of the presidency.

III

Harding was in a unique position regarding appointments at secondary levels in his administration. The party had been out of power for eight years, and he intended to Republicanize the bureaucracy. He believed the party in power had the right and duty to reward supporters. He spent an enormous amount of time and energy dealing with the most minor appointments. Even Daugherty was not free from Harding's scrutiny in matters of political appointments.

Appointments were based on a curious combination of merit and spoils. Under pressure from Republicans for positions, Harding encountered far more job seekers than jobs. Progressive elements in the party wanted the bureaucracy Republicanized, but on a merit basis. Other elements demanded that the test be support for the party. This divergence reached the cabinet. Hoover, Mellon, Hughes, Hays, and Wallace supported merit appointment while Davis, Fall, Weeks, Denby, and Daugherty believed in spoils. As time passed, Harding leaned more toward the position of the "best minds," but he never entirely accepted the principle of merit.

Harding placed many close friends and associates in jobs. As he once allegedly remarked, "God, I can't be an ingrate." His appointments demonstrated he was far from one. He made the Marion homeopathic physician Charles Sawyer "the suddenest brigadier general in history," lending prestige to Sawyer's position as White House physician. His good friend and drinking companion, Ed Scobey, became director of the Denver Mint. His brother-in-law, the Reverend Heber H. Votaw, an erstwhile missionary, became the superintendent of federal prisons. He made Daniel R. Crissinger, a Marion banker and close friend, comptroller of the currency, later moving him to governorship of the Federal Reserve Board. Another Marion resident, Henry Hane, became a bank examiner, and a former *Marion Star* newsboy who had attended West Point and risen to the rank of major in the army air service, Ora Baldinger, was elevated to the position of presidential military aid. The adventurer

Charles R. Forbes headed the Bureau of War Risk Insurance and later directed the newly formed Veterans Bureau.[18]

The quality of these appointments was spotty at best. Votaw proved ineffective as a prison administrator; there were rumors of drug traffic throughout the prison system. Crissinger, a business-man-lawyer, never performed well in the sensitive positions entrusted to him. Conservatism and thrift failed to make up for his lack of qualifications. Scobey was the archetypal political hack but did little damage during his tenure. Baldinger proved a competent soldier, and Sawyer an increasingly valued friend and adviser, though his medical credentials left something to be desired. Forbes was a disaster of the first magnitude and provided the first major scandal of Harding's administration.

Harding was usually circumspect in the use of patronage. He worked closely with the Civil Service Commission and moderately expanded the merit system, contrary to the record of his predecessor. In 1923 Harding supported the passage of the Government Classification Act. This forward-looking legislation granted a pay raise for civil service workers and also provided for standard rates of compensation, more consistent personnel practices, and precise job descriptions. This act went a long way toward creating a more efficient and responsive federal civil service. Even so, this caused Harding difficulty with the cabinet and with Republican senators and representatives.

Serious fights over the spoils positions came in the Postal and Treasury departments. Mellon believed the Treasury was a business and should be so run, staffed by men intimately acquainted with business practice. The focus of dispute turned out to be Elmer Dover, who had been appointed assistant secretary in charge of customs and internal revenue. Formerly Mark Hanna's secretary and a friend of Daugherty's, Dover wanted to "Hardingize" the Treasury. He clashed with the commissioner of Internal Revenue, David H. Blair, a Mellon appointee who believed in competent men, even if Democrats. Dover viewed such opinions as heretical, took his case to Daugherty, and ultimately it reached the president. Harding realized that Mellon was prepared to back Blair to the point of resignation, and so the merit system was protected within the Treasury.

The results were mixed in the postal service. Hays believed in a merit system but was forced to compromise. When Wilson took office in 1913, he had proceeded to replace the first three classifications of postmasters with deserving Democrats. In 1917 he placed these positions on the civil service list, removing some 12,000 jobs from the patronage rolls. Harding was under pressure from members of his party to revoke Wilson's executive order. A compromise was worked out under which a postmaster was chosen from the top three candidates taking the civil service examination. For all practical purposes this meant that a Republican could be installed in almost all vacancies. This compromise did not prevent Harding from appointing the Marion postmaster by executive order or telling Mary Lee to take the civil service examination but promising her the position in advance. "It will not be necessary for you to study up in order to prepare for the test," he wrote. "Most of the grading is based on business reputation and general standing in the community. . . . Please do not have any worries about coming into the realization of the promise made to you. I should be disappointed in the discriminating power of the Executive if he could not choose a post office appointee."[19] Nor did it prevent the president from coming to the aid of a friend in Bedford, Virginia, whom he wanted awarded the local postmastership. So, a merit system of sorts was allowed to stand in the postal service, but not when it inconvenienced the chief executive.

If Harding made several important diplomatic appointments, Hughes was usually left alone in his placement of diplomatic personnel. The secretary of state put together a professional overseas staff. Work was begun on the Rogers Act to modernize the foreign service, which was passed finally in 1924. The bill had Harding's support. Harding's other "best minds," largely untouched by the spoils system, maintained professional staffs.

Harding entered office on the promise that he would reduce the federal budget, and this provided the opportunity to appoint Dawes director of the Bureau of the Budget, created soon after the president came to power. The Bureau of the Budget for the first time allowed the executive to prepare a federal budget on a rational basis. Harding had wanted Dawes to become secretary of the treasury for the purpose of saving a billion dollars. Dawes had maintained that a cabinet officer would not have authority to enforce unpopular budgetary decisions on other cabinet-level officers. They would tell him to mind his own business. Dawes argued for creation of a Bureau of the Budget with the director responsible to the president. Then he would be in position to ensure budgetary plans. The acerbic Dawes believed in operating the government in a businesslike manner, including a budget. Dawes's arguments impressed Harding, and when the Bureau of the Budget was created the Chicagoan was asked to take the position.[20] Dawes agreed to serve for one year, maintaining that by that time he would have made so many enemies he would no longer be effective. He was effective and saved more than a billion dollars, to the dismay of many enemies.

Closely tied to Harding's desire to economize in government was his hope to reduce the size of the federal government to pre–World War levels. In 1916 approximately 400,000 persons were employed by the federal government, with slightly less than a quarter being military personnel. At the peak of the war—in 1918 —over 900,000 civilians were working in federal bureaus. The number of civilians working for the government by 1921, when Harding assumed control of the government, was approximately 25 percent higher than in 1916, and the Harding administration failed to reduce this figure. To be sure, because of cuts in defense personnel, the number employed by the government dropped to a low of 536,000 in 1923, only to begin to grow gradually throughout the remainder of the decade. The Post Office Department, as an example, had 212,000 employees in 1916, compared to 268,000 in 1923. Harding discovered that it was difficult to reduce a well-entrenched bureaucracy.

Harding also had the opportunity to restructure the Supreme Court by appointing four new justices. William Howard Taft had appointed six Supreme Court judges during his four years in office, compared to only three for Wilson. It was clear that the winning candidate in 1920 would be able to reconstitute the Court. When Chief Justice Edward D. White died on May 19, 1921, the first opportunity appeared. In talks with the president-elect, Taft noted that "many times in the past the Chief Justice had said he was holding the office for me and that he would give it back to a Republican administration." Harding understood Taft's lifelong ambition, but the former president was still "nonplussed at the way in which he took me into his confidence and was nearly struck dumb when he asked me if I would go to the Supreme Court." Complications occurred because Harding had made the same promise to George Sutherland. Taft campaigned in earnest. The suggestion that the matter wait for a second opening so the president could send both names forward at the same time did not sit well with Taft, who was sixty-four years old and while president had established the rule that no person over sixty years of age should go on the Court. His campaign succeeded, and his appointment became official on June 30, 1921.

Taft's qualifications for the Supreme Court were unique. Pursuing a position on the Court as early as 1889, he had a lifelong interest in the Court. He had served as a federal judge, law professor, governor-general of the Philippines, and secretary of war, not to mention being elected president in 1908. During the 1920 campaign, he had maintained that "there is no greater domestic issue in this election than the maintenance of the Supreme Court as the bulwark to enforce the guaranty that no man shall be deprived of his property without due process of law."[21] Taft was to pursue this philosophy with a vengeance while chief justice. The Court during the 1920s reflected the social, economic, and political views of the dominant political party.

Harding's opportunity to change the Court did not end with Taft's elevation to chief justice, and Harding was to appoint three more conservative, property-oriented lawyers—George Sutherland, Pierce Butler, and Edward Sanford. Sutherland, an ex-senator from Utah, would write the majority opinion in the case of *Adkins* v. *Children's Hospital*, which held invalid an act of Congress establishing a minimum wage for women and children in Washington, D.C. Taft urged Harding to appoint Butler, although he was a Democrat, because the chief justice knew the Minnesotan had conservative views on property. Butler had the distinction of voting to overturn sixty-nine federal statutes after Franklin D. Roosevelt became president. Sanford, a conservative from Knoxville, Tennessee, would write the majority opinion in *Gitlow* v. *New York*, upholding a New York statute under which Gitlow was convicted for publishing Communist propaganda. He wrote a similar opinion in the case of *Fiske* v. *Kansas*. These justices were to have a profound effect on the judiciary and the nation long after Harding had disappeared from the scene.[22]

It fell to Harding to appoint sixty federal judges at various ranks, and nearly all were Republicans. His appointments Republicanized the federal bench but not at the cost of quality, as the credentials of these individuals were viewed as high.[23]

With return of the Republican party, the personnel of regulatory commissions took on a decidedly conservative cast. One of Harding's first appointments to the Interstate Commerce Commission was John J. Esch, an author of the Esch-Cummins Transportation Act of 1920, long a friend of railroad management. From a progressive standpoint such an appointment was a disaster. Other agencies such as the Federal Reserve Board, the Federal Trade Commission, and the Tariff Commission suffered the same fate.

Crissinger, as mentioned, was appointed in 1922 to head the Federal Reserve Board. Harding's first appointment to the Federal Trade Commission was an Indiana Republican, V. W. Van Fleet, who had been an assistant to Daugherty. His second appointment to that commission was a conservative Iowa farmer, C. W. Hunt. The Tariff Commission failed to escape the conservative tide. Harding's first appointment was T. O. Marvin, the long-standing secretary of the Boston Home Market Club, as well as editor of an appropriately named journal, *The Protectionist*.[24]

Under Harding the government thus took on an increasingly probusiness appearance. He started reshaping the regulatory commissions, a process that continued through the 1920s. Commissions were staffed by people from the very sectors of the economy they were intended to control. The progressive concept of regulatory commissions as policemen was scrapped. The commissioners became the advocates of the groups they were to regulate. The vestiges of progressivism passed from the scene.

As had been the case with many Republican presidents, Harding hoped to strengthen the Republican party throughout the South by judicious use of patronage. Like other Republicans before him, Harding was not successful. Racial prejudice and turncoat Democrats buried his hopes. "Alas," he lamented, "I grow discouraged whenever I contemplate the question of patronage in a state like that of Georgia. I sought to encourage the organization of a new party down there, and I thought we had brought into it a number of people who would give us some hope of Republican success and at the same time help us to bring high-grade men into the public service."[25]

The president gave little attention to minority group appointments. The NAACP had asked for blacks as assistant secretaries in the Departments of Labor and Agriculture. Not only did Harding ignore this request, but he was slow to appoint blacks to positions they traditionally had held, at least before Wilson. He responded to pressure by requesting that his cabinet find "a couple of suitable places for colored appointees."[26] It was not until June that Harding made his first significant black appointment, Henry Lincoln Johnson, as recorder of deeds for the District of Columbia. Indifference to placing blacks in the administration may have stemmed from the attempt to rebuild the Republican party in the South. For whatever reason, blacks found little cheer in Harding.

Women had more cause for hope as Harding rewarded electoral support with several substantial appointments. Helen Gardner was named to the Civil Service Commission, while Grace Abbott was placed in charge of the Children's Bureau within the Department of Labor. Harding refused to fire married women from government service as an economy measure. He opened the foreign service to women, with Lucille Atcheson passing the examinations in July 1922. The process of women reaching the upper echelons of government started under Harding. Thus Harding responded to the success of the suffrage movement. Women could find no real cause for complaint on the treatment they received during the Harding administration.[27]

The personnel of the federal bureaucracy changed significantly. The quality of Harding's appointments varied from excellent to awful. On the whole, however, he was conscientious in the way he picked personnel. His appointments reflected his conservative viewpoint, which was to be expected. He was eminently successful in Republicanizing the bureaucracy. As time passed, he placed more emphasis on merit. Unfortunately, the weakness of a few appointments plagued the reputation of his entire administration.

3

★★★★★

DOMESTIC AFFAIRS I: CONTENTION WITH CONGRESS

I

Harding was sworn in as president by Chief Justice Edward D. White at 1:18 P.M., March 4, 1921. Immediately thereafter, from the east portico of the Capitol, the president delivered his inaugural to a large crowd gathered for the occasion. The first address to be electronically amplified, it could be heard as far away as the Senate office building. Harding was proud of his ability to please a crowd and had worked hard on his address. The new president, referring to his speaking style, would sometimes say that he "bloviated." He certainly did on that March day:

> When one surveys the world about him after the great storm, noting the marks of destruction and yet rejoicing in the ruggedness of the things which withstood it, if he is an American he breathes the clarified atmosphere with a strange mingling of regret and new hope. We have seen a world of passion spend its fury, but we contemplate our Republic unshaken, and hold our civilization secure. . . .
> Standing in this presence, mindful of the solemnity of this occasion, feeling the emotions which no one may know until he senses the great weight of responsibility for himself, I must utter my belief in the divine inspiration of the founding fathers. Surely there must have been God's

53

intent in the making of this new-world Republic. . . . We have seen the world rivet its hopeful gaze on the great truths on which the founders wrought. We have seen civil, human, and religious liberty verified and glorified. In the beginning the Old World scoffed at our experiment; today our foundations of political and social belief stand unshaken, a precious inheritance to ourselves, an inspiring example of freedom and civilization to all mankind. Let us express renewed and strengthened devotion, in grateful reverence for the immortal beginning, and utter our confidence in the supreme fulfillment.[1]

In spite of archaic language, Harding emphasized that the war was the main cause of problems in the country. "Our supreme task is the resumption of our onward, normal way," he orated. "Reconstruction, readjustment, restoration—all these must follow. I would like to hasten them." His task was to settle problems the war had created, but which the Wilson administration had left untreated. Normal business and labor patterns had been disrupted badly by the war. The goal was to restore efficiency to government, to make sure that government ran in a businesslike manner. In this way war-related problems of business could be dealt with.

The business of government was clear. The new president wanted to reduce tax burdens, create sound commercial practices with adequate credit facilities, examine agricultural problems sympathetically, end unnecessary government interference with business, and establish business practices throughout the federal government. It was apparent to Harding that American standards of living could not be maintained without substantial tariff barriers. "There is a luring fallacy in the theory of banished barriers of trade," he stated, "but preserved American standards require our higher production costs to be reflected in our tariffs on imports." Harding emphasized that his administration was going to be orthodox— America first. He wanted to return the United States to the days of McKinley, not to the days of Roosevelt and Wilson.

Harding set about establishing his administration. On March 7 he met with Republican congressional leaders to discuss which problems should be attacked first. At once he faced a bewildering diversity of opinions—tax reform, emergency tariff measures, and many other problems were suggested for top priority. While no agreement was reached, the consensus was that tax reduction and an emergency tariff were the most pressing issues. Congressional leaders suggested that a special session of Congress be summoned to deal with these problems.

The following day Harding began to get acquainted with his cabinet and announced that the cabinet would meet every Tuesday and Friday at 10:00 A.M. Cabinet meetings were to be kept simple, with no secretaries to take down debates or record votes. All discussions were confidential, with Harding keeping the privilege of revealing any decisions. At the meetings Harding spoke first, followed by a brief report from each secretary. Finally, the meeting turned to a discussion on subjects of general concern, usually led by the president.[2] Even though Harding had not settled on priorities of the administration with his cabinet and congressional leaders, on March 14 he called for a special session of Congress on April 11, 1921.

Harding lacked decisiveness. He was caught between forces demanding instant action on an emergency tariff and groups which believed that tax reduction was of prime importance. Characteristically, he tried to please both groups, indicating that he favored tax relief first but hoped Congress would act "within forty-eight hours" on an emergency tariff to protect agriculture. An agreement with congressional leaders was reached that action would begin simultaneously on both issues. The House of Representatives would start on the tariff, while the Senate would consider tax relief.

By early April, Harding had established his priorities for policy after wide consultation with his cabinet, the leadership of the Republican party, and business and community leaders. Results of these consultations were laid before Congress in a message on April 12. Harding declared that "first in mind must be the solution of our problems at home, even though some phases of them are inseparably linked with our foreign relations. The surest procedure in every government is to put its own house in order." His address was wide-ranging; its breadth took many observers by surprise. Returning to the theme of his inaugural—that many of the country's problems were creations of the war—the president called for lower taxes, more efficiency in government, lower railway rates, improved highways, encouragement of civil and military aviation, careful regulation of the air waves, a veterans bureau, and a department of public welfare.[3] While not a call for national reform, this second address stood in contrast to his "bloviation" on inaugural day. Harding, as an example, thought consumer prices too high and wondered if they resulted from "'open-price associations,' which operate, evidently, within the law, to the very great advantage of their members and equal disadvantage to the consuming public." He hoped Congress would investigate such practices "without the spirit of hostility or haste in accusation of profiteering."

Harding began the listing of his proposed measures by emphasizing the pressing need to restrict national expenditures to match national income, which would enable the lifting of "the burdens of war taxation from the shoulders of the American people." He proposed to quicken this task by implementing tax relief and by introducing a general budgetary system to enable the executive branch rigorously to control spending. In his mind, these two items deserved immediate attention from Congress.

The next item on Harding's priority list was an emergency tariff. He argued that "one who values American prosperity and maintained American standards of wage and living can have no sympathy with the proposal that easy entry and the flood of imports will cheapen our costs of living. It is more likely to destroy our capacity to buy." He believed that the American marketplace was being offered too cheaply to foreign producers. According to Harding, the farmer was the hardest hit by an influx of foreign farm products. He wanted to provide relief for the farmer.

Transportation was another area of the economy that Congress needed to examine closely. The railroad system was in poor condition because of "ill-considered legislation, the war strain, Government operation in heedlessness of cost, and the conflicting programs, or lack of them, for restoration." This difficult situation was made even worse by the economic depression. Harding argued that high freight rates discouraged commerce and that these railroad rates had to be reduced. The president's solution was not more regulation but less regulation: "the remaining obstacles which are the heritage of capitalistic exploitation must be removed, and labor must join management in understanding that the public which pays is the public to be served, and simple justice is the right and will continue to be the right for all of the people."

While perhaps not quite as important as railroads, highways were also an integral part of the transportation industry. The principle of federal aid to state highways had been established in 1916 but not pursued vigorously because of the war. The "large federal outlay demands a Federal voice in the program of expenditure," Harding stated. "Congress cannot justify a mere gift from the Federal purse to the several States, to be prorated among counties for road betterment. Such a course will invite abuses which it were better to guard against in the beginning." In conjunction with his plan for the federal government to oversee highway construction, Harding realized that highway maintenance was an equally important part of any well-developed road program. The president was distressed by the waste of millions on highways because there was no maintenance policy. Therefore, he recommended that all future federal funding for highways be tied to an adequate maintenance program.

The American merchant marine was identified as another problem area for the United States. "It is not necessary to say it to Congress," Harding noted, "but I thought this to be a fitting occasion to give notice that the United States means to establish and maintain a great merchant marine." He argued that "our differences of opinions as to a policy of upbuilding have been removed by the outstanding fact of our having builded." The merchant fleet was a fact, and in his opinion it was necessary to coordinate the enormous fleet produced during the war with the various forms of inland transportation. Harding believed America would be strengthened by a strong merchant marine, "because carrying is second only to production in establishing and maintaining the flow of commerce to which we rightfully aspire."

It was equally important, according to Harding, to regulate radio and cable communication systems. Because of strategic, commercial, and political considerations, he wanted to encourage the development of American-owned cable and radio services. He was particularly interested in creating facilities for adequate press coverage of the world. For practical reasons, it would be necessary to license radio stations, as well as cable systems. This would ensure orderly development of the air waves and would protect "American interests."

Another technological advance that Harding felt compelled to encourage was civil and military aviation. He was particularly interested in civilian development of aviation, which would relieve the government of a potentially expensive undertaking. With the increase in aircraft, it would be necessary to regulate air traffic; and he recommended setting up a bureau in the Department of Commerce for that purpose. Military personnel would be used, along with personnel of other agencies of the government, to establish national airways and landing fields in cooperation with the states.

Turning to social concerns, Harding noted that the World War had added enormously to the number of veterans in the United States. He was deeply concerned with the plight of soldiers injured in the war. Since the veterans faced a bewildering number of agencies in the federal bureaucracy, Harding recommended that a veterans bureau be established to bring together the conflicting agencies in one unit. In this manner, the veterans would receive more effective aid from the country for which they had made many sacrifices.

In the same vein, Harding discussed other social issues, recommending that a department of public welfare be established. This agency would be charged with coordinating government activities in "education, public health, sanitation, conditions of workers in industry, child welfare, proper amusement and recreation, the elimination of social vice," and other functions. By bringing together the numerous agencies dealing with these concerns, Harding argued that "increased effectiveness, economy, and intelligence of direction" would result. Harding demonstrated some concern for the racial difficulties in the country, declaring that "Congress ought to wipe the stain of barbaric lynching from the banners of a free and orderly, representative democracy." He thought progress could be made by the creation of a biracial commission to study the question of racial adjustment, and he was convinced that in "mutual tolerance, understanding, charity, recognition of the interdependence of the races, and the maintenance of the rights of citizenship lies the road to righteous adjustment."

The remainder of Harding's address was devoted to defense spending and foreign relations. He believed that the defense establishment should be reduced to the minimum necessary for national security. In foreign relations, he argued for a formal end to the war with Germany and made clear that his administration wished the League of Nations well but would not take a role in the endeavor.

Conspicuously absent from his address was any well–thought-out program to deal with the agricultural crisis in particular and the deepening economic depression in general. It was Harding's belief that these matters would be adjusted naturally, without substantial government interference. The government could best aid the situation by cutting taxes, limiting expenditures, and providing tariff protection. Reducing, not enhancing, the government's role in the economy was the goal. The government's responsibility was to aid business rather than shackle it by federal regulations. Competition and nature would ultimately solve the major economic problems facing the nation. Harding was sincere in his desire to have less government in business as well as more business in government.

This, the unspoken part of his message to Congress, became the basis for the Harding administration's policy in domestic matters.

So Harding laid his suggestions before Congress. The new president—to the surprise of many—did not sit back and allow Congress to dictate a program. Instead, in what was probably his best presidential speech, he presented a comprehensive program to Congress. But, given his conception of the presidency, Harding was unwilling to provide executive leadership and guidance for Congress. It was not his place to cajole Congress, to force it down the path of priorities he had established. Congress, in Harding's opinion, was its own master, and only with great reluctance would Harding attempt to intervene in congressional affairs.

II

The Sixty-seventh Congress, which met for the first time on April 11, 1921, was overwhelmingly Republican. The House seated 303 Republicans out of 435, the largest majority in party history. This group, however, lacked cohesiveness. Ninety Republican congressmen had not served in the Sixty-sixth Congress, and many owed election to local issues. These first-termers were not disciplined. The only thing they had in common was that they had defeated Democrats. The Republican majority in the Senate was equally awesome, fifty-nine Republicans facing thirty-seven Democrats. Despite these majorities the Republicans often found it difficult to work together. Republican unity during the Sixty-seventh Congress seemed to suffer because of the surplus of Republicans, and the party was not nearly as effective as during the preceding Congress.[4]

Harding's conception of executive-congressional relations contributed to the lack of Republican unity. He believed it was the duty of the party leadership to push his program through Congress; his own role was slight. Harding preferred that Congress work out details of legislation, with the aid of cabinet officers. He believed, at least at the beginning of his presidency, that it was not the executive's place to propose legislation; broad outlines of policy, yes, but providing the details of the program was the business of Congress. But the old guard leadership, which emphasized probusiness policies, was not up to such a task. Henry Cabot Lodge's prestige had been damaged during the battle over the League. Boies Penrose and Philander C. Knox, long powerful in Senate affairs, were both ill and would die before the end of the year. Eleven Republican "irreconcilables" remained in the Senate and were as obdurate as ever, refusing any measure that hinted at altering their nationalistic stand. The House also lacked leadership, and Republican dissidents were numerous. Increasingly independent Republican representatives from large metropolitan areas were making their presence felt. Perhaps the most divisive element in Congress was the emerging farm bloc, led by two Republicans from Iowa, Senator William S. Kenyon and Representative Lester J. Dickinson. These men brought together a coalition from the South and Midwest which cut across party lines. On important issues they held the votes. Consequently, the large Republican majorities had little meaning on many important issues.[5] Congress was factionalized; there was little party unity.

Even with these disabilities, Congress was able to act on three issues left from the Wilson administration—an emergency tariff, immigration restrictions, and budget procedures. Wilson had disliked immigration restriction and had let a bill pertaining to it die with a pocket veto. The Democratic president had been hostile to high tariffs and had sent an emergency tariff measure back to Congress with detailed objections. He had vetoed the budget bill in June 1920 because of a constitutional question. All these items were revived in the special session of the Sixty-seventh Congress.

Nativism was certainly not new in the United States, but in the postwar era it took on new dimensions. Many southern Europeans had come to the United States shortly before World War I. To many Americans these people were strange, even dangerous. The new immigrants seemed unwilling to accept American ways, and some had trouble learning rudimentary English. Pressure for conformity had been enormous during the war, with so-called hyphenate Americans suspected of anti-American activities and placed under close watch. The Red Scare heightened fears concerning these new citizens. They were often viewed as socialists or, even worse, Bolsheviks. Many people argued that the influx of these groups had to be stopped. Anglo-Saxon immigrants were acceptable, but Italians, Jews, Slavs, Russians, Orientals, and others were considered dangerous.

The new immigration bill was clearly a stopgap; its passage took only four hours, and Harding signed it on May 19, 1921. Even though the House sponsor, Representative Albert Johnson of Washington, would have preferred that all immigrants be excluded, immigration quotas were established at 3 percent of a country's nationals residing in the United States in 1910. The law discriminated against people from southern and southeastern Europe and cut immigration from over 800,000 in 1920 to slightly more than 300,000 in 1922. Refinement of the act had to wait until 1924, when new legislation excluded some nonwhites from the United States, to the particular distress of Japan.

Republican leaders turned to an emergency tariff. The collapse of farm prices in 1920 had created intense pressure for relief. Agriculture had been the first sector of European economies to recover from the war, and that recovery contributed to the collapse of American agriculture. The farmer could see his equity vanishing while country banks were failing. For this reason, as well as the need for unity within the party, the Republicans had to act. The farmers were demanding higher tariffs on raw and processed foodstuffs. In the face of stiff competition in citrus fruits from Italy and Spain, the California Fruit Growers Exchange called for a tariff of two cents a pound for lemons. This request, along with others, was incorporated into emergency legislation. Not every sector of agriculture benefited from this protection, with American fruit growers probably gaining most from the tariff.

The emergency tariff was more than an attempt to alleviate the woes of thousands of failing farmers. Industry sought and received protection. Some American manufacturers feared that European industry would dump products on the American market because of Europe's need for exchange. An antidumping clause was added to the increased agricultural duties. Industries using foreign patents, acquired by Americans through the Alien Property Custodian, also sought protection. Dyestuffs, explosives, and coal-tar derivatives were excluded from the American market. The emergency tariff was signed by Harding on May 27, with a provision that it would extend for only six months, time to allow Congress to prepare a permanent tariff.

Congress turned to budget procedure. While Harding wanted to reduce expenditures, the idea of a federal budget system was not original with him. "The pressure for the adoption of an orderly procedure in the expenditure of public money was essentially not political." Indeed, "it did not originate among politicians, and although it met with less open resistance from them than did the earlier movement for civil service reform they accepted it without full devotion or understanding."[6] The first president to recommend a system to Congress was William H. Taft. During the Wilson administration, businessmen and economists became proponents of a system. The shift from duties on imports to income taxes as the

61

source of federal funding made those who paid the heaviest taxes more interested in an economic way to run the government. Because of heavy deficit spending during the war, the idea gained support, and by 1920 both political parties endorsed the idea.

Congress had sole authority to raise and appropriate money under the Constitution. By 1885 most attempts to keep a balance between receipts and expenditures—the job of the House of Representatives' Committee on Ways and Means—had failed; happily, in the half century following the Civil War, receipts ran far ahead of expenditures. Government departments and bureaus lobbied Congress in their own interest, with little or no executive coordination. But even Congress was ready for reform by the time of the Harding administration.

On June 10, 1921, Harding signed the Budget and Accounting Act, which provided for two agencies—the General Accounting Office and the Bureau of the Budget. The General Accounting Office was intended to be the congressional watchdog to ensure that public funds were not mishandled. It was headed by a comptroller general, who was appointed to a fifteen-year term to free him from political pressure. He was subject to removal only by joint resolution. The Bureau of the Budget was part of the executive branch, reporting to the president. The budget director was not to take instruction from cabinet officers but only from the president, which gave the director the authority to plan a responsible budget without constant interference. The Senate and House placed sole authority to present bills calling for expenditures in the respective committees on appropriations, while leaving responsibility for revenue bills in the House Committee on Ways and Means and the Senate Finance Committee.

Congress retained the power to control the direction of financial policy. But as time passed it became evident that a new, nonpolitical arbiter of financial policy had been created in the Bureau of the Budget. To secure appropriations an advocate first had to secure approval of the director of the budget to get an estimate into the budget. Once approval was gained and funds appropriated, the General Accounting Office ensured compliance through authorization before an expenditure could be made, as well as by audits afterwards. This procedure placed the finances of the government on a more sensible basis.

Harding turned to Charles G. Dawes as his first director of the budget. Earlier Dawes had turned down appointment as secretary of the treasury, but the Chicagoan agreed to take the budget post for one year on condition that Harding would support him in attempts to economize in government and rationalize federal expenditures. Dawes's first act was to explain his detailed concepts to the cabinet. He made clear that he was concerned with mundane affairs of day-to-day government; his bureau was not concerned with policy except when it involved economy and efficiency. Dawes realized that without the cooperation of government bureau chiefs his efforts would be for naught. So one of his first recommendations was that a system of promotions and salary increases be instituted for bureau chiefs who were economizers. With Harding's blessing Dawes called a meeting of bureau chiefs. Over 1,200 people trooped into the Department of the Interior auditorium, including the president and cabinet, to hear Dawes lecture in soft tones on the necessity of economy and efficiency. At a second meeting of similar size Dawes demonstrated his well-known acerbic qualities. He made known his irritation with the practice of the army selling surpluses for low prices to contractors who in turn sold the same items to the navy at inflated prices. Brandishing two brooms above his head he rasped: "This may look like a stage play, but it is not, because things like this have got to stop. Here is a Navy broom made in accordance with Navy specifications. Here is an Army broom made in accordance with Army specifications. Now, the Army had 350,000 of these brooms surplus. The Navy needed 18,000 brooms. It could have had the Army brooms for nothing but, because they were wrapped with twine instead of wire, the Navy wouldn't take them as a gift. So the Navy went into the market and bought brooms at top prices." Such practices would no longer be tolerated. He pointed out that in the business community the "mere knowledge of it in the body of a business organization would drive the guilty man out of his position in disgrace." There is no record of the fate of the naval officer involved in the Great Broom Fiasco.

Even though appropriations for fiscal 1921–1922 were to go into effect within a week after he took office, Dawes made an effort to prepare a new budget that reduced expenditures below the authorized level. Bringing in such former army associates as Colonel Henry C. Smithers, designated coordinator general, the new budget director slashed everything in reach. The navy was forced to return over $100,000,000, while the Agriculture Department found itself shorn of over $25,000,000. While Dawes perhaps underestimated the stubbornness and guile of bureau chiefs in resisting reform, he achieved notable success in his efforts to bring economy and efficiency to the government. In December 1921, Harding was able to present Congress with the first complete federal budget for fiscal 1922–1923. An estimate of $3,505,754,727 was set before Congress; when the books closed on that year in 1923, there was an unspent surplus. Dawes saved the government well over one billion dollars in his attempts at retrenchment. On leaving office in June 1922 he noted: "I am carrying back as souvenirs of this experience the handwritten pasteboard sign in the office door: 'Bureau of the Budget,' and two brooms. I wish I could take back some of the secondhand furniture which we raked up in the Treasury cellars. One cannot successfully preach economy without practicing it. Of the appropriation of $225,000, we spent only $120,313.54 in the year's work. We took our own medicine."[7] Harding's desire to bring a businesslike approach to government was carried out through the Bureau of the Budget, and the system remained in effect throughout the 1920s.

III

Congress's fast action on immigration, a tariff, and the federal budget did not head off trouble between the administration and Capitol Hill. Differences appeared quickly. Harding's commitment to economy in government led him into one of his more persistent debates with Congress. In July 1921 the Senate, because of inability to agree on other problems, decided to consider a soldiers bonus. While the soldiers who fought in the World War were paid better than their compatriots from other nations, their wages were not anywhere near those paid to workers fortunate enough to stay home. With postwar unemployment, there was intense pressure to redress the balance through a bonus. The bill in the Senate proposed a bonus of $1.00 a day for service during the war ($1.25 if overseas). Money was to be paid out in quarterly installments of $50.00 or commuted to an insurance policy with a face value of 40 percent above the balance due. The estimated cost of such a program was enormous—several billion dollars.

This program alarmed Harding, who saw that it would shatter all attempts at budget reduction and debt repayment and that it would increase the national debt. The administration began a campaign to kill the legislation. On July 6, 1921, Secretary of the Treasury Mellon sent a letter to the Senate asking that consideration be deferred until tax reduction had been settled. Lunching with his former colleagues on Capitol Hill the next day (a practice

Harding carried out throughout his presidency as a means of maintaining contact with Congress), the president requested that the bonus bill be delayed and informed senators that he would soon address them on the subject. In an uncharacteristic move he attempted to intervene directly in the affairs of Congress by personally delivering his message to the Senate on July 12, 1921. The president scolded Congress for slowness on tax reduction and made it clear that tax revision should be the Congress's first priority. While expressing sympathy with the veterans, he stated his fear that a bonus would be a financial disaster. "We may rely on the sacrifices of patriotism in war," he advised, "but to-day we face markets, and the effects of supply and demand, and the inexorable laws of credits in time of peace. . . . A modest offering to the millions of service men is a poor palliative to more millions who may be out of employment."[8] Harding was against subsidizing individuals, no matter what the disguise. His campaign proved successful, at least to the extent that the bill was recommitted to committee by the Senate on July 15. The issue was not dead and was to cause the president great trouble before the congressional elections of 1922.

The demand for adjusted compensation for veterans was sometimes confused with the attempt to bring together the bewildering number of federal agencies handling veterans affairs, a matter over which there was no controversy between the administration and Congress. Dawes had chaired a commission in the spring of 1921 which recommended that agencies dealing with veterans during and after the war be under one bureau. A senator called the conflicting agencies "a sort of fungus growth upon other acts which had already been put into effect."[9] The law to provide soldiers with insurance was supervised by the Bureau of War Risk Insurance, created to insure merchant vessels against war damage. The bureau was attached to the Treasury Department, and its new mandate meant it had to establish records on every person in the military, based on files in the Adjutant General's Office. Responsibility for hospital care was centered in another bureau in the Treasury Department, the Public Health Service, which had been created to prevent persons with contagious diseases from entering the United States. Retraining and rehabilitating soldiers was vested in the Federal Board of Vocational Education, established in 1917 to help young people prepare for a productive future. While the confusion of divided responsibility was probably no worse than in the rest of the government, Congress was willing to deal with this problem because of the sacrifices the veterans had made for their country.

Harding signed the Sweet Act on August 9, 1921, which created the Veterans Bureau, made it responsible to the president, and gave it control of the agencies dealing with veterans affairs. Harding appointed Charles R. Forbes, chief of the Bureau of War Risk Insurance, as head of the new agency. One of Forbes's first duties was to organize a hospital system across the country to treat veterans. The resulting fiasco was to haunt Harding. Shortly before his death, Harding appointed another head of the Veterans Bureau, General Frank T. Hines, who was charged with straightening out the mess left by Forbes. Hines fulfilled his duties admirably.

Another source of discord during Harding's presidency was, as mentioned, the farm bloc, the loose amalgam of senators and representatives from the Midwest and South led by Senator Kenyon and Representative Dickinson. Kenyon was an able parliamentarian and floor manager and could count on between twenty and twenty-five votes in the Senate, while Dickinson controlled a hundred votes in the House. This bloc primarily promoted agricultural interests. The bloc made a shambles of hoped-for Republican dominance of Congress. Faced with the worsening crisis in agriculture, the bloc's members demanded action. The bloc was not satisfied with the emergency tariff. This group had the power to bring Congress to a standstill if the administration refused to meet at least some of its demands for relief. Secretary of Agriculture Wallace proved to be an able proponent of the farm bloc in the cabinet. Much to the distress of Secretary of the Treasury Mellon, Wallace argued that relief measures should take precedence over reduction in taxes. This was the kind of dispute that made Harding intensely uncomfortable, as both secretaries sought his support. The scales were tipped in Wallace's favor because of the power of the bloc.

Shortly after the special session of Congress convened, a concurrent resolution was introduced to create a committee to investigate the worsening agrarian crisis. Approved on June 7, 1921, the Joint Commission on Agriculture Inquiry was to include members of the House and Senate to be appointed by the president. Harding's appointees, largely from the farm bloc, held hearings in July and August to gather background information. Though originally limited to a ninety-day inquiry, the commission was unable to make its first report until January 23, 1922. The commission made three more reports, finally winding up its business in 1923. Recommendations stressed the need for farm cooperatives, more credit, freight rate reductions, increased agricultural research, better wholesale facilities, and improved roads to move products to market. These efforts, however, would be time consuming and were not enough for the impatient farmers. They wanted more immediate action.

To Harding's dismay it became obvious that he would have to scrap the administration's priorities or face the wrath of the farm bloc. The extent of the bloc's power was revealed when Lodge's motion to adjourn the Senate for a month starting July 5 was defeated by bloc senators, who were not interested in a vacation while thousands of farms were failing. The idea behind the motion for adjournment was that time was needed to prepare tax reforms as well as a permanent tariff. Farm bills were then near completion, and the farm bloc was not in a conciliatory frame of mind. It had pushed through an amendment to the Farm Loan Act which became effective July 1, 1921. Mellon had opposed the amendment as "not sound in principle," though he conceded that some relief was necessary. The amendment passed. It provided for more capital for federal land banks, which enabled farmers to overcome some of their short-term financial problems by increasing mortgage indebtedness. Still, the amendment meant only marginal relief to farmers, and the farm bloc wanted much more.[10]

If the administration desired tax reduction, it first would have to grant agricultural relief. Harding was forced to reconsider his priorities, if in fact farm relief was ever part of his program. In a meeting with farm-bloc leaders, arranged by Wallace in early July after failure of the plan to adjourn the Senate, the president agreed to relief. The bloc agreed to adjournment, but only after legislation for farm relief was passed. A further amendment to the Farm Loan Act on August 13, 1921, increased the interest on Farm Loan Bonds from 5 to 5.5 percent to investors, leaving the interest paid by farmers unchanged. In combination with the earlier amendment, long-term credit became more easily available. The Packers and Stockyards Act, signed on August 15, 1921, enabled the secretary of agriculture to provide modest supervision over packers. The act made it more difficult for interstate packers to control prices paid to farmers. The bill did not provide for controls on refrigerator cars and cold-storage plants, and it excluded licensing procedures for the packers. But rural America viewed it as a step in the right direction.

A more complex and controversial measure dealt with the speculative grain trade. Farmers long had viewed that trade as part of a conspiracy to deprive them of their rewards, and to a certain extent they were right. Hearings in Congress brought out that the grain trade was a complicated business involving such terms as "futures," "short-selling," "puts and calls," "bids," and "takes." "The narrow agrarian view was that the grain market was a haven for 'hordes of parasites,' who sold and resold grain, each time adding to its price after it had left the farms, and engaging in price manipulations."[11] On August 24, 1921, Harding approved the Capper-Tincher Grain Futures Act (Futures Trading Act), which placed a prohibitive tax of twenty cents per bushel on grain sold for future delivery unless the grain was owned by the farmer or producer. This method of regulating futures-trading in grain came under attack in the courts and was invalidated by the Supreme Court nine months later. It was replaced in September 1922 by the Grain Futures Act which based regulation on the interstate commerce clause.

All was not unity in the farm bloc. The fate of the Norris Farm Relief bill demonstrated that. The senator from Nebraska was more liberal than many of his Republican agrarian colleagues. As chairman of the Senate Committee on Agriculture and Forestry, he wanted a public export corporation capitalized at $100,000,000 to purchase farm surpluses for cash and sell them overseas on extended credit. The plan was a roundabout way of providing price supports for farmers. This plan received widespread support in agriculture but was opposed by individuals within the administration, especially Mellon. Wallace opposed the bill because it would have involved the government directly in business and, perhaps more important, because it would have made the secretary of commerce chairman of the export corporation. After testing the wind Hoover opposed the bill because of proposed government involvement in business. An alternative had to be developed quickly by the administration or there was danger that the farm bloc would force Norris's proposal through.

The result was that Senator Frank B. Kellogg from Minnesota, a mild member of the farm bloc, on July 26, 1921, substituted the Meyer-Hoover Bill for the Norris measure in a complicated parliamentary maneuver. The substitute bill used the existing War Finance Corporation to carry the credit needs of farmers, while extending credits to exporters of farm products. Norris was enraged, launching a three-day tirade on the floor of the Senate that ended only with his collapse from exhaustion. He pointed out that the War Finance Corporation also put the government into business, but "the Government is all right in business if the middleman and the banker and the trust company can get their rake-off. If they are eliminated it is a crime . . . it is populistic."[12] This bitter attack was to no avail, and Harding on August 24 signed the Meyer-Hoover Bill (Emergency Agricultural Credits Act), splintering the farm bloc on this measure.

The bloc nonetheless had forced the administration to consider farm relief before tax revision. Harding was sympathetic to the farmer and generally took the advice of his secretary of agriculture. The president was uncomfortable with much of the proposed legislation, and only political reality caused him to support farm relief. Harding's ordeal with the bloc was not over. He was able to blunt the bloc, however, by appointing Kenyon to a federal judgeship. Kenyon was replaced as leader of the Senate farm bloc by Arthur Capper from Kansas, an able publicist who had little of the skill of Kenyon in managing bills on the Senate floor. Even so, the bloc remained a force throughout Harding's tenure.

The farm problem extended into Harding's cabinet and became the basis of a prolonged struggle between Wallace and Hoover. The problem was largely prices, distribution, and markets, and a clash between a strong secretary of agriculture and a strong secretary of commerce was almost inevitable. Farming was changing from a way of life to a business, and farmers were demanding more government attention. The farm industry in the postwar world required expanded government services, and the extensive commercial aspects of agriculture created problems of department jurisdiction. Hoover and Wallace were interested in providing increased services. Both were expanding their departments, and much time and energy were consumed in a clash of personalities. Harding was not the type of person to intervene in such a dispute, and it lasted much longer than necessary, ending only with Wallace's death in 1924. In the beginning Harding tended to lean toward Wallace, probably because Wallace was a golfing, drinking, and poker companion, a fact the secretary of agriculture exploited to his advantage. But Hoover was a crafty bureaucratic enemy, as Wallace discovered.[13] Hoover's appointment had been well received by the farm bloc. The secretary of commerce began to build his small department into a giant agency charged with rationalizing American business. Securing considerable autonomy from Harding, Hoover pushed his department to the limit of its authority and beyond, and ultimately Harding came to rely on his secretary of commerce. In a short time Hoover developed an extensive information service and was bringing in top business talent to administer the many new programs initiated to assist business. Julius Klein, a professor of Latin American history and economics at Harvard, was appointed director of the Bureau of Foreign and Domestic Commerce, while Christian Herter, many years later secretary of state in the Eisenhower administration, was placed in charge of publicity. Commerce expanded its employees, as well as its appropriations. Hoover's department was acquisitive, taking over the Bureau of Custom Statistics from the Treasury Department and lifting the Mines and Patents Office from the Department of the Interior. Hoover was quick to justify such actions on the ground that he was aiding business and industry, the principal aim of government in the Harding administration. But Hoover's bureaucratic imperialism brought him into conflict with another expanding department, provoking a long-term cabinet wrangle.

Wallace believed Hoover was "stuffy" and "opinionated" as well as too quick to argue over minuscule points. Hoover's never-ceasing raids on the Department of Agriculture gave Wallace cause to dislike his fellow cabinet member. But the dispute between Wallace and Hoover was more than personal and territorial; it was philosophical. The secretary of commerce opposed subsidies for farmers. As the agrarian crisis deepened, Wallace was inclined toward subsidies. Hoover opposed Wallace's attempts to lower railway freight rates for farm products because Hoover believed that such plans would injure business. Both secretaries believed in more efficient, scientific farming. Which agency was to provide such expertise was another matter. Hoover perhaps had a broader notion about modern agriculture, seeing it as a part of the economy rather than the major national enterprise. But he could not match Wallace's ability to articulate the needs of the farmer. In the end Wallace perhaps proved to be the more perceptive observer.[14] Whoever the winner in the Hoover-Wallace struggle, and no matter what the outcome of the battle between the farm bloc and the administration, agricultural policy remained an issue of contention between 1921 and 1923.

Yet another source of contention was tax reform. Business, represented by Mellon and Hoover, maintained that tax reductions were necessary to restore the economy. When Mellon became secretary of the treasury, he resigned from directorships in over sixty corporations with an aggregate wealth of more than two billion dollars. He understood the views of business and was listened to in the cabinet with deference. Harding accepted Mellon's views, as he had respect for wealth and social position. Even Hoover was cowed by Mellon. The secretary of the treasury pushed to end a legacy of the war—the excess profits tax. He wanted to reduce the maximum surtax from 65 to 32 percent. Surtax levels started at 1 percent on income in excess of $5,000, increasing to 65 percent on incomes of $1,000,000 or more. Mellon believed that as much capital as possible should be in the hands of the wealthy, because these people were the main risk-takers in society. They provided for expansion of the economy, which would result in an increase in jobs for the less fortunate. Mellon contended that the general tax-rate levels of 4 percent on incomes under $4,000 and 8 percent on the remainder should be unchanged. And Mellon proposed that the corporate tax of 10 percent should be lowered. To recover lost revenue the secretary suggested doubling the tax stamp on documents, placing a two cent tax on bank checks, increasing the price of postal cards, and placing a federal tax on automobiles. He argued that as a result of high surtax rates the wealthy were putting money into tax-exempt, "safe" investments, not taking risks needed to aid recovery. In short, Mellon believed that middle- and low-income people in the United States should bear a disproportionate share of the cost of government and that the rich should not be penalized because they were wealthy. Mellon pushed this philosophy with a vengeance. The House Ways and Means Committee substantially supported Mellon's view in its tax bill, though dissidents forced a 12.5 percent corporate tax, rather than a reduction, and increased tax exemptions for lower-income families, as well as raising personal exemptions. Even so, the Ways and Means bill created a furor when it reached the House floor, with Democrats —and even a few Republicans—making dire predictions about corporations gaining control of the country. It was passed on to the Senate, despite the protests.

In the Senate the bill for tax reduction became entangled with the farm bloc and the soldiers' bonus bill. Harding understood little about the tax issue, confiding to his secretary, Judson Welliver, "I can't make a damn thing out of this tax problem. I listen to one side, and they seem right, and then—God!—I talk to the other side, and they seem just as right."[15] Lack of understanding did not prevent him from scolding the Senate on July 12, 1921, for inaction on tax reduction, or from supporting Mellon's position. When the Senate took up the tax-reform measure in September, there were arguments within the Finance Committee. Senator Penrose, suffering from cancer, made the tax bill his final crusade and acted as Mellon's spokesman. He ruthlessly defended the bill, and ultimately his committee endorsed the House bill. The only real defeat for Mellon and Penrose was retention of a House compromise to retain the excess profits tax until January 1, 1922.

Once the bill reached the Senate floor it sparked acrimonious debate. The attack was led by Democrats, but many Republican farm-bloc members sided with them. The bloc viewed the tax bill as another attempt by large business interests to discriminate against rural sectors of the country. The Senate passed the bill on November 7, 1921, the chief difference between the Senate and House versions being that the House accepted Mellon's surtax rate (32 percent) while the Senate imposed a surtax of 50 percent. Harding agreed to a compromise of 40 percent, but in a surprise move the House reversed itself and accepted the Senate version, probably an indication of unhappiness with Mellon's tax rates. This reversal on surtax rates could not conceal the Republican bias toward the rich. Harding signed the Revenue Act of 1921 on November 23, providing substantial tax savings for the wealthy.

The act ended the special session of the Sixty-seventh Congress. Because of the power of the farm bloc, Congress accepted some farm relief. Generally, Congress in special session had followed the proposals of the administration. It had adopted a tax reduction on terms generally acceptable to business. Additionally, Congress had restricted immigration, established a Veterans Bureau, and provided for a national budget, though it had failed to agree on a permanent tariff. The probusiness orientation of the administration and most of Congress had been obvious. Progressivism, at least in the government, appeared dead in Washington in 1921.

In the long run, the administration's tax and economic policies proved ill considered. Normalcy, as Harding called it, consisted of prewar solutions to postwar problems. Harding wanted to return the country to an earlier era. The tax cuts, along with the emphasis on repayment of the national debt and reduced federal expenditures, combined to favor the rich. Many economists came to agree that one of the chief causes of the Great Depression of 1929 was the unequal distribution of wealth, which appeared to accelerate during the 1920s, and which was a result of the return to normalcy. Five percent of the population had more than 33 percent of the nation's wealth by 1929. This group failed to use its wealth responsibly, as Mellon had maintained they would. Instead, they fueled unhealthy speculation on the stock market as well as uneven economic growth. Consequently, normalcy, with its probusiness orientation, planted at least some of the seeds for an economic disaster of unheard-of dimensions.[16]

IV

The contention and disunity of the special session continued through the Sixty-seventh Congress, and the tariff issue did little to better relations with the administration. The emergency tariff signed by Harding in 1921 had a six-month limit, so action was necessary. Tariff bills originated in the House, and it became the responsibility of Joseph W. Fordney, chairman of the Committee on Ways and Means, to initiate discussion of the tariff. He held a series of public hearings, followed by secret meetings from which Democrats were excluded. By the end of June 1921 Fordney had a bill ready for the floor. The bill was protected from revisions by a voting deadline and a limit to amendments that could be attached. The House version passed on July 21, 1921, but the procedure had left many congressmen unhappy.

The Senate stood in contrast to rapid House action. It was not until April 11, 1922, that a bill was reported out of the Committee on Finance, now under Porter J. McCumber of North Dakota, who had succeeded Penrose. Business had bombarded both the administration and Congress with protectionist arguments. The Senate version included more than two thousand amendments to the House bill, mostly calling for stronger tariff protection. Debates over the tariff in the Senate were long and often bitter. The farm-bloc members argued against the embargo on dyes and chemicals, industries created from "captured" German patents, because of their belief that imported dyes and chemicals would lower prices of these products on agrarian markets. Ultimately the bloc accepted the embargo because the bill reflected the tariff schedule agriculture desired. When the bill passed the Senate by a vote of 48 to 25 on August 19, 1922, only two Republicans opposed it. Democrats were not against protection, but their negative votes resulted because of details of the act. Tariff schedules had been debated, but the Democrats were probably as protectionist-minded as their Republican antagonists.

The House-Senate conference committee was a welter of interest groups, all scrambling for preferential treatment. Businessmen brought intense pressure for action to give them the best treatment possible. Agricultural interests, in particular, resented this seemingly preferential treatment and demanded equal consideration.

Senator Kellogg complained that such high rates for industry would be resented in rural areas of Minnesota, possibly affecting his re-election—to which Representative Fordney reportedly commented: "Well, I would rather see the Senate lose you than American industry suffer."[17] When the conference measure was reported to the House, there was much dissatisfaction with it. John N. Garner, Democrat from Texas, enlivened the debate by playing off Republican industrialists against rural elements of the party. He succeeded in recommitting the bill to committee, which placed potash on the free list and eliminated the embargo on dyestuffs and chemicals, because the duties on imports accomplished the same purpose. After these successes, Garner tried to recommit the bill again but the Republicans regrouped and overwhelmed him and his tactics.

After months of debate among interest groups, the bill passed both House and Senate, and Harding signed the Fordney-McCumber Tariff on September 21, 1922. The act included a provision that allowed the president some discretion in establishing the tariff. The president could raise or lower rates by as much as 50 percent, if deemed necessary. The Tariff Commission, headed by a protectionist, was to provide information to guide the president in applying the sliding tariff scale. This feature failed in practice, and Harding and Coolidge together made only thirty-seven tariff changes, of which thirty-two resulted in higher rates.[18]

The Fordney-McCumber Tariff was one of the highest in American history; little more could have been provided for American industry in the way of protection. Harding had made known his feelings about high tariffs in his inaugural address, and generally Republicans and Democrats believed in protectionist policies. There is little doubt that the tariff was ill-considered. It wrought havoc in international commerce and made the repayment of war debts more difficult. Harding, his administration, and members of Congress apparently did not understand the damage their tariff policies would do to world commerce. Harding believed his policies were a necessary part of his campaign pledge to aid business. American business was at stake, and a high tariff seemed the best remedy. The Coolidge and Hoover administrations continued such practices.

Although the tariff took up most of the Senate's time during 1922, Harding sought to push subsidies for the merchant marine through Congress, albeit unsuccessfully. In 1920 the Merchant Marine Act had been passed to straighten out wartime chaos in the maritime industry by strengthening the Shipping Board created in

1917. Little could be done to implement the act because Wilson's appointees to the Shipping Board were not confirmed by the Senate. After considering several candidates Harding finally settled on Albert D. Lasker, a Chicago advertising executive who had done extensive publicity for the Republican party in 1920. Lasker knew little, if anything, about shipping, but he was an able advertiser and a first-rate executive. His most immediate problem was the more than one thousand vessels acquired by the government during the course of the war. How could the government get out of shipping? Harding realized that Lasker faced difficulties, writing him, "To be honest about it, I have doubts about whether anybody who gets on the Shipping Board is entitled to congratulations, because you have now got tangled up with the 'damndest' job in the world."

Lasker faced a problem of magnitude. He employed the best legal and shipping talent he could find, offering salaries as high as $25,000 a year. At the same time he was drastically reducing the Shipping Board's staff. He began the tedious process of examining contracts between the previous board and private industry, finding some of them "the most shameful piece of chicane, inefficiency, and of looting of the Public Treasury that the human mind can devise."[19] Lasker must have been embarrassed when his first attempt to reduce the government inventory of ships in August 1921 brought only $430,500 for 205 wooden ships, less than it cost the government to build one of the vessels. Such sales invoked heavy criticism of the Shipping Board in Congress, particularly from farm-bloc members. Lasker's problems were accentuated by the business depression which hit the maritime industry hard. It became all the more difficult to reduce the large operational deficit caused by maintaining the fleet of government vessels. There were few buyers for government ships, even at greatly reduced prices. Such ships cost more to run than privately owned vessels, and foreign-owned ships could be operated more cheaply than both. The result was a Shipping Board deficit of fifteen million dollars a month. Lasker tried to make travel attractive on American-owned passenger ships by offering first-run movies, unlimited caviar, free golf balls to practice drive into the sea, and well-known entertainers. All these features failed to make up for prohibition, which prevented the sale of liquor on government-run vessels.

With no positive results to their efforts, the Shipping Board and Lasker were coming under heavy criticism by the autumn of 1921. The board's fleet was still in existence, with its heavy operating deficit. Despite Lasker's desire to end government involvement in shipping, he seemed to be involving the government more heavily, particularly in passenger travel. Though there appeared no clear-cut decision regarding shipping, Harding supported Lasker publicly, maintaining that the problem would take time to solve. At the same time, he placed pressure on Lasker to produce a solution. The head of the Shipping Board became a frequent visitor at the White House for consultation with the president. Because of these conferences Lasker was later to claim that "the ship subsidy plan, from beginning to end, was President Harding's personal plan."[20] The claim was probably overdrawn. But Harding did believe that a strong merchant marine was a necessity for reasons of defense as well as for the strength and for the well-being of business. The president had made his opinions known on the need for a merchant marine.

Lasker and Harding concluded that the only solution to the problem was to provide direct subsidies to private shippers at an annual cost of around thirty million dollars.[21] Harding unfolded his ship subsidy plan in a special message to Congress on February 28, 1922. He reminded Congress that "we have voiced our concern for the good fortunes of agriculture, and it is right that we should. We have long proclaimed our interest in manufacturing, which is thoroughly sound, and helped to make us what we are. . . . But we have ignored our merchant marine. The World War revealed our weakness, our unpreparedness for defense in war, our unreadiness for self-reliance in peace." He saw little difference between a ship subsidy bill and a tariff or limited aid to agriculture. He was surprised at the intense opposition to his proposals, especially by those people who charged that they were antiagriculture. While Hoover supported the bill, Wallace was troubled by it and had a running battle with Lasker over details. These proposals were different from the tariff or aid to agriculture, despite Harding's inability to see the difference. The president was proposing direct cash payments to private shipowners, while opposing any direct cash payment to farmers in need of relief or to soldiers who had fought the war. The farm bloc understood the similarity, even if Harding did not.

Harding and Lasker attempted to push the issue throughout the spring and early summer of 1922. Opposition in the House was intense, and Harding was continually warned by congressional leaders that insistence on the measure would split the Republican party in an election year. Even so, he wanted to force the issue. The president believed in his plan for a strong merchant marine, notwithstanding that sentiment in the Midwest was running heavily against a ship subsidy plan. Apparently Harding failed to understand that a shipping bill might contribute to the defeat of many Republican congressmen at the polls. They understood the ground swell of opinion, and Harding had to wait.

After the election, with disastrous losses for the Republican party, Harding appeared even more determined to force his merchant marine proposals through Congress. He convened a special session of the lame-duck Congress on November 20, 1922. Appearing before Congress the next day, he demanded action. Without a subsidy the United States would face a deficit of more than $150,000,000 a year, and more importantly, face loss of supremacy on the seas. In a thinly veiled criticism of the farm bloc, he commented: "Frankly I think it loftier statesmanship to support and commend a policy designed to effect the larger good of the nation than merely to record the too-hasty expressions of a constituency."[22] Harding's determination to force the bill through the special session of Congress succeeded in the House. On November 27 the House voted 208 to 184 for the bill, with Lasker keeping a list of Republicans who voted against the bill and were seeking favors from Harding. But time ran out on the special session, as the fourth and last session of the Sixty-seventh Congress met on December 4, 1922. The bill was soon entangled in other legislation in the Senate, and opponents used this to advantage. In February 1923 opponents began a filibuster that lasted more than five days. Harding had to capitulate. In private Harding was not a graceful loser, writing to Lasker that "it is a curious thing that men are almost universally opposed to a subsidy without realizing how many subsidies they are enjoying in the accepted things in government service."[23]

Why Harding had pushed so hard for the ship subsidy was open to question. His actions raised doubt about the president's political sagacity. Perhaps he believed his prestige was on the line because of his involvement in the plan. Also, he had stated in the April 1921 address that the carrying trade was the second most important business in the United States, behind industry, placing it in a position for preferential treatment. His persistence hurt his party in an election year, a time when Harding's well-known penchant for conciliation and compromise inexplicably disappeared. If Harding chose the issue of the ship subsidy to demonstrate political strength and ability, he decided upon a poor issue. Harding's attempt at strong executive leadership ended in failure. Eventually the United States government got out of the shipping business by

77

writing off its merchant fleet, and private business was left to carry the American colors in merchant and passenger shipping.

Although the tariff and ship subsidy bills occupied much of Congress's attention during 1922, the soldiers bonus continued to plague the administration. In July 1921 Harding had intervened to stop Senate consideration of the bonus; he hoped the measure would not be brought up again. The bill was revived early in December and received enthusiastically by both congressmen and senators. Republican legislators wanted to return home in an election year having approved a bonus measure for the veterans of the World War. It was apparent to many congressmen in marginal districts that their political future probably depended on such a bill.[24]

With Mellon's support, Harding again made plain that he would not accept a bonus that was not adequately financed. It is doubtful that Harding would have accepted an adequately financed bonus either, because it would have ruined his program of tax reduction. In 1922 the Republican Congress was determined to pass some bonus, even at presidential displeasure. Harding remained firm, and ultimately the House passed an unfunded bonus by a vote of 333 to 70. Senator McCumber took the measure under his wing, but his Senate committee failed to provide funding. McCumber solicited Harding's support on the ground that it was necessary to ensure the reelection of many Republicans. Harding was convinced the bill was unwise and continued to resist. Finally, the Senate in August passed its version of the bonus bill, and in conference the House and Senate versions were merged. On September 14, 1922, the House passed the measure by overwhelming vote in twenty-five minutes; next day the Senate passed the bill by a vote of 36 to 17. Many Senators decided it was better not to make their positions a matter of public record. The measure provided that each honorably discharged veteran would receive a certificate worth $1.00 a day for service ($1.25 for the days overseas). The certificate would triple in value if held for twenty years, with a full value of over $1,800.

Observers expected Harding to give up and reluctantly sign the measure, especially in view of the tremendous political stakes. Harding went through with his veto on September 19, six weeks before election day. He noted that he was sympathetic to the plight of veterans but argued that it was unfair to increase the national debt "for a distribution among less than 5,000,000 out of 110,000,000, whether inspired by grateful sentiment or political expediency, would undermine the confidence on which our credit is builded and establish the precedent of distributing public funds whenever the proposal and the numbers affected make it seem politically appealing to do so."[25] These were interesting words for a president who was trying to force a ship subsidy on Congress.

Congress responded swiftly to Harding's veto. Only two days before adjournment the House voted to override the veto by a substantial margin. That afternoon the Senate sustained Harding's veto by a vote of 44 to 28, four votes less than the necessary two-thirds majority to override.

Harding was opposed by most of the leadership of the Republican party, many of whom campaigned against the veto. He was widely praised in financial and business circles for his "responsible" action. He was not about to allow the American Legion to disrupt his plans for tax reduction, efficiency, and economy. The program of normalcy had to be maintained. It was not important if a few Republican congressmen were sacrificed. Indeed, his attitude harked back to the earlier remark supposedly made by Fordney— Harding would rather see some Republicans lose than American business suffer.

Two years later, during the 1924 election year, Congress passed the Adjusted Compensation Act over Calvin Coolidge's veto. The final bonus system had no direct cash payments, but rather insurance policies. The insurance holders could borrow up to one quarter of the face value of the policy.[26] Veterans were far from satisfied, but they had their bonus.

V

The winter of 1921–1922 was unhappy for many people. The postwar depression was lingering, with about 11 percent of the labor force unemployed. Undercapitalized firms and manufacturing concerns were going under by the thousands. The agrarian crisis showed few signs of abatement. Approximately 10 percent of the farmers in the country had lost their land. Unions were responding to pay-cuts, loss of membership, and unemployment in a series of increasingly violent strikes in the summer of 1922. The country was restless with normalcy, and conditions were creating a threat to Republican dominance of Congress.[27]

As the November 7 elections neared, Republican leaders realized that some defeats were inevitable. It was traditional for the party in power to suffer losses during midterm elections, but it was hoped that Democratic gains could be minimized. However, the overwhelming Republican victory two years before had been largely a reaction to Wilson, rather than an endorsement of normalcy. Such protest votes could evaporate without leadership, and Harding was not providing the necessary leadership.

The record of the administration in 1921–1922 was by no means one of failure; it had accomplished much that it had set out to do. But many of Harding's "accomplishments" would have occurred with or without Harding—the budget act being an example, although it might not have been implemented so rigorously under another president. It proved difficult for Republicans to run on a record of reduced taxes for the rich while holding the line on taxes for middle- and low-income groups. The Republicans were vulnerable on the tax bill and other issues, such as seating Truman H. Newberry in the Senate. Newberry had spent several hundred thousand dollars to defeat Henry Ford in a 1918 Michigan senatorial campaign. Newberryism became synonymous with purchase of political office. The Republicans seemed to have done their share of that between 1920 and 1922. Most of all, normalcy—with its limited antidepression measures—had failed to return prosperity.

The election was more than a slight move away from the party in power. The seven million majority the Republicans had enjoyed two years before vanished in an unparalleled off-year defeat. In the House of Representatives the Sixty-seventh Congress had seated 303 Republicans and 131 Democrats. The Sixty-eighth Congress would seat only 221 Republicans, while there would be 212 Democrats. Republican losses in the Senate were also devastating, reducing the 59–37 majority to 51–43. Dominance of the Senate was precarious because two senators were elected on the Farmer-Labor ticket. Frank Kellogg's uneasy feeling about high tariff rates were borne out by his defeat in Minnesota. Old guard members and friends of Harding, such as Senators Joseph S. Frelinghuysen of New Jersey and Harry S. New of Indiana, went down to defeat. Even Harding's choice for governor of Ohio, Carmi Thompson, lost. The only Republicans who ran well were those who emphasized more radical social policies. The defeat for the Republicans was blamed on the tariff, the bonus, the labor policies of Attorney General Harry Daugherty, and disunity.

There had been signs that Harding was modifying his conception of the presidency. His earlier philosophy of "the president proposes, the Congress disposes" was not working. Harding's party was leaderless, without direction. The election results probably changed the president's ideas, and he attempted to use his newly

80

acquired conception of the presidency in forcing the ship subsidy bill through Congress. The attempt failed. His choice of an issue upon which to exert his authority cast further doubt on his ability to lead. He appeared unable to read the mood of Congress, which any successful leader must do.

On March 4, 1923, the Sixty-seventh Congress adjourned. Fate was to dictate that Harding would not survive to greet the new Congress, but it is unlikely that he would have had any better luck than Coolidge in preventing a bonus from passing in 1924. And there is no evidence that Congress, or the American people, wanted aggressive leadership in the White House in the 1920s. Memories of Wilson were too strong, and it is probable that any "new Harding," at least the sort suggested by some recent historians, would have met the same fate as did the "old Harding" on the ship subsidy bill.[28]

In his brief term, Harding had faced a faction-ridden Congress and was unable to master the situation. There was no reason to believe he would have performed any better with the Sixty-eighth Congress, had he lived. Prosperity returned to much of middle-class America by 1924 and saved the Republicans from another humiliation. That does not mean that relations with Congress would have improved after 1923. Indeed, it is hard to imagine how relations between an overwhelmingly Republican Congress and a popularly elected Republican president could have been any better than they were between Harding and Congress in early 1921. Two years later the hopes had gone sour.

4

★★★★★

DOMESTIC AFFAIRS II: NORMALCY AT WORK

I

Harding informed Congress on April 12, 1921, that one of the policies of his administration was "to have less government in business as well as more business in government." Then, and on other occasions, the president made clear that the new administration would do all in its power to advance the interests of business. In Harding's mind the business community provided the identity of the United States. His administration established a trend that was to last through the 1920s, as large-scale government intervention in the economy passed from the scene. Business became dominant in government, demanding and receiving preferential treatment.

Business exercised its greatest influence over the fortunes of the country during the 1920s. President Harding wanted to do everything in his power to promote business. Harding called for tax reductions and attempted to soothe labor unions; but, when necessary, he took action against labor. Harding desired to return to normalcy, as he defined it—government would do all within reason to serve American business.

To make government more responsive to business, Harding determined to reorganize the executive branch and establish business methods of efficiency. During the last months of the Wilson administration a joint congressional committee on reorganization had been established. Harding appointed his old friend Walter F. Brown as his representative. When Brown discovered that most of the executive departments were hostile to reorganization, he developed his own plan. Brown submitted a tentative plan to Harding in January 1923 which proposed ten executive departments: State, Treasury, Justice, Agriculture, Interior, Commerce, Labor, Communications (in place of the Post Office), Defense (replacing War and Navy), and Education and Welfare, a new cabinet department. The plan set off a series of bureaucratic intrigues which seemed to perplex Harding. After the president's death the attempt to restructure the executive branch collapsed, as Coolidge did not share Harding's belief in reorganization.[1]

The failure of the plan did not prevent individual departments from establishing modern business methods as a basis for operation. Harding set lines for policy but cared little about how such lines were followed. This provided the ambitious and energetic Hoover, one of the leading advocates of business philosophy within the administration, with broad areas in which to operate. The secretary of commerce used his position to promote all types of business-related activities. He viewed the government as a coordinator for business interests. The government was not an initiator of new policies but the fulcrum on which business activities could move. Hoover became one of the American heroes of the 1920s. He represented the "new" commercial civilization developing in America, an economy that stressed productivity—under private guidance. The government would provide informational services, technical aid, and other services. Government was to be the servant; and, in turn, business would create a happy, prosperous, contented America.

Hoover expanded the Department of Commerce to make it more responsive to business. The Commerce Department collected mountains of statistics, which were published weekly in 160 newspapers around the country and were of great help to businessmen and trade associations. Hoover believed in trade associations because of their ability to encourage research, their aid in gathering statistics, and efforts to standardize products; and by 1923 businessmen viewed them as essential. Trade associations deserved support because they could make businesses more efficient, with agencies like Commerce providing economic information to the associations. Hoover reminded businessmen that the administration had their interests at heart and that trade associations and chambers of commerce across the country could expect a respectful hearing in the Commerce Department on their problems.

Henry Wallace, hardly an admirer of the secretary of commerce, thought along similar lines. He recognized the need to reorganize the Agriculture Department to make it more responsive to the farming community. A partial reorganization was begun during the Wilson administration, with the department grouped into three areas: regulation, research, extension. Wallace named full-time directors in each area. The secretary focused on scientific aspects of the department, emphasizing research. In July 1922 he combined the Office of Farm Management, the Bureau of Crop and Livestock Estimates, and the Bureau of Markets into a single office, the Bureau of Agricultural Economics. He appointed a professor from the University of Wisconsin, Henry C. Taylor, to direct the new office. Taylor, a pioneer in scientific collection and interpretation of agricultural data, soon made the Bureau of Agricultural Economics one of the best research agencies in government.[2]

Taylor distributed the results of his research to farm leaders, county agents, and legislators. His bureau prepared "outlook reports" on domestic markets. Claiming that the Bureau of Foreign and Domestic Commerce of the Department of Commerce was not performing adequately, Wallace had Taylor expand his reports to foreign market trends, which added to the tension between Wallace and Hoover. All these activities were not to regulate the farmer but to inform him about conditions so he could make decisions. One of the results of the new bureau's activities was to change the focus from the individual farmer to broader problems. As the farm crisis persisted, Wallace moved into fixing prices and controlling production, attempting to make agriculture equal to industry in gaining the attention of the government. Harding supported Wallace, and especially the work of the Bureau of Agricultural Economics. The president did not understand the farm crisis but hoped the farm experts would find solutions to ease it. So while Hoover was making Commerce more responsive to businessmen, Wallace was making Agriculture more responsive to farmers.

Harding further emphasized his commitment to efficiency in government by support for the Bureau of the Budget, a development that heartened the business community. Dawes had led the way as first director of the budget, cutting more than a billion dollars from the budget. Dawes stayed only a year and selected his replacement, General Herbert M. Lord, convincing Harding that the chief financial officer of the army was the best man for the job. Not as flamboyant as his predecessor, Lord inherited an able staff and continued to stress economy. In the fiscal year ending June 30, 1923, federal expenditures were $3,294,000,000, a two billion dollar saving from the last year of the Wilson administration.[3] While such a comparison was not fair, because the Wilson administration had expenses as a result of the war, Harding had demonstrated a commitment to business in government.

To further the commitment to businesslike practices in government, the administration made a concerted effort to lower the national debt. Under Mellon's guidance, the debt fell from $23.1 billion in 1921 to $21.8 billion in 1923. This trend continued until 1929, with the debt falling to a low of $16.5 billion in Hoover's first year as president.

Also symbolic of the business-minded ethos of the administration was the fate of regulatory agencies created or strengthened by progressive reformers.[4] During the Progressive era the theory had developed that the government had the duty to regulate business on behalf of the public. The Interstate Commerce Commission was strengthened. In 1913 the Federal Reserve Act created the Federal Reserve Board to overlook affairs of banks and bankers. This was followed by the Federal Trade Commission, to regulate other business activity. These agencies were to regulate excesses of businesses and were an important part of Wilson's New Freedom. The commissions had broad powers and were feared by business on the ground that they might fall under the influence of powers inimical to business. During the Wilson era, the boards attempted to carry out their public charge. Business leaders wanted this type of regulation to cease, and under Harding the process of reconstituting the boards with personnel more favorable to business began. The president wanted to change the philosophy of the Interstate Commerce Commission. Although the process was not complete until the Coolidge administration, the commission took on a probusiness viewpoint. The Federal Reserve Board moved in the same direction, as Harding appointed more conservative personnel to the board. These appointments represented banking interests primarily, the group the board had been created to control. Soon the board was dominated by a conservative ethic, which had much to do with deflation of the economy in the Harding years. Harding was able to make two appointments to the five-man Federal Trade Commission, but the commission clung to its progressive leaning by a three-to-two majority. Completion of reconstitution did not come until Coolidge appointed to its chairmanship William E. Humphrey, a former congressman from Washington and lobbyist for lumbering interests. A long-time critic of the commission, Humphrey helped transform the FTC into a powerful advocate of business. The regulatory agencies thus were made to conform to normalcy, and the vestiges of progressive control in federal government ended.

The six-member Tariff Commission had been dominated by Wilson appointees who were low-tariff advocates. Harding was able to appoint four new members who shared his belief in protectionist policy. Thomas O. Marvin, the new chairman, was an outspoken advocate of high tariffs. One of the appointees was a holdover on the commission, William S. Culbertson, a moderate Republican from Kansas, who often expressed his opposition to high-tariff policies to Harding. Harding tried to be fair, but he made clear that he wanted the commission to reflect the conservative view of the tariff structure. So the progressive philosophy of maintaining low tariffs to enhance domestic competition disappeared from the commission at the same time Congress was raising record tariff barriers.[5]

The Supreme Court was reconstituted to conform to normalcy. Harding appointed four conservative, property-oriented lawyers to the Court, and it took on a conservative cast in a series of decisions. The Court moved away from social litigation, and the "Brandeis Brief" suffered accordingly. Consequently, cases concerning child labor, freedom of the press, and minimum wages received little sympathy from the Court. The conservative justices believed that the government should not have much power over property, nor should it be involved in the regulation of private business affairs and individual rights, and their influence remained long after Harding's death. There was only one new appointment to the Supreme Court between 1923 and 1930, and normalcy continued to influence the Court until late in the 1930s.[6]

The Harding administration was involved in the important transportation and communication revolution sweeping the country. Although Harding never learned to drive, he had purchased his first car in 1905, and he became a supporter of the development of good roads. The Federal Aid Road Act of 1916 allowed the secretary of agriculture to aid states in building and maintaining roads over which the mails passed. Harding believed this was not enough support and suggested to Congress the need for a nationwide program. Farm groups and the American Automobile Association helped persuade Congress to pass the Highway Act of 1921, which allowed states to designate a network of interstate and intercounty roads for federal funds. Federal outlays jumped from $19.5 million in 1920 to $75 million in 1921, rising to $88 million by 1923. As a result of Harding's action a network of highways developed which played a part in the economic prosperity of the decade.[7] The growth of highways in turn assisted the growth of the leading business of the 1920s, the automobile industry.

Harding was interested in radio and aviation. When he took office, there were only two radio stations. A year later over three hundred stations were on the air, broadcasting to more than three million homes. Harding believed that government should regulate all radio transmitters, for both domestic and foreign broadcasting. Hoover moved into the field and formulated policies for regulation and development. He sponsored a meeting of radio broadcasters in 1922 to discuss frequencies. The broadcasters agreed to a voluntary system of licensing through the Commerce Department, as well as to the distribution of frequencies in the 500 to 1,500 kilocycle range. Hoover and Harding understood that something more than a voluntary association was needed, and a bill was introduced in Congress for broad regulatory powers for the Commerce Department. The Sixty-seventh Congress adjourned before its passage, and it was not until 1927 that statutory government control began.

Harding was concerned about aviation. Again Hoover seized upon this interest, sponsoring a national conference on commercial aviation. The conference of 1922 focused on emergency procedures, development of air routes and airports, inspections of planes and pilots. The White House pressed Congress for legislation, but nothing was done until 1926 when the Air Commerce Act provided a Bureau of Aeronautics in the Commerce Department.

It was plain that normalcy entailed commitment to business methods at all levels of society. The administration was not out of step with the country, for in the 1920s businessmen assumed dominance in American society. From the biggest baron on Wall Street to the smallest merchant in a little town, businessmen were listened to with respect and looked to for leadership. Local chambers of commerce grew rapidly throughout the decade and exerted considerable influence on local affairs.

Henry Ford became a symbol of the 1920s. The epitome of the American success story, he had risen from a poor farm boy to become one of the wealthiest men in the country. He was one of the initiators of the modern industrial society that came to dominate the United States in the 1920s. While maintaining that history was bunk, Ford devoted much of his enormous energy to preserving the values of old-fashioned America. The *New Republic* in 1923 editorialized that "the average citizen sees Ford as a sort of enlarged crayon portrait of himself; the man able to fulfill his own suppressed desires, who has achieved enormous riches, fame and power without departing from the pioneer-and-homespun tradition." Ford was a living example of the tension between the old and the new. While perhaps one of the architects of the destruction of old values, dislocating people through the automobile, he sought to preserve those very values. He was efficiency at its best and worst. A group of college students of the decade rated him the third greatest figure of all time, behind Christ and Napoleon.[8]

Even the culture of the 1920s reflected the business outlook of American society. Most Americans were not familiar with the writings of F. Scott Fitzgerald, Henry L. Mencken, or Ernest Hemingway. Popular culture maintained an old-fashioned belief in work. Novels emphasized success—Horatio Alger–type stories. Zane Grey, Harold Bell Wright, and Edgar Rice Burroughs dominated the fiction lists. Bruce Barton in *The Man Nobody Knows* enthralled a generation by recasting the image of Christ in business terms to make Christianity more understandable. The 1920s witnessed a mania for sports, for sports heroes. The country fawned over "Babe" Ruth and "Red" Grange, individuals who succeeded against great odds in the sports world. Most people wanted to be assured that the United States was not casting off its mores during an uncertain age, and they found such assurance throughout the country. The America of the 1920s was rooted in tradition; the small group known as the "lost generation" was truly out of place during the decade.

II

The probusiness attitude of the administration did not mean an end to problems from the war. The country faced a profound agricultural and industrial depression. Yet seemingly there was little the government would do to alleviate the suffering. Harding encouraged national conferences to make recommendations on how to handle the farmers and the unemployed. There was the appearance of action to alleviate suffering, while in fact there was little or no relief. Perhaps another way to describe this policy is "normalcy in action."

Wallace had proposed the idea of a national conference on the problems of agriculture during the campaign. He brought up the idea shortly after the election, but Hoover and Mellon counseled against it. They feared such a conference would make it appear that the administration favored agriculture over industry. In December 1921 Harding agreed to a conference to consider the immediate problems facing agriculture and to provide an intense examination of the future of agriculture, gathering information in the process.[9]

The conference opened on January 23, 1922, for five days of meetings. A diverse group, the 336 delegates represented 37 states and included farmers, representatives of farm organizations (even the National Negro Farmers' Association), political leaders, and agricultural economists. Harding delivered a statement to open the conference, noting that the country was concerned about conditions. Agriculture was "truly a national interest and not entitled to be regarded as primarily the concern of either a class or a section." He departed from his text to note critics, "or a bloc," in Congress.[10]

The conference divided into twelve committees to consider aspects of problems facing agriculture. Controlled by Wallace, these committees produced moderate proposals dealing with symptoms rather than cures. The conference approved the emergency farm legislation passed by the special session of Congress and advocated a new permanent tariff. The conferees recommended construction of a St. Lawrence Seaway and farm-to-market roadways. Farmers were sagely advised to diversify, not to depend on the export of staples. It was suggested that farmers cut costs, decrease acreage, develop cooperatives. The conference called for strengthening the War Finance Corporation, placing a farm representative on the Federal Reserve Board, and general lowering of railroad freight rates. None of the recommendations was a threat to Republican farm policy.

There was one other topic—agricultural price parities—discussed at the conference. Perhaps the essential difference between industry and agriculture during the 1920s was that industry could regulate its inventories by controlling production, while farmers, due to the nature of their enterprise, were unable to control output. So, farmers increasingly had sought a means to dispose of surpluses. George N. Peek, president of the Moline Plow Company of Illinois, brought to the conference a plan to provide the farmer marketing equality with industry. With the help of Hugh S. Johnson he had worked out a proposal for a two-price system for commodities. Peek and Johnson hoped to create high domestic prices by dumping surpluses abroad at bargain rates. The domestic price was to be pegged to the same ratio that farm commodities had borne to industrial commodities before 1914. The two men had developed the "parity" principle. Peek understood that his company would sell few farm implements to farmers during a depression. The Harding-sponsored conference, however, was not interested in providing direct price supports to farmers. The Peek-Johnson proposals were tabled, only to be taken up by two members of Congress, Senator Charles L. McNary of Oregon and Representative Gilbert N. Haugen of Iowa. In the mid-twenties McNary-Haugenism was to be a source of contention between Harding's successor, Coolidge, and agricultural interests, and Coolidge vetoed several McNary-Haugen bills.[11] There were weaknesses in the bills, one particularly being that the bills were based on the principle of dumping surpluses abroad while providing for no production controls at home. That was not the overriding reason for Coolidge's vetoes, however. He believed the government should not subsidize farmers, directly or indirectly. There was no reason to think that Harding's response (had the occasion arisen) would have been any different.

The administration did respond to many recommendations made by the conference. Congress passed the Capper-Volstead Act, which provided legal protection for cooperatives. This gave farm cooperatives advantages that trade associations and corporations were unable to secure. The administration supported extension of the War Finance Corporation for another year, to underwrite farm credit, and made money available for farmers to buy seed in areas suffering from crop failures. Reluctantly, the administration supported expansion of the Federal Reserve Board to include a farm member. The agricultural community had claimed that the board was not responsive to farm credit needs. With a farm member, the board would hear about agricultural problems.

One of the major recommendations was that the government force the railroads to lower rates. Hoover was against such treatment, while Wallace supported it. Harding faced a dilemma, because to lower rates would mean lowering railway profits or wages of railway workers, or both. Harding came to favor preferential freight rates for the farmer, even though it was increasingly clear that such rates would not help the farmer much. The decision to support lower rates played no little part in the railway strike of 1922.

By 1923 the combination of the legislation the farm bloc had engineered and the recommendations of the agricultural conference that the administration had accepted had helped to ease the economic crisis in the American countryside. But the Harding policy had not brought prosperity to rural America, and the farm problem remained throughout the 1920s, mainly because of the unwillingness of the Republicans to intervene in the agricultural economy.[12] Attempts to provide genuine farm relief were shunted aside because they would have involved government action that few Republicans were willing to consider. Direct government intervention on behalf of the agricultural community was simply unacceptable.

Much the same situation existed regarding industrial unemployment. The most troublesome issue in 1921 was unemployment, which rose to 11.9 percent. Conditions showed few signs of abatement, and long-term suffering was a real possibility. The first person in Harding's administration to demonstrate concern for the unemployed was Hoover—not, as one would suppose, Secretary of Labor James Davis. Hoover suggested a national conference on unemployment. Harding agreed.[13]

Hoover began recruiting academic experts, businessmen, labor leaders, and engineers. Edward Eyre Hunt, one of his aides, served as secretary and enlisted such men as Owen D. Young of the General Electric Company, James P. Noonan of the AFL Brotherhood of Electrical Workers, and John Donlin, president of the AFL Building Trades Department, along with Otto Mallery, who was with the Industrial Board of Pennsylvania. With economists and efficiency engineers, these individuals supplied energy and direction to the conference that met on September 26, 1921.

Much of the work of the conference was carried on by advocates of industrial efficiency. The Taylor Society and the American Engineering Society offered advice and suggestions. The focus was on reduction of unemployment, but the implications of the conference were of longer range. Hoover understood that this was the first federally sponsored effort to reduce unemployment and that as a precedent it could have long-term effects. The secretary believed the conference would demonstrate that a democratic society could solve problems of modern industrial development through voluntary efforts. Consequently, the conference "was to be a unique blend of private initiative, federal leadership and persuasion, and engineering know-how."

An "uplifting" spirit ran through the conference. It was believed that confidence in the future and cheerfulness in adversity needed to be instilled in the unemployed. One suggestion was that the unemployed be grouped into clubs to inculcate self-respect, "through the spirit of song in the midst of good cheer, and whole-some communion every Sunday morning." Despair would be lightened by fellowship, food, and religion. The public had to be convinced of the need to help those unfortunates without work, for joblessness was not necessarily the fault of the individual. Local communities and organizations were urged to use slogans like "Improve the Home Town and Give Work to Workers," and to "use 'four minute men,' movies and community singing and other war-time methods in raising funds," as well as using dramatic presentations to tell "the story of unemployment and the possibilities of success."[14]

Harding opened the conference with a warning not to expect relief from the "public treasury." Hoover followed with a longer oration telling his audience that the only way to alleviate the problem was through voluntary, local action, not the federal government. The government would not accept suggestions such as the one made by Otto Mallery—that, if all other initiatives failed, the federal government should provide ten dollars per week to the unemployed as a minimum standard of living. "Unless we would destroy individual initiative and drive ourselves straight into nationalism or paternalism," Hoover had stated in July, "the Government can not undertake to reduce or raise wages, or fix prices, no matter how it is camouflaged."[15]

Given this view, it was not surprising that the conference decided that the government was "an adviser, coordinator, and supporter, not initiator." The major relief for the unemployed had to be carried out at the local level. It was suggested that local self-help projects, such as home repairs, be initiated to alleviate unemployment. Emphasis was placed on individual good works, because public works could only partially solve the problem. These suggestions, along with recommendations for an increased tariff rate, lowered railway rates, lowered government spending, and aid for agriculture and the coal industry, were the major accomplishments of the unemployment conference.

The conference produced no large legislation, although tariff rates were raised, railroad rates lowered, and federal public works projects were speeded up. The government did set up federal-state-local committees to fight unemployment and encouraged a work-sharing program in which the employed voluntarily rotated their jobs with the jobless. A proposal was submitted to Congress in 1922 to adjust the rate of public works projects to the state of the economy with "execution of about 80 per cent of the usual annual average of federal public works during years of active industry and the postponement of about twenty per cent for execution during years of depression." This "safety valve" bill received widespread support in the press, among labor leaders, and from engineers who considered it a dramatic step. The bill did not pass, despite attempts to revive it throughout the 1920s.

Notwithstanding these considerable limitations, the conference was a political plus for the administration. The activities of the conference were widely and favorably publicized. Even Harding's detractors, such as Samuel Gompers, approved the conference. "In all its procedure," Gompers reported to the AFL, "the conference was guided by the fact that it was not authorized to attempt to overturn existing theory and practice but was expected to meet the problem . . . through existing agencies." Within these limits, the "conference was rich with results."[16] Hoover agreed. Indeed, the limited program had gone beyond any previous federal effort or relief. In the view of the secretary of commerce, the government had done what was necessary and nothing more. When prosperity returned, there would be no large bureaucracy to dismantle, nor would the government be left with additional functions.

The economy started moving again during 1922. The findings of the conference on unemployment had little, if anything, to do with this. Perhaps the only contribution was to rivet attention on unemployment. Given the economic knowledge of the time, it was not surprising that few people understood the role of the consumer in an industrial society. There was no emphasis on public works, deficit spending, or tax cuts to stimulate growth. Cuts were made, but to relieve businessmen from "unfair" burdens of wartime taxation rather than to start growth.

The unemployment conference was yet another example of the importance of Hoover in the administration. The conference was properly within the jurisdiction of Secretary of Labor Davis. Davis, however, was not even in Washington for the opening of the conference, because he was "obligated" to attend fraternal conventions in the Midwest. While he was given a minor role by Hoover, his tardy appearance led one observer to comment, "At the conference on unemployment, which was Mr. Hoover's, the best and only example of the unemployed present was the Secretary of Labor."[17]

Hoover's activities in the field of labor did not end with the unemployment conference. He provided the major initiatives in the fight to eliminate the twelve-hour day in the steel industry by persuasion rather than regulation. The strike of 1919 had exposed archaic labor practices in the mills, particularly the twelve-hour shift. The strike had failed to gain the changes workers demanded, and Hoover realized that conditions might well cause further upheaval. Most observers recommended reform, but operators ignored such pleas. Early in 1922 it appeared that some of the more moderate operators were willing to consider reform in the industry, particularly elimination of the two twelve-hour shifts, to be replaced by three eight-hour shifts.

Hoover advised the president that Elbert H. Gary, head of United States Steel, would probably comment on the twelve-hour day at a company meeting on April 17, 1922. The secretary of commerce recommended that Harding send Gary a letter expressing hope that the twelve-hour day would be abolished. Harding followed Hoover's advice, but the letter had no apparent effect, as Gary remained silent on the issue. Hoover urged the president to call a meeting of executives at the White House to discuss the matter. Hoover wanted to publicize the meeting, to put pressure on the steel managers, but Harding was reluctant. Along with forty other steel executives, on May 18 Gary attended a dinner at the White House with no announcement of the purpose. Harding told the gathering he was in earnest about abolishing the twelve-hour shift. Hoover was more blunt in presenting the administration's case, citing statistics that the abolition of the twelve-hour day would result in an increase in efficiency. Angered, the corporate leaders threatened to walk out of the meeting. Harding's skill at applying balm emerged, and he even extracted a face-saving promise that Gary would head a committee to study the matter and make a recommendation.

The secretary of commerce was angry at the treatment he had received. He understood that the steelmen would not act unless pressed, a fact that Harding was reluctant to accept. Against Harding's wishes, Hoover leaked the contents of the meeting to the press. As expected, the story received widespread and sympathetic coverage. He asked the Federated Engineering Societies (of which he was president) to examine the twelve-hour shift, and the resulting report supported Hoover's conclusions. Under this public campaign the steel industry remained silent, hoping the issue would go away. But the energetic secretary had no intention of allowing the agitation to die.

By the spring of 1923 signs appeared favorable. Owen D. Young and Dwight Morrow were convinced of the efficacy of the eight-hour shift and were bringing pressure on steel executives.

95

Hoover's aides had been successful in keeping the issue before the public, and many businessmen seemed interested. The steel operators on May 23, 1923, rejected the eight-hour day, in a report by a committee chaired by Gary. They insisted the workers were not in favor of it and argued that the changeover to three shifts a day would require sixty thousand additional workers. They suggested that if the administration wanted to change to an eight-hour day in the steel industry all restrictions on immigration would have to be lifted.

The industry decision, after more than a year of work, was a shock to the administration. Hoover maintained that the report revealed "an inability to grasp the great ground swell of social movements among our people" and advised the president not to "allow this matter of fundamental social importance to drop." He drafted a letter for Harding to the steel executives, reiterating that the twelve-hour day should end. The letter implied the threat of legislation, stating that the president hoped the problem would be "solved by action inside the industries themselves." This letter, along with Hoover's campaign, resulted in victory. Late in June the industry capitulated. Speaking in Tacoma, in a speech drafted by Hoover, Harding congratulated the magnates for their "important step" which would "heal a sore in American industrial life which has been the cause of infinite struggles and bitterness over a generation."[18] Hoover had demonstrated that an aggressive government could bring substantial social change on a "voluntary" basis.

Hoover's activities in both the unemployment conference and the campaign against the twelve-hour shift reflected favorably on the administration. It is true that the unemployment conference's accomplishments were not far-reaching and the steel industry was unpopular, but changes had been wrought with a minimum of government interference. These activities had benefited the American worker, even if the administration lacked a burning passion for social justice. Normalcy at work in the agricultural and unemployment conferences and in the twelve-hour shift controversy had generated favorable comment and some progress. While soon dimmed, these accomplishments were not completely forgotten even during the mishandling of the coal and railroad strikes during 1922.

III

During the World War organized labor had made tremendous gains. Union membership stood at an all-time high of more than

5,000,000 in 1920, almost a fifth of the labor force. Management, determined to change this situation, had held firm in a series of strikes in 1919 and 1920. Business became more confident about redressing its relations with labor. Using the depression as an excuse, many business enterprises set about reducing wages, and some, favoring the "American plan," hoped to destroy organized labor. By 1923 union membership had dropped to slightly more than 3,440,000. This trend continued throughout the 1920s.[19]

During the spring and summer of 1922, the administration was beset by the most far-reaching strikes of the decade. Over a half-million coal miners walked off their jobs in April 1922 and in July more than 400,000 railroad workers struck. Coal stocks declined, while violence appeared across the country. The nation's industries seemed on the verge of collapse. Harding by nature sought to avoid confrontation. He was under intense pressure, particularly after the railroad strike started on July 1. He found the strikes complex and his cabinet divided on policy. Hoover and Davis counseled moderation, while Attorney General Daugherty was anxious to break the strikes. Harding equivocated, but he realized that inaction was impossible.

The United Mine Workers, headed after 1920 by the pugnacious John L. Lewis, was the largest union in the United States. But the coal industry was in trouble because of the end of wartime expansion, as well as the rapidly increasing use of oil. Miners were fortunate when they had three or four days' work each week. The operators wanted to reduce the price of coal by cutting wages, in some cases by as much as 45 percent. They wanted to end the hard-won union practice of nationwide negotiation and replace it with local contracts, hoping wages would fall. The mine workers wanted employment, with a six-hour day and five-day week, though they were reconciled to wage cuts. The issue of the strike seemed to be the belief that operators were attempting "to break" the union.

In the fall of 1921 the administration hoped to bring the parties together. It was apparent that operators were not going to honor the 1920 contract which had established contract negotiations on a nationwide basis; a strike was inevitable. On April 1, 1922, the workers struck. The early administration response to the strike was largely formed by Hoover: the government declined to intervene. To put pressure on the workers, Hoover encouraged the production of nonunion coal, while attempting to get nonunion operators to restrain prices. He told West Virginia miners that price restraint and continued production were patriotic because of the public need.

Hoover's policies of private and public pressure might have prevailed, had not violence erupted in Williamson County, Illinois, where the owner of the Southern Illinois Coal Company, William J. Lester, was anxious to make a profit from selling coal during the strike.[20] Even though his mine was in the heart of an area controlled by the United Mine Workers, Lester imported strikebreakers to work his mine near Herrin, Illinois. On the morning of June 22 the miners killed eighteen strikebreakers who had surrendered. The nation was stunned by the massacre, as well as by the unwillingness of local authorities to bring the strikers to justice.

Initially, Harding reacted sympathetically toward the striking miners. As coal supplies dwindled and violence flared, pressure mounted for action. Early in July the government sponsored a meeting of operators and miners because Hoover had concluded that no solution was possible between the parties unless the government made some proposals. Hoover recommended regional negotiation and arbitration. The union resisted arbitration because it wanted representatives of the major coal fields to comprise the basic bargaining unit. To provide for long-range solutions to the coal problem, Hoover suggested a coal commission. The negotiation in Washington collapsed, and the president blamed the miners. Harding began a determined public assault on the mine workers. On July 18 he telegraphed the twenty-eight governors of the soft-coal–producing states, asking them to provide assurance to coal operators of the right of men to work. In short, Harding was attempting to encourage strikebreaking on a massive scale. The governors and the public supported Harding, but there were few miners to act as strikebreakers. The mines failed to open, and Harding throughout August maintained his assault on the union. He believed a few selfish union officials were responsible for the failure to settle: "I cannot believe that the thoughtful, loyal mine workers throughout the country mean to imperil the welfare of the people of the United States."[21]

Lewis ultimately agreed to settle on terms that maintained the old wage scales and called for a federal commission to investigate the mines. The Coal Commission, created by Congress on September 22, 1922, was composed of seven members, all appointed by the president. It investigated conditions in the industry and prepared a report which did not recommend complete unionization of the field but did call for compulsory arbitration. The report pleased no one. While the strike was settled on grounds reasonably favorable to miners, the situation of the United Mine Workers worsened through the decade, as the union declined in members and influence. The mines were operating, much to the administration's relief.

Over 400,000 railway craft workers walked off their jobs on July 1, 1922, the first nationwide railway strike since 1894. The workers were striking as much against the Railway Labor Board as the railroads. In the Transportation Act of 1920, Congress had established the board with a membership of nine—three each from labor, management, and the public—and authority to set wages and working conditions for railroad employees, although its pronouncements lacked the force of law. Shortly before Harding took office, the board had granted a 22 percent increase in wages. The board was usually not sympathetic to railway workers. It negated the national contracts that had covered train-service workers and had provided for much of the expansion of the nonoperating employee unions. The board ordered two pay-cuts for railway workers, in 1920 and 1921, on the ground that railway employees should share in postwar economic dislocation. The unions reluctantly accepted most of the board's decisions. The Railway Labor Board occasionally decided against the railroads, but powerful carriers ignored the decisions without penalty. The inability or unwillingness of the board to force railroads to accept its rulings created a sense of outrage among employees, who had been forced to abide by the board decisions. When the Railway Labor Board recommended a further wage reduction in June 1922, a strike seemed likely. The four biggest unions, which were affiliated with the AFL and consisted of the operating employees, came to terms with the carriers and declined to join the strike by the craft workers. Without the support of these powerful elements, the shopcraft workers were in a tenuous position from the beginning of their walkout on July 1.

Harding immediately reacted to the railroad strike. Mistakenly, he believed the decisions of the Railway Labor Board were legally binding, and he wanted to make both the workers and the railway executives adhere to board decisions. Spokesmen for Harding attacked the strike as an affront to the public and the government. Harding supported a board resolution which declared that strikers were labor "outlaws" who should be stripped of seniority rights, and he encouraged the carriers to hire strikebreakers. Even so, the president recognized that the railroads' failure to carry out board decisions lent legitimacy to the workers' claims.

The cabinet was divided on the strike. The attorney general saw no justice on the side of the railway workers and advised the president to take drastic action. He clung to the conviction that Bolshevik agents were responsible and ordered Justice Department agents to gather information. The secretary of labor did not accept this interpretation and spoke on behalf of the strikers. Davis met with labor leaders and protested that it was unfair to punish railway workers for rejecting one decision of the Railway Labor Board, while the railroads ignored all board decisions. At the same time, Hoover launched a campaign to secure the aid of sympathetic railroad executives. Hoover sought the role of conciliator and avoided direct intervention.

Harding was in a difficult position and, characteristically, temporized. He was committed to lower freight rates, and the carriers had made plain that this course would require wage reductions. He wavered between positions advocated by Daugherty and Davis. At first it appeared that Davis had reached a compromise as a result of discussion with labor leaders. The administration proposed that workers resume work on a status quo basis, with unions accepting the pay-cut and carriers dropping their position that strikers had lost their rights of seniority. The sides were to promise to obey decisions of the board. The unions agreed early in August, even though this proposal was unfavorable. Without the support of the major unions, the strikers were desperate for a settlement. Hoover was sent to New York to secure the agreement of railroad managers, but, sensing victory, they flatly refused.

Harding was not angry at the refusal of the railway executives, and by August 7 he gave up the pretense of being an impartial arbiter. The president attacked the unions. On August 19, he wrote Daugherty: "At any time you have an intolerant situation, where it is desirable for the federal government to intervene with armed forces please let me know so that the matter may be immediately taken up." Late in August, without informing the cabinet, he directed his attorney general to seek an injunction against the strikers. Daugherty sought out Federal Judge James Wilkerson in Chicago and secured a restraining order. The injunction Wilkerson handed down on September 23, 1922, was perhaps the most far-reaching in the stormy history of American labor. The judge ordered union officials to cease "picketing or in any manner by letters, circulars, telephone messages, word of mouth, or interviews encouraging any person to leave the employ of a railroad."[22]

During a cabinet meeting, Hoover, Davis, Hughes, and even Albert Fall angrily denounced Daugherty's injunction. Harding was taken aback and ordered the attorney general to modify some of the more obnoxious parts of the injunction. But the injunction had been Harding's decision, and his action was to stand behind it. Harding thus needlessly antagonized labor, which came to evaluate the record of the administration on the basis of the injunction. The pressure of two strikes apparently had caused Harding to make a mistake that was to haunt the Republican party. Ironically, at the time Daugherty was seeking the injunction the strike was collapsing. The unions could not hold out against the odds and were willing to settle on any terms. The injunction had done nothing more than wipe out the last pockets of resistance.

The industrial crisis of 1922 was over, and the administration's handling of it provided little for the president on the credit side of the ledger, a fact obvious in the elections of that year. The administration's actions in both the coal and railroad strikes had illustrated two aspects of the policy of normalcy: the unwillingness of the government to intervene against businessmen, and the general probusiness bias that the Republicans brought to government in 1921. These two characteristics were to continue to dominate government policy throughout the 1920s. Normalcy, as a result, did not end with Harding's death in 1923.

IV

If the purpose of the administration was service to business, that did not mean that other individuals and groups did not receive consideration.

Harding was a compassionate man, and one of the first who benefited from the president's warm nature was Eugene V. Debs. Debs had been sentenced to ten years in prison for antiwar activities during World War I. Woodrow Wilson, who never suffered opposition lightly, vowed that Debs would not leave prison as long as he was president. Harding viewed the situation differently and soon after his inauguration agreed to meet a group concerned about Debs's fate, which included such notables as the editor of the *Nation*, Oswald Garrison Villard, Monsignor John A. Ryan, and William Allen White. After the pleas, Harding responded that he would give the case immediate attention. One of the more militant members of the group demanded a "yes" or "no" answer. White was shocked by this outburst but pleased by Harding's dignified retort: "My dear woman: you may demand anything you please out of Warren G. Harding. He will not resent it. But the President of the United States has the right to keep his own counsel, and the office I occupy forbids me to reply to you as I should like to do if I were elsewhere!"

Debs was allowed to come to Washington for an interview with Daugherty, and the president decided to release him on July 4, 1921. He faced opposition from both his wife and the attorney general. Both thought it politically unwise. Groups like the American Legion discovered the president's plan and protested, and Harding temporarily hesitated. In the end his sympathy for a fellow midwesterner from a common background won out, and in December 1921 he pardoned Debs, along with twenty-three other political prisoners. He asked Debs to stop by the White House on his way from the Atlanta prison. Debs kept his word never to reveal the substance of his presidential interview, but the day after Christmas told reporters: "Mr. Harding appears to me to be a kind gentleman. We understand each other perfectly."[23] Harding gradually released those political prisoners who had not engaged in violent or destructive behavior. As a result, he even freed twenty-seven members of the Industrial Workers of the World in June 1923.

Debs was not the only unpopular American to sense President Harding's kindly nature, though political considerations blocked the attainment of some of Harding's desires. Perhaps the most persistent social problem in the United States has been the position of black citizens in a supposedly democratic and equalitarian society. Before the First World War much of the racial problem was localized in the South. But with massive migrations of blacks to northern urban centers, tension extended nationwide. It produced bloody race riots in Chicago, Detroit, and elsewhere in 1919. Blacks were demanding equal political, economic, and social rights and using groups like the National Association for the Advancement of Colored People to seek those rights. During the Wilson administration, blacks in the federal government had faced segregation on a nationwide scale, and social circumstances had steadily deteriorated for all blacks. Blacks looked to the Republican party to advance their interests and hoped the new Republican president would alleviate some of their more pressing problems.

There was little evidence that before taking office Harding gave any thought to the position of blacks. As a candidate he listened during audiences with black leaders, and his demeanor aroused hope that he would act, but he was unwilling to make commitments. During one preinaugural discussion of racial problems in the South between Harding and black leaders in Florida, however, it was embarrassingly clear that he thought his visitors were job-seeking politicians. During a long, rambling discourse it became plain that he had never heard of the Tuskegee Institute nor of its famous founder, Booker T. Washington. The meeting led one participant to remark, "If you'd eliminate damn from that fellow's vocabulary he couldn't do anything but stutter."[24]

After the inauguration, Harding met again with black leaders and was provided with a proposed program to gain full citizenship for blacks. They requested antilynching legislation, investigation of peonage in the South, a national commission to study race relations, black assistant secretaries in the Departments of Labor and Agriculture, an end to the occupation of Haiti, and an executive order ending segregation in government service. They were encouraged by his April 1921 message to Congress in which he called for the country to "wipe the stain" of lynching from American society and made a proposal for the creation of a biracial commission.[25] Despite Harding's vagueness, even W. E. B. Du Bois was excited by the "strongest pronouncement on the race problem ever made by a President in a message to Congress."[26] It appeared that the years of labor by the NAACP and other groups were finally bearing fruit.

Harding's fullest statement on racial issues was in Birmingham on October 26, 1921, before a carefully segregated audience of thousands of blacks and whites. During the oration, the president made positive statements about political, educational, and economic equality for blacks. He cautioned blacks not to seek social equality, as it was unattainable. The speech received a mixed response. Many liberals praised the president for courage in the heart of the South, but hard-core segregationists were outraged. Some southern congressmen castigated the president. Many blacks were disappointed because of the comments on social equality but still hopeful.

Words were one thing. Action proved more difficult, and by the end of 1921 the hopes black leaders had entertained for Harding were fading. The president was unwilling to support the Dyer antilynching bill in Congress. To be sure, lynchings were declining; but from 1889 to 1918, at least 3,224 people were lynched. Before 1900 slightly less than four out of five (80 percent) were black; after 1900 the proportion of blacks increased dramatically. Of sixty-nine lynchings in 1921, fifty-nine were blacks (92 percent). For black citizens at that time, this stark reality was probably the single most disturbing fact of American life. The NAACP engaged in a campaign to stop lynching. The Dyer bill died in the Senate, the victim of a filibuster. But the publicity provided relief, as the number of black victims fell to twenty-nine in 1923 and sixteen in 1924. Throughout the remainder of the decade the number of lynchings remained fairly constant. This decline was a hollow victory, as it was evident that in the South less than 1 percent of the lynchers were ever brought to justice.

Harding's record in regard to abolishing segregation was also disappointing. He apparently had indicated to some black leaders that he was prepared to abolish segregation in the federal government by executive order. If so, he crassly ignored his promise, and in some cases prejudice against blacks appeared on the increase. The president failed to make important black political appointments. He ignored the request to appoint black assistant secretaries in the Departments of Agriculture and Labor and was slow in naming blacks to posts traditionally held by them. Eventually, Harding appointed a few blacks.

Harding was unwilling to commit himself even on the resurgence of the Ku Klux Klan. The Klan of the 1920s was different from its post–Civil War predecessor, in that it had broadened its targets to include Catholics and immigrants. In the South the focus remained the blacks. The president received inquiries asking if he were a member of the Klan, and privately he had his secretary respond: "In some quarters it has been represented that the President is a member of this organization. Not only is this untrue, but the fact is that the President heartily disapproves of the organization and has repeatedly expressed himself to this effect."[27] The House Rules Committee held a hearing on the Klan early in October 1921, but the investigation provided a forum for the Klan leadership. There were hints in the press that Harding favored a Justice Department investigation, but none was forthcoming. It became apparent that the administration was allowing politics to guide its policies toward the Klan.

The record of the administration regarding blacks was unsatisfactory, and many blacks began considering abandoning the party of Lincoln. Perhaps Harding's sympathetic hearing early in his administration made disillusionment the more bitter. The president's words were not matched by deeds. Given the times, it was perhaps unfair to expect more of Harding, but he missed an opportunity for understanding between the races.

Harding's record regarding women—the other active social group of the 1920s calling for social, political, and educational equality—was better. In 1922 he signed the Cable Act, which changed citizenship requirements. An American woman no longer lost her citizenship by marrying a foreign national eligible for citizenship. The Cable Act nonetheless had severe defects in that it reflected racist attitudes of the 1920s. An American-born white woman who married a foreigner ineligible for citizenship because of race was stripped of citizenship and could not regain it as long as the marriage lasted. More odious, American-born black and oriental women lost their citizenship permanently if they married foreigners ineligible for citizenship. Even with these defects, the bill was a step toward equal rights.[28]

The administration supported the Sheppard-Towner Maternity and Infancy Protection Act of 1921, a significant move by the government in social welfare. Taft in 1912 had created the Children's Bureau with Julia Lathrop as director. This agency launched an investigation of maternal and infant mortality and soon discovered that for an advanced industrial society the United States had an unusually high rate. In 1918 more than 16,000 women died of maternally related causes. More than 250,000 infants failed to survive their first year. It was discovered that around four-fifths of the women in the country failed to receive proper prenatal medical attention. The Children's Bureau discovered, not surprisingly, a relationship between economic level and mortality rates; but even in the higher income levels, the mortality rate compared unfavorably to that of such countries as New Zealand.

The Children's Bureau argued that the two ways to overcome this problem were to ensure adequate income levels for all people and to provide instruction in hygiene. To accomplish the latter, Lathrop suggested a law similar to the Smith-Lever Act of 1914 in which the federal government made funds available to the states for county agricultural agents. The proposal was introduced in 1918, with the stipulation that the government would provide matching funds for the states to supply prenatal and postnatal instruction. The bill made little headway.

After his election, Harding actively encouraged passage of a similar bill. Despite opposition of the American Medical Association, which feared involvement of the states in medical care, the bill passed and Harding signed it on November 23, 1921. It provided a small attack on a major medical problem, with an appropriation of less than $1,500,000 for its first year, falling to $1,250,000 for the next five years. But it was a start toward better maternal and infant care. During the Coolidge administration, provisions of the Sheppard-Towner Act were allowed to lapse because Coolidge hoped for "gradual withdrawal of the federal government from this field, leaving it to the states."[29]

The newly acquired right of suffrage for women made the Harding administration more receptive to appointing women to responsible positions within the federal government. Harding named Mabel Walker Willebrandt as assistant attorney general, a precedent-shattering move. He opened the diplomatic service to women, appointed women to head three bureaus, catered to the women's movement by attempting to create a department of social welfare, and refused to dismiss women from the government service as an economy measure. All in all, the women's movement found promising advances under the administration.

The Harding administration had a mixed record regarding groups not in the mainstream of American society. Harding had released Debs but supported immigration limits, and he remained silent on nativist movements. Blacks found comfort in his words but became disillusioned with the Republican party. Uncertain as to the extent of women's political power after 1920, Harding was more prepared to meet at least some of the demands of the newly enfranchised women.

Normalcy at work provided an uneven picture. It was clear that the emphasis of the administration was on creating a business-like government. Harding believed business the prime function of the nation and government. The theme of domestic policy followed by the administration was to facilitate business, which would bring peace and prosperity. The Bureau of the Budget—one of the Harding administration's more significant achievements—was a case in point. By a commitment to rational planning of the federal budget, while preaching and practicing economy, the administration demonstrated to the business community that it was serious about reorienting the national government. As a result, the programs of Wilson's New Freedom were substantially altered, though the regulatory agencies so painfully created by the Progressives were not dismantled.

Harding was a conservative. Aiding business was acceptable, but helping the individual citizen in need lay outside of the framework of Harding's view of the role of government. If nonbusiness elements of the community benefited from the government policies, it was well and good. But events proved that many people remained apart from the benefits accrued by business, and the administration was unwilling to use its power to alter society in a way to help its less fortunate members. The conservative bias toward wealth was all too apparent during the presidency of Harding.

5

★★★★★

FOREIGN POLICY I:
STRUCTURES AND REVOLUTIONS

I

President-elect Harding announced to the press on February 21, 1921, that Charles Evans Hughes had formally accepted an offer to become secretary of state. Asked by the press whom to consult on matters relating to the State Department, Harding responded: "You must ask Mr. Hughes about that. That is going to be another policy of the next Administration. From the beginning the Secretary of State will speak for the State Department."[1] With that he retired, leaving Hughes with the reporters.

Harding generally kept to his statement, but he was not without knowledge about foreign affairs. In his years as publisher of the *Marion Star* he had exhibited more than normal interest in international relations, generally supporting the emergence of the United States on the world scene. He had traveled widely, for a political figure of the time, first going to Europe in 1907, returning in 1909, and yet again in 1911. In 1909 he made a side visit to Egypt. In 1911 he visited in the Caribbean. In 1915 he traveled to Hawaii, and between his election and inauguration as president he journeyed to Panama. He had traveled more than many of his predecessors. Further, he had served as chairman of the Senate's Committee on the Philippine Islands, where he opposed Wilson's plan for independence, and on the Committees on Naval Affairs,

Pacific Islands, and Territories. He was also a member of the Foreign Relations Committee. While these experiences did not make him an expert on foreign affairs, they made him aware of their complexities. But he was not comfortable in dealing with diplomatic problems. Because of this feeling and because of his administrative theories, developed by watching the Wilson administration, he was glad to leave Hughes in charge. This represented a departure from Wilson, who had used Bryan, Lansing, and even Bainbridge Colby largely as clerks and kept control of foreign policy in the White House.

Hughes had first met Harding in 1916 when the then senator from Ohio presided at the meeting at which Hughes accepted nomination as the Republican presidential candidate. He did not see Harding again until he visited Marion during the 1920 campaign. The two men were not close friends but developed effective working relations. From the start, Hughes knew he would have control of foreign affairs. As he later noted, concerning dealings with Harding: "I realized that I must take a full measure of responsibility when I felt definite action should be taken. I did not go to him with a statement of difficulties and ask him what should be done, but supplemented my statements of the facts in particular cases by concrete proposals upon which he could act at once, and to which he almost invariably gave his approval."[2]

Hughes kept the president informed on just about every activity of the State Department. He saw him, or talked with him on the telephone, almost every day. He sent dispatches to the president, provided papers on problems, and brought returning mission chiefs to the White House. Hughes at first tried to work through the cabinet, giving detailed summaries about diplomatic problems. He found there were too many leaks to the press. Harding, for his part, had respect for and even awe of Hughes's ability and contented himself with giving the secretary advice on how to get along with Congress and how to work within the public mood of the country. For Hughes, who liked Harding, this was a fine relationship. In contrast to other members of the administration, Hughes was not comfortable in giving advice outside his field of authority. He had accepted the position as chief foreign-policy–maker in the Harding administration and wanted to give advice only on that subject.

Hughes did not have much background in foreign affairs. He was a graduate of Brown University and Columbia Law School, with experience in the law and in state and national politics as well as on the nation's highest court. His formal training consisted of teaching a course in international law during two years at the Cornell University Law School in the early 1890s. Still, it was clear from the first day that he settled in on the south side of the second floor of the State, War, and Navy Building, now the Old Executive Office Building, next door to the White House, that he meant to control the department. Arriving at work promptly at 9:00 A.M. and rarely leaving before 7:00 P.M., he stayed on top of every phase of the department's activities. He demanded frequent reports, took his own pen to revise department papers, and expected immediate responses when he summoned officials. It was Hughes who made or approved all the decisions of the department.

While such a style could have earned Hughes hostility, his reception in the department was positive. Department officers were impressed. One recalled: "I have never worked with a man who could go over papers as rapidly as he could, know what was in them, and know accurately." Even more important in gaining respect and affection of officials was his reliance on the diplomatic and consular services. From the start, he made every effort to staff the offices of the department, in Washington and abroad, with career officers. He asked the outgoing undersecretary, Norman Davis: "Please tell me who are the incompetent Division Chiefs because I want to get rid of them. Tell me who are the competent ones, because I want to keep them."[3]

Hughes appointed Henry P. Fletcher as undersecretary, Fred Dearing as assistant secretary, and Robert Woods Bliss as third assistant secretary, and retained Alvey A. Adee as second assistant secretary and Wilbur J. Carr as head of the consular service. His division chiefs were mostly officers of the diplomatic service: John V. A. MacMurray for the Far East, Sumner Welles for Latin America, Allen W. Dulles for the Near East, DeWitt C. Poole for Russia. Fletcher later became envoy to Belgium, and Hughes replaced him with William Phillips, who had served as minister to the Netherlands. Hughes was forced by Harding to make some patronage diplomatic appointments: Richard Washburn Child, editor of *Collier's Weekly*, became ambassador to Italy; Myron T. Herrick, former governor of Ohio, returned to Paris (he had served there during the Taft administration); Alanson B. Houghton, chairman of the board of the Corning Glass Works, went to Berlin; and George Harvey, editor of the *North American Review*, went to London. Hughes especially fought the last appointment and gave in only when Harding insisted that he was obligated to Harvey.

There were other such appointments, but Hughes supported them: Jacob G. Schurman, president of Cornell University, to China; Charles B. Warren, a Detroit lawyer with diplomatic experience, to Japan; and Cyrus E. Wood, who had served as Taft's minister to Portugal, to Spain. And Hughes made appointments from the diplomatic service: Joseph Grew went to Switzerland, Hugh Gibson to Poland, Charles S. Wilson to Bulgaria, Edwin V. Morgan to Brazil, William M. Collier to Chile. Six of the 9 ambassadors the Harding administration appointed had diplomatic experience, as did 14 of the 30 ministers. Hughes's policy was carried on at all levels, with 87 of 102 appointments in the consular service going to men with an average of ten years of experience.

Hughes lectured to the United States Chamber of Commerce in 1922 on the necessity for a trained foreign service. It was flattering to believe that the average American could easily represent his country abroad, but this idea was costly in the long run. "The patent fact is that you cannot have an efficient Foreign Service without having trained men," Hughes admonished, "and you cannot secure trained men without an adequate system for their selection and maintenance."[4] He stressed promotion from within and raised salaries in the diplomatic and consular services so they would not become the domain of the financially well-off. He supported the Rogers Act of 1924, which rotated personnel between Washington and the field and integrated the diplomatic and consular services, ending long-time dissension. In all these actions he gained Harding's support. The Civil Service Reform League commended Hughes and the administration. There is little question but that Hughes and Harding had a much better record in this field than their Democratic predecessors. Most important of all, the morale of the diplomatic service and the quality of its applicants improved, and the beginnings of the modern professionalism of the diplomatic corps were set in motion.

In still another area Hughes proved effective. His relations with the press, like Harding's, were excellent. He viewed public opinion as the ultimate source of foreign policy and believed the State Department had to educate the public. One of the most effective methods was through the press. Hughes or his undersecretary saw the press twice each day, except in the slow summer season, and the secretary spoke freely, without notes. Usually he would not allow himself to be quoted, but he was candid and solicitous. He worked at establishing good relations with some of the more prominent newsmen, such as Walter Lippmann of the *New York World* and Rollo Ogden of the *New York Times*. His conferences proved lively, and reporters crowded in to hear him. This was in marked contrast to the Wilson years. In addition, Hughes carried his views to the American public by means of speeches. There was no question as to who was the spokesman of the administration on international relations.

While Hughes had not had much experience, by 1921 he had developed his views on foreign policy. He had concluded that "foreign policies are not built upon abstractions" but resulted from international cooperation which recognized "divergent national ambitions." He believed that war was a continuing feature of international relations and thought the most important task of the diplomat was to avoid war. He held little hope for the repression of armed conflict by radical revision of international law. He saw no point—and here his disagreement with Wilson was clear—in formulas "which would require states to act contrary to their vital interests." This led him to the "most distinctive" enterprise of his era—"development of institutions for the promotion of international arbitration, adjudication, and conciliation, as well as the codification of traditional international law."[5] He stressed international law and diplomatic accommodation. He believed in progressive development of the world order.

Hughes lacked bold imagination and kept coming back to law as the major factor in international relations. His attitude toward diplomatic recognition, important in relations with Russia and Mexico, was an example of the influence of law upon his policy. In dealing with recognition, he did not judge it by European but by American standards, and he looked for precedents to guide him. He recognized the right of revolution and maintained he would not attempt to interfere with internal concerns of any country. He quoted Thomas Jefferson who, when secretary of state, wrote that America could not deny any nation the right "whereon our own government is founded"—to govern by whatever form it pleases, change forms at will, and transact business with nations through whatever organ it thinks proper: king, convention, assembly, committee, president, or anything else.[6] To Jefferson the will of the nation was the only essential. Hughes saw this policy throughout the history of recognition of foreign governments by the United States. He quoted Secretary of State James Buchanan to the effect that the United States always had recognized *de facto* governments. Buchanan maintained that nations had the right to reform political institutions, but a government had to be capable of maintaining itself and "then its recognition on our part inevitably follows."

Hughes's ideas on recognition came from these precedents, as well as others. Secretary of State William H. Seward had introduced the idea that the United States would not recognize a government established by force in violation of constitutional principles until the people approved the regime: a new administration had to be "sanctioned by the formal acquiescence and acceptance of the people." Hughes admitted it was difficult to determine the will of the people, which could be manifested by continued acquiescence. In any case, Hughes stated, a wise precaution was to allow enough time to enable any new regime to prove its stability and the apparent acquiescence of the people.

McKinley's secretary of state, John Hay, had added another requirement to the recognition policy of the United States. He believed that a new government should be able to fulfill its international obligations, as well as to be in control of the administration of the country. David Jayne Hill, who was acting secretary of state in 1900, had written that the rule of the United States was to defer recognition until a government was in possession of the machinery of state, with the assent of the people, and was also "in a position to fulfill all the international obligations and responsibilities incumbent upon a foreign State under treaties and international law."

Hughes agreed that the ability to perform international obligations was important, though not enough. There had to be both ability and action. Harding's secretary again cited precedent. Wilson had refused to recognize the government of Victoriano Huerta in 1913 in Mexico; and although he had conditionally recognized Venustiano Carranza, Mexican assurances with respect to international obligations had not been fulfilled. Consequently, Wilson withheld recognition from Álvaro Obregón in 1920.

For Hughes, the two criteria for recognition—present and future stability (including acceptance by the people), as well as ability and willingness to fulfill international obligations—were part of American policy before he took control of the department. These criteria became the basis of his policy. In the instance of recognition, as well as in other areas, the law had great influence on Hughes.

While Harding gave Hughes responsibility in foreign policy, Hughes faced competition for control from two different sources. The Harding administration was clearly at the beginning of the process that ended the State Department's primacy in foreign affairs.

The first of the competitors was, of course, Congress. When Harding announced Hughes's appointment, Senator Boies Penrose from Pennsylvania commented: "I do not think it matters much who is Secretary of State. Congress—especially the Senate—will blaze the way in connection with our foreign policies."[7] Hughes did run into a good deal of difficulty with Congress. The Senate's Committee on Foreign Relations, headed by Henry Cabot Lodge, proved troublesome. Flushed with victory over Wilson's treaty, this committee looked with suspicion on Hughes and the department, questioning almost every effort at international cooperation. Recognizing the lesson of the Wilson years, and with Harding unwilling to challenge his former colleagues, Hughes set out to woo the Senate. He frequently consulted members of Congress, avoided any direct challenge, used unofficial representatives at certain diplomatic gatherings, appointed members of Congress to represent the United States at international conferences, and on occasion bypassed Congress through executive agreements. He thought Congress's role was limited by the Constitution and believed that Congress had a duty to appropriate funds for the executive to carry out foreign policy. Nonetheless, he constantly found himself contending with Congress over foreign policy.

A second competitor came from within the executive branch, in the form of Herbert Hoover's Department of Commerce. That department's Bureau of Foreign and Domestic Commerce (BFDC), under Dr. Julius Klein, challenged the State Department for control of economic aspects of American foreign policy. To be sure, this was not a new phenomenon. In previous years, especially in wartime, other agencies took an interest in foreign affairs. In World War I, agencies like the War Trade Board and the Committee on Public Information became competitors of the State Department. Conflict continued into the Harding administration and, in fact, increased during those years, setting in motion a process that eventually led to the creation of the National Security Council in 1947.

Hughes got on well with his rival Hoover. They respected one another and were clearly two of the strong members of the Harding cabinet. But Hoover was appointed secretary of commerce with a commitment from Harding that he would be involved in economic policy. He thus came to think of himself as secretary of commerce and assistant secretary of everything else. He believed the government had to be changed to facilitate large-scale American involvement in international economic relations. Hoover reorganized the Bureau of Foreign and Domestic Commerce along commodity and regional lines and built a network of fifty offices all over the world, reporting on trade and investment. He staffed these offices with trade commissioners and commercial attachés who competed with State Department officers. He expanded publications and created new ones to report findings of his overseas personnel. Hoover understood that it could become profitable for American business to exploit foreign economic opportunities. Consequently, he used Department of Commerce resources to point out existing opportunities and also to aid those engaged in foreign economic endeavors.[8] He worked with business leaders and heavily influenced policies dealing with loans, trade treaties, war debts, reparations, unstable currencies, armament expenditures, capital outflows for investment, and tariff revisions.

Since America's presence on the world economic scene was recent and no rules existed for the division of responsibility between State and Commerce, the aggressive Hoover was able to increase his authority, especially since Hughes seemed reluctant to do battle. Hoover expanded his consular service and received all economic reports submitted to the Department of State. By 1923 Commerce had clearly gotten the best of the battle and, by the end of the Harding presidency, had established its supremacy in international economics.

Notwithstanding these rivalries within the executive branch and between that branch and Congress for control of foreign policy, Hughes remained a dominant force in foreign policy during the administration. But, it must be repeated, he was not the only force.

II

Of all the many problems left unsettled by Wilson in international relations, perhaps the most troublesome, and in the long-run the most significant, concerned relations with the Soviet government created by the Bolshevik revolution in Russia in late 1917. Interestingly, Hughes lost control of policy toward Russia to Hoover, who had experience in dealing with Russians.

The Russian Revolution had troubled American policy since the moment of the Bolshevik takeover. Americans reacted with euphoria to the overthrow of Tsar Nicholas II in March 1917, concluding that democracy had replaced autocracy. But the provisional government, as the government that replaced Nicholas was called, proved unable to consolidate its power while continuing to fight in the World War. There were frequent changes in leaders, and finally the Bolsheviks, led by Lenin and Trotsky, took over. The Soviets began negotiating with Germany and eventually signed a separate peace at Brest-Litovsk in early 1918, ending Russia's role in the great struggle. The United States meanwhile remained undecided as to its policy toward Russia. Pushed by Secretary Lansing, who feared bolshevism, Wilson decided not to recognize the Soviet government, following the precedent set in 1913 in regard to Mexico. Later, pushed again by Lansing as well as France and especially Great Britain, he consented to send troops to North Russia and Siberia.[9] The limited purpose for the dispatch of these troops was soon lost sight of, and they became, planned or not, part of an army of intervention that sought to overthrow the Bolsheviks. The Allies failed, and the Russian problem remained unsettled as the negotiators convened in Paris to conclude the war.

Hoover had watched the Bolshevik revolution and American policy toward Russia with a good deal of concern. His interest in Russia had begun at the turn of the century and was quickened by trips in pursuit of mining concessions. These visits affected the way he looked at the revolution and convinced him well before 1917 that there was trouble ahead. He had been struck with the contrasts of the country, the extremes of wealth and poverty, the "hideous social and governmental" structures. Hoover had become convinced that "some day the country would blow up." He was not surprised when Nicholas was overthrown, but he told the journalist Will Irwin, "This revolution will be difficult to stabilize. There have been centuries of oppression. There is no large middle class. There is almost total illiteracy in the people. There is no general experience in government. Russia cannot maintain a wholly liberal republic yet. Revolutions always go further than their creators expect. And in its swing, this one is more likely to go to the left than to the right."[10]

Hoover's reaction to the Bolshevik takeover several months later was both specific, in view of his experiences, and general. He looked on with dismay as the Bolsheviks encouraged workers to take over plants, expropriate private property, dismissed management, and dramatically increased wages. He knew that untrained workers could not supply the technical and administrative skills an industrially developing Russia needed. On a more general level he was concerned with the international policies followed by the Bolsheviks: withdrawal from the war, the hostile attitude toward the Allies, the treaty which allowed the Germans to move troops to the Western front.

During the months between November 1917 and March 1919, when Hoover emerged as the dominant figure in American-Russian affairs, he had a good deal of time to come to some conclusions about bolshevism and Soviet Russia. Hoover became convinced that bolshevism flourished where starvation existed—bolshevism and starvation went hand in hand. It was a simplistic explanation, but with Hoover's background it was natural. As he watched the Bolsheviks control European Russia and withstand the anti-Bolshevik movements, all he read seemed to prove his analysis. He became alarmed about bolshevism beyond Russia and worried about the people of Austria, Serbia, Bulgaria, and Turkey.

At the Paris Peace Conference where Hoover served as director-general of relief, his views and actions concerning the Russian question were based on two themes. He believed in the Russian people, and his compassion was genuine. The second theme was his strong opposition to bolshevism. Yet he felt that the Western Allies could not succeed militarily in overthrowing bolshevism. In Paris he proposed to feed Russia, as a humanitarian undertaking and the most effective antidote to bolshevism; to protect the emerging independent countries from bolshevism; and to assist Russian prisoners held in Germany. All these activities, especially the attempt to extend relief by means of a neutral commission, proved a searing experience. Even as the conference came to a close, Hoover remained convinced, as he told Wilson, that the Bolshevik government would fall of its "own weight or it will have swung sufficiently right to be absorbed in a properly representative government."[11] He thought the foundation of any government was economic stability, relating especially to currency, transportation, and the production and distribution of goods, and he pointed to economic chaos in Soviet Russia.

Hoover's activities and ideas about Russia at Paris were a curious combination. He had had as much experience with Russia as any of the major figures at the conference. He at times showed great insight in Russian affairs and at other times seemed naïve. Better than most statesmen, he understood the roots of bolshevism and its power. He had seen prewar Russia and knew that oppression had brought revolution. He realized that the country might move from one extreme to the other and that military intervention could never succeed. At Paris he worked against the plans for intervention. He believed bolshevism was not limited to Russia. But he clung to linking bolshevism with starvation, and perhaps more than anyone else was responsible for the belief that full stomachs would eliminate bolshevism. All this meant that the Allies waited for the Bolsheviks to be overthrown, one way or another, and did not grapple with the problem. Hoover was rigid in his outlook, believing the socialist structure in Russia made economic activity impossible.

Hoover's views were important both at Paris and in the years that followed. As head of the American Relief Administration, he supplied gasoline, food, and clothing to the anti-Bolshevik army moving against Petrograd in late 1919, and he offered to feed starving children in the Bolshevik-controlled area of Poland in 1920. He also offered the Soviet government supplies on condition that American prisoners held by the Soviets be released. In all these efforts success eluded him.

Meanwhile, the Wilson administration made formal its policy toward the Soviet government in August 1920 with publication of the so-called Colby Note. The note adopted the nonrecognition policy, which was supported by an American populace alarmed over the spread of bolshevism to the United States. Secretary of State Colby stressed friendship between the American and Russian people and stated the American government's belief that the Russians would "overcome the existing anarchy, suffering and destruction." While they had the right to adopt "any particular political or social structure," the United States believed "the existing regime in Russia is based upon the negation of every principle of honor and good faith and every usage and convention underlying the whole structure of international law—the negation, in short, of every principle upon which it is possible to base harmonious and fruitful relations." The United States government was not able to find "any common ground upon which it can stand with a power whose conceptions of international relations are so alien to its own, so utterly repugnant to its moral sense." Hence it refused to recognize the Bolshevik government. The note announced opposition to the dismemberment of Russia. The United States would not recognize the independence of new countries, such as Georgia, created out of Russian territory. It included no mention of trade, repudiation of tsarist debts, or property nationalized after the Soviet takeover, and thus the possibility of trade remained. This note proved important and throughout the 1920s remained the basic statement of American policy toward Russia. Wilson's policy became institutionalized by Republican administrations in the 1920s. Hoover found himself in complete agreement with it.[12]

There is evidence that before his inauguration Harding was

willing to reopen the question of recognition, as well as discuss the possibility of trade. But his willingness soon disappeared. In fact, in his inaugural Harding had made note of revolutions, referring to the Soviet experience:

> If revolution insists upon overturning established order, let other peoples make the tragic experiment. There is no place for it in America. When World War threatened civilization we pledged our resources and our lives to its preservation, and when revolution threatens we unfurl the flag of law and order and renew our consecration. Ours is a constitutional freedom where the popular will is the law supreme and minorities are sacredly protected. Our revisions, reformations, and evolutions reflect a deliberate judgment and an orderly progress, and we mean to cure our ills, but never destroy or permit destruction by force.[13]

Within three weeks of taking office in March 1921, the administration publicly announced its Russian policy, and the individual who announced it was Hoover. The secretary of commerce issued a widely publicized release noting that trade was limited by communism. He stated that the question of trade with Russia was far more a political than an economic question as long as Russia was controlled by the Bolsheviks. "Under their economic system, no matter how they moderate it in name, there can be no real return to production in Russia, and therefore Russia will have no considerable commodities to export and consequently, no great ability to obtain imports." Hoover called on the Soviets to abandon "their present economic situation," for trade credits could not be extended to "a government that repudiates private property." Responding to inquiries he had received from trade associations, he said that trade with the Bolsheviks had to be limited to Soviet gold reserves, estimated between $60,000,000 and $200,000,000. Even trade in that amount would not help production, until the Russians abandoned communism. Hoover apparently released his statement before clearing it with Hughes, an extraordinary action, though he later wrote Hughes he hoped his statement reflected the views of an "earlier conversation."[14]

The Soviets meanwhile were active. The day after Hoover's press release the Soviet representative in Estonia, Maxim Litvinov, sent an appeal from the president of the All-Russian Central Executive Committee, Mikhail Kalinin, calling for reversal of the recognition policy and an improvement in relations. This appeal was discussed at a cabinet meeting on March 25, 1921, where both Hoover and Hughes spoke against it. It received no support and was answered that same day by Hughes. The American government was "unable to perceive that there is any proper basis for considering trade relations," and recognition would be discussed only after "the safety of life, the recognition by firm guarantees of private property, the sanctity of contract, and the rights of labor" were agreed upon by the Bolsheviks. The United States hoped for fundamental changes. Hughes followed this up with a letter to labor leader Samuel Gompers, noting that "the attitude and action of the present authorities of Russia have tended to undermine its political and economic relations with other countries."[15]

What did these statements of March 1921 mean to Soviet-American relations? They clearly accepted the Wilsonian doctrine of refusing to recognize the Russian Soviet Federated Socialist Republic, which became the Union of Soviet Socialist Republics in 1922. The Republicans agreed with their Democratic predecessors about the ideological reasons for nonrecognition. Hoover was convinced of the need to proclaim an American ideology, because bolshevism, more than any ideology, threatened American individualism, mobility, private property, equality of opportunity, democracy, and economic expansion. For Hoover, relations with Russia were unacceptable.

These March statements, especially by Hoover and Hughes, went beyond the Colby Note by tying commerce and ideology to recognition. Indeed, the Republican leaders were so opposed to the Soviet system that they "sometimes suspected all commercial propositions from Russia of being nothing more than propaganda tactics aimed at obtaining recognition." Initially, the Harding cabinet was unanimous in its negative reaction. The way to counter bolshevism was to prohibit both diplomatic and commercial relations. The linkage of trade and ideology created contradictions in formulating a policy toward Russia. Both Hoover and Hughes believed it was vital for America to increase its world trade, yet "they found it difficult to decide whether to take advantage of what Russian market there was or to use economic pressure against the Soviets."[16]

The final point that became clear in March 1921 was that Hoover had preempted the role of spokesman for policy with Russia. Hughes shared Hoover's view of the Russian problem, and may have been even more alarmed by bolshevism than was Hoover. Even so, it was Hoover, not Hughes, who articulated policy.

The American response to the famine in Soviet Russia in 1921 only increased Hoover's preeminence in Russian policy. By early summer, 1921, Russia was in the grip of one of its worst famines, the result of a prolonged drought in the Volga region, the effects of the civil war, and the economic breakdown the revolution had brought. Lenin recognized that "war communism" had caused turmoil and introduced the "New Economic Policy" (NEP), a limited return to capitalism. But the summer raised the possibility of starvation of millions. With the government in danger of being overthrown, Lenin permitted the author Maxim Gorky to issue an appeal to "All Honest People" to aid the famine-stricken parts of Soviet Russia. Describing the suffering, Gorky appealed for food, medicine, and clothing.[17]

The only country capable of responding was the United States, and the only individual in a position to coordinate such an effort was Hoover. While Gorky's appeal was not directed at Hoover, the secretary was interested in it. Seeing an opportunity to carry on humanitarian work, modify bolshevism or possibly even help bring the downfall of the Bolsheviks, alleviate agricultural surpluses in the United States, and bring the release of American prisoners from Soviet Russia, Hoover worked to gain support from both President Harding and Secretary Hughes. Harding and Hughes consented, with the president giving "fullest approval of the action on the part of the American Relief Administration in initiating an effort to mitigate the famine in Russia, particularly to save the lives of children." Thus Hoover responded to Gorky, announcing his willingness to render aid but only under certain conditions: freedom must be given to Americans imprisoned in Russia; and any relief plan would be conducted without interference, on a nonpolitical basis. After negotiations the Soviet Union and Hoover's American Relief Administration (ARA) signed an agreement at Riga on August 20, 1921, which met most of Hoover's demands.[18]

The agreement, which the Soviets termed a treaty and hoped would lead to better Soviet-American relations, proved to be an instrument to aid famine victims. Hoover moved to start the relief program. He consolidated his position within the government, getting the president to announce that all relief had to go through ARA, and he began to plan the relief as well as seek funds to pay for it. In the end, by mid-1923, more than 200 Americans had helped set up some 18,000 stations in Russia which fed approximately 10,000,000 people. About $78,000,000 was expended, of which $10,000,000 came from Russian gold. Of the rest, approximately $28,000,000 was American government money and the remainder came from public charity. There were difficulties with Soviet officials, but generally the relief went smoothly. The food (some 540,000 tons), clothing, and medical supplies were much appreciated. Foreign Minister Georgi Chicherin spoke of "grandiose, disinterested aid rendered by the American people through the ARA, the self-sacrificing activity of the personnel of the ARA, and the splendid organization of its entire work." One of the ironies of this mission was that the ardent anti-Bolshevik Hoover may have played a role in reversal of the course of the Russian economy in 1921–1922 and "contributed significantly to the maintenance of the Bolshevik regime."[19]

ARA activities in Russia made Hoover preeminent in Soviet-American relations. Without the secretary of commerce the ARA would not have become involved in the Russian operation. Hoover was able to bring together diverse groups in America for "what was simultaneously a self-aggrandizing, humanitarian, anti-Communist, anti-depression effort." The ARA was the first channel of communication between the United States and Soviet Russia and could have served as an instrument for reconciliation. But because of Hoover's continued opposition to bolshevism, he still fought recognition of Russia. With the refusal of the administration to alter its policy, a unique opportunity for a significant change in Soviet-American relations was lost.[20]

Hoover's continued support of nonrecognition proved important during the years of the Harding administration, for his view fortified that of the secretary of state. The two cabinet officers were able to keep Harding in their corner. The American non-recognition policy resulted in a refusal to participate in a conference of European powers in April 1922 in Genoa to discuss Central and Eastern European reconstruction. The American government feared that political questions, especially recognition of Russia, would be discussed. The State Department did permit Richard Washburn Child, ambassador to Italy, to attend as an "unofficial observer." The conference divided over the Russian question. Germany's decision to sign the Rapallo agreement to restore diplomatic and trade relations with Russia brought the meeting to a close, though another took place at The Hague in June, with similar results. Again the United States refused to participate.

These difficulties intensified Hoover's and Hughes's belief in nonrecognition. Despite some Senate pressure, which included the introduction on May 15, 1922, of a resolution "that the Senate of the United States favors recognition of the present Soviet Government of Russia" by Senator Borah of Idaho, the administration stood firm. Throughout 1922 and 1923, Hughes and Hoover opposed recognition. In a March 21, 1923, speech to the Women's International League for Peace and Freedom, Hughes said "the fundamental question in the recognition of a government is whether it shows ability and a disposition to discharge international obligations." When the Soviets recognized tsarist debts, gave safeguards for life and property, abided by international conventions, and stopped propaganda activities, the United States would consider recognition. As late as July 19, 1923, several weeks before Harding's death, Hughes wrote Gompers that the United States accepted "the right of revolution and we do not attempt to determine the internal concerns of other States." But recognition also meant a need to fulfill international obligations, and the Soviets had repudiated that responsibility. "What is most serious," Hughes said, "is that there is conclusive evidence that those in control in Moscow have not given up their original purpose of destroying existing governments wherever they can do so throughout the world." Thus the United States would not recognize the Soviet Union. It is possible that the Republicans might have reversed the policy had it not been for the "confiscation of private property, repudiation of debts, and world revolution, all of which were even more distasteful to Republican conservatism than to Democratic liberalism."[21]

If Hoover agreed with Hughes about continuing nonrecognition, the secretaries of commerce and state came to have differences over the American embargo on trade with Soviet Russia. Initially, American business supported the no-trade, nonrecognition policy proclaimed in March 1921. Hoover's first statement was endorsed by a group of businessmen, including the presidents of United States Steel, the National City Bank of New York, and the Baltimore and Ohio Railroad, as well as by the executive board of the International Longshoremen's Association. Soon the pressure to end the trade embargo began, as some businessmen feared they would be frozen out of Russian markets and called for separation of trade and recognition policies. Hoover was much more sensitive to this thinking than Hughes, and by late 1921 work with famine relief had convinced him of the trade potential with Russia. He began to argue within the administration for permission for companies to enter Russia. Using some arguments made by former Indiana governor James P. Goodrich, who had served with the

ARA, Hoover recommended that Hughes approve an American trade mission. He publicly suggested such trade. Hughes reluctantly agreed to Hoover's suggestion for the trade mission, but the project fell through when the Soviet government demanded a reciprocal arrangement. Neither Hoover nor Hughes could approve a Bolshevik mission to the United States.

The conflict between Hoover and Hughes over trade with Russia continued throughout 1922 and 1923. It was only part of a larger dispute as to whether State or Commerce should control American foreign economic policy. State and Commerce disagreed over credit being granted to the Soviet government by American businessmen, the purchase by Americans of Soviet bonds, the acceptance of Russian gold for purchase in the United States, and the use of German middlemen in Soviet-American trade. Many of the controversies that began in the Harding administration continued into the Coolidge years. Hoover often supplied American businessmen information from the Slavic Section of the European Division of the BFDC and privately encouraged them to exploit Russian trade opportunities.[22] By 1921 many division chiefs of the BFDC were sending information to businessmen who inquired about conditions in Russia; and the next year *Commerce Reports* and *Supplements*, publications of the Commerce Department, began listing Russian figures.

With the end of general internal disorder in the Soviet Union by 1922, the possibility of Soviet-American trade increased. Until that time banking, financial, and export-import groups were in agreement with the nonrecognition, no-trade policy. In 1923 trade increased and so did the significance of Hoover and the Department of Commerce, who were sympathetic to trade. At the time the Harding administration ended, the issue of trade was still unresolved. But Hoover's policy of nonrecognition while privately encouraging trade had gained the upper hand.

There were other pressures on Soviet-American relations. Some reached Harding directly. Even before he had been inaugurated, he had been pressed to change the Russian policy of the Wilson administration by recognizing the Soviet government. Privately and in public, some politicians and some of Harding's friends tried to change America's policy. Among the most active was Senator Joseph I. France of Maryland. Senator Borah carried on his battle on the Senate floor and in correspondence with the president. But Hughes and Hoover were against any change. On several occasions Hughes funneled reports to Harding describing conditions in Russia. One such report was by Francis B. Loomis, the former assistant secretary of state, after a three-month trip to Russia. Hughes wrote to Harding about Loomis's observations: "I fear that Mr. Loomis, despite his recent contact with various Russians, has not gained a just understanding of the situation."[23]

The pressure by 1923 had become so great that, apparently without the knowledge of either the secretary of state or the secretary of commerce, Harding approved visits to Russia by former Secretary of the Interior Albert Fall and by Borah's progressive ally Raymond Robins. Fall's trip began in May 1923 after the New Mexican saw the president, who allegedly wanted to "get the truth of Russian conditions." But Harding was to die before Fall, who came to favor recognition, could return. In the summer of 1923 Harding granted permission for Robins to investigate conditions in Russia but died while Robins was en route.

A pattern of pressures emerged during the Harding years that appears to show that the president and his secretaries of state and commerce were not in agreement as to relations with Russia. Some historians have concluded that the president would have changed America's Russian policy, approving trade and possibly even recognition. The conclusion that the Fall and Robins trips would have led to a reversal of policy had Harding lived does not seem warranted, especially since Harding again stated his support of nonrecognition in a speech written for delivery in San Francisco on July 31, 1923, but canceled because of the president's fatal illness. Harding's approval of the trips probably was an attempt to mollify critics rather than a prelude to change. Hoover and Hughes would have tried with all their power to prevent such a change, for "both were irrevocably committed to the waiting game."[24] It seems likely that Harding would have approved the expansion of Soviet-American trade that Hoover supported. There is no evidence that Harding was willing, or able, to reverse nonrecognition. Had Hoover and Hughes come to support recognition, such a reversal might have been possible. The Harding years represent a missed opportunity to better Soviet-American relations, which have been a problem for much of the twentieth century. Much of the responsibility for the missed opportunity must fall to Herbert Hoover, who more than any other individual made sure that the troubled Soviet-American relationship remained troubled throughout the 1920s.

III

If the Harding administration was unable to work out a satisfactory policy for the United States to follow in regard to the Russian revolution, the Republicans proved more effective in dealing with the Mexican revolution. The Mexican situation was inherited from the Wilson administration. Washington had found it difficult to deal with events in Mexico after the 1910 overthrow of long-time dictator Porfirio Díaz. Francisco Madero's succession was looked on with hope but his presidency was short-lived, with Huerta taking over in 1913. Huerta earned Wilson's opposition and eventual intervention at Veracruz. Then Huerta fell, with an American push, to be succeeded by Carranza. Conditionally recognized, Carranza was opposed by Francisco ("Pancho") Villa, and Carranza became a problem. Wilson sent General John J. Pershing chasing Villa around Mexico in 1916. Then there was the 1917 Mexican Constitution which affected American interests. In the United States some Republican senators led by Fall began to look into relations with Mexico. In a long report of May 28, 1920, the Fall committee indicated that Mexico under Carranza was no safe place for American citizens or investment. The United States should withdraw recognition until a government came to power capable of maintaining stability and willing to comply with international obligations, which included responsibility for American lives and property, an understanding that certain provisions of the 1917 Constitution did not apply to Americans, and the appointment of commissioners to decide claims and solve disputes concerning the international boundary. Only after these stipulations were met should the United States extend recognition. If unfavorable conditions continued, the report recommended that the American government act forcefully against Mexico.

Before the Fall committee had completed its investigation and recommendations, the United States was relieved of further contention with Carranza. There had been increased Mexican dissatisfaction with him; and Mexico's military hero, General Álvaro Obregón, gained control of Mexico City in early May 1920. Carranza fled to the mountains where he was slain. Obregón's supporter, Adolfo de la Huerta, became provisional president. There was consideration of recognition by the Wilson administration. Soon Secretary Colby announced the conditions for recognition, which included a mixed claims commission, nonenforcement of retroactive provisions of the 1917 Constitution, and servicing of the

Mexican foreign debt. Both de la Huerta and Obregón stated that Mexico would pay all it owed to citizens of the United States and would not apply retroactive aspects of the Constitution, but they felt that their government should be recognized without any agreement. They turned down Colby's offer. The State Department then hesitated, and the Mexican government became convinced it could not afford to deal with an outgoing president. Though de la Huerta did not obtain American recognition, his administration had suppressed the revolts of General Pablo Gonzalez and Pancho Villa and had brought internal peace.

With Mexico at peace and at the tasks of rehabilitation, an election was held, and Obregón won a four-year term, beginning December 1, by an overwhelming majority. After the inauguration there was increased pressure to recognize the Mexican government. The ceremony was attended by governors of Texas and New Mexico and other Americans favoring relations. Wilson received messages urging recognition from the governors of Arizona, California, Illinois, Michigan, and Oklahoma, as well as from Chambers of Commerce of such cities as St. Louis, Los Angeles, and San Francisco. All were concerned with trade and alarmed over further confiscations by the Mexican government if the United States did not extend recognition. Wilson and Obregón refused to reconsider their positions. Mexico waited patiently for Harding to become president. After Harding's victory, Obregón announced his pleasure with the results and declared American-Mexican problems at an end. He described Wilson as Mexico's "most terrible enemy" and March 4, 1921, as a "day of deliverance."[25]

The day of deliverance from nonrecognition did not come so quickly. The Mexican problem that confronted Secretary Hughes was compounded by Harding's announcement that the new secretary of the interior was none other than Fall. During the Huerta era Fall had proposed that an army of 500,000 men should occupy Mexico to open up communications between the seaports and Mexico City and to establish a constitutional government. Fall indicated that there would be no change of policy concerning recognition under the Harding administration. He said that so long as he had anything to do with the Mexican question no government would be recognized which did not enter into a written agreement to protect American citizens and their property rights in Mexico. Many people believed that Fall's ideas would influence his friend the new president.

To the new secretary of state there was a more important and necessary condition to recognition than Obregón's pledge to protect American interests, or for that matter than Fall's demand for immediate indemnity for losses and injuries since 1910. Hughes had studied diplomatic recognition and the Mexican situation and had come to the conclusion that the program of reform in Mexico constituted a threat to American interests. Prior to recognition the Mexicans must sign a pact furnishing safeguards. The United States presented Obregón with a Draft Treaty of Amity and Commerce on May 27, 1921, intended to promote commercial intercourse and remove differences between the countries. The proposed treaty called for assurances against confiscation and expropriation, except for public purposes and then only with prompt payment of just compensation, and for a guarantee that neither the 1917 Mexican Constitution, which included the right to impose on private property such limits as the public interest might demand, nor the Carranza agrarian decree of January 6, 1915, would apply retroactively. The United States asked for restoration, where possible, of all that Americans had lost since 1910, compensation for that "which it is not possible to restore," and reciprocal guarantees for nationals of either country of freedom to worship. For Hughes, "Whenever Mexico is ready to give assurances that she will perform her fundamental obligation in the protection both of persons and of rights of property validly acquired, there will be no obstacles to the most advantageous relations between the two peoples." When Mexico proved willing to discharge international obligations by treaty, recognition would take place.

Hughes's decision was controversial, and he defended his position vigorously. Before the Chamber of Commerce in Washington on May 26, 1922, he declared that no state was entitled to a place within the family of nations if it destroyed honorable intercourse by confiscation and repudiation. In addition to public defense, Hughes and his department worked to keep the president's support. Undersecretary Fletcher in November 1921 wrote Harding that difficult as the Mexican problem appeared it was one of "common honesty and fair dealing, and should be squarely met." Harding agreed, content to leave the State Department in charge of Mexican policy. Nothing arose for a time to change his mind about the proper American attitude. The president replied to Fletcher that policy was "quite in harmony with all that I said during the political campaign of 1920, and it is quite in harmony with everything which has been said directly or indirectly to President Obregón." In March 1922 public demands for a change induced Hughes to write the president that the United States was "simply insisting that, as a *sine qua non* of international intercourse, property rights and obligations shall be secure and when it appears that a regime is adopting a confiscatory policy, we cannot enter into relations with it until we are satisfied that valid titles and rights acquired under its own laws will be respected." Hughes thought it a simple operation but important. Harding again agreed.

Hughes did much more than argue, privately and in public, against recognition. Using the economic difficulties foreigners faced as a result of the 1917 Constitution and suspension of payments on the $600,000,000 Mexican external debt, about a quarter of which was owed Americans, as justification, he closed the capital markets of the United States to Mexican loans. The Mexican government needed between $50,000,000 and $100,000,000 to stabilize the currency, establish a central bank, and finance internal reconstruction and development without increased taxation. The United States enjoyed the greatest capital surplus in the period after the World War, and "Hughes believed that by withholding American loan funds from Obregón, he could compel the Mexican leader to sign the treaty of amity and commerce."[26] In cutting out loans to Mexico, Hughes worked with Thomas W. Lamont, senior partner of the J. P. Morgan Company and chairman of the American section of the International Committee of Bankers in Mexico, a committee to get the new government to recognize the Mexican debt and resume payments on it. Hughes persuaded Lamont's committee to refuse to lend money to Mexico until Obregón accepted Hughes's treaty. The secretary of state also pressed the Oil Executive Committee, a group of oil men considering a loan to Mexico, to fall in line with department policy.

While Hughes was building support for nonrecognition, Obregón was far from inactive. Obregón made it clear that Mexico would never sign the treaty to gain recognition and said it was neither possible nor expedient for Mexico to sign a convention or treaty before being recognized. He did much more than merely issue statements. Realizing that Mexico needed American recognition for both prestige and economics, he set out to use propaganda to convince the American public that recognition would result in large commercial benefits. Obregón's government set up excursions to Mexico for businessmen; used an agency of the Mexican government in New York City as a clearing house for literature distributed in the United States; employed journalists such as the veteran correspondent of the *London Daily Telegraph*, Emile J.

Dillon, to write of the virtues of Obregón's government; hired a former state senator from Arizona, J. L. Schleimer, to lobby state legislatures to send to Washington resolutions supporting recognition (more than twenty eventually did); and used contacts to try to change the American government's position—with retired army general James A. Ryan, a friend of Harding's, the most important. This campaign, which one American official claimed cost nearly $2,000,000, proved effective, as businessmen, chambers of commerce, labor unions, state and national politicians, and newspapers called for a change in policy.[27]

Obregón took steps to lessen the fears businessmen had concerning the Mexican revolution. He announced his intent to settle claims and protect investments in Mexico; called for a commission to handle claims resulting from the revolution; and had his finance minister, former President de la Huerta, sign an agreement with the International Committee of Bankers, the Lamont–de la Huerta Agreement of June 1922, which recognized a Mexican external debt of over $500,000,000, plus interest of more than $200,000,000. Payments, with low interest, were to spread over forty-five years.

Obregón's activities increased the pressure for recognition, and so did the decisions by the Mexican Supreme Court which guaranteed rights of investors. One decision ruled that "petroleum properties in the process of development before May 1, 1917, when the present constitution took effect, are protected from a retroactive application."

While the department and Hughes remained committed to a treaty, other officials, including Harding, began to have doubts. Harding realized something had to be done. Letters, resolutions, memoranda, and personal visits, all calling for a change in policy, could not be ignored. Additionally, Fall, the opponent of recognition, had left the cabinet. Harding had suggested in July 1921 that the United States send a commissioner to Mexico to negotiate a settlement. By early 1923 the proposal was revived by General James A. Ryan, who represented the Texas Oil Company in Mexico. Ryan had returned to Washington in late March, had received Harding's permission for a conference, and had cleared the proposal through the State Department. He issued an invitation for direct negotiations to his friend President Obregón, who accepted, saying he was pleased to appoint two delegates to the conference.

It was announced that Mexican and American delegates would meet in Mexico City. Harding appointed Charles Beecher Warren, former ambassador to Japan, and John Barton Payne, former secre-

131

tary of the interior and then president of the American Red Cross, telling them *very emphatically* that he wanted a way to be found whereby the Government of the United States might recognize the Government of Mexico."[28] Known as the Bucareli Conference because it was held at the Mexican Foreign Affairs Ministry at No. 85 Avenida Bucareli in Mexico City, the meetings began in mid-May 1923 and lasted until August. The Mexicans made few concessions. The special and general claims conventions, which proved to be the heart of the settlement, could have been signed two years earlier. The special claims convention covered damages through revolutionary acts between November 20, 1910, and May 31, 1920, and the general claims convention covered both countries after July 4, 1868. Both conventions established commissions, with delegates appointed by each country and the Permanent Court of Arbitration at The Hague. In the end the long–drawn-out settlements of the claims were disappointing to the United States, but they ended temporary problems, and the United States formally accorded recognition on August 31, 1923.

In final analysis the Americans had backed down. From the outset the Mexican government had said it would never buy recognition at the cost of dignity. As pressure in favor of recognition increased, the American government had to abandon its position. A legal-minded secretary of state was bypassed by a president conscious of public opinion. Harding accepted the idea of a conference to discuss problems, and his successor accepted its decisions, although many questions were left unresolved. This controversy displayed many of the ideas that dominated Hughes's foreign policy and also their limits and indicated the difficulty the secretary had in keeping control of American foreign policy. The controversy was unique, for Harding, a president who generally stayed out of the making of foreign policy, played a decisive part in it.

IV

Relations between Mexico and the United States were only one part of the Latin American policy of the United States. Wilson's diplomacy between 1913 and 1921 had perhaps caused more controversy there than anywhere else in the world. Even Harding, not greatly interested in controlling foreign policy, had felt compelled to speak about Latin American policy during the 1920 campaign. Harding had criticized Wilson for intervening in both the Dominican Republic and Haiti, attacking the Democratic vice-presidential candidate, Franklin D. Roosevelt, for his part in the Haitian intervention:

> If I should be elected president . . . I will not empower an Assistant Secretary of the Navy to draft a constitution for helpless neighbors in the West Indies and jam it down their throats at the point of bayonets borne by the United States marines, nor will I misuse the power of the executive to cover with a veil of secrecy repeated acts of unwarranted interference in the domestic affairs of the little republics of the western hemisphere, such as in the last few years have not only made enemies of those who should be our friends but have rightfully discredited our country as their trusted neighbor.[29]

While these charges were partly political, an appeal to black Americans, Wilson's record in Latin America had been poor. Wilson's two interventions in Mexico had caused difficulty in Mexican-American relations, and Harding entered office with troops stationed in the Dominican Republic, Haiti, and Nicaragua. Other countries such as Cuba and Guatemala were fearful of intervention. Wilson had sounded a hopeful note in Latin American relations in 1913 by pledging cooperation between the United States and its southern neighbors, but other events had taken attention from the Western Hemisphere. After the war, with increased involvement in Latin America, especially through investment, the administration had turned its attention south of the border but made little progress.[30] Wilson and the American government remained distrusted.

From the beginning of the Harding administration, there was a division of authority in Latin America. The president generally stayed out of relations with Latin America. Aside from his activities regarding Mexico and his unfortunate appointment of a friend, E. Mont Riley, as governor general of Puerto Rico, Harding left policy to Hughes. But the State Department was not supreme, as the Department of Commerce was also involved in expanding United States economic influence. Conflict between State and Commerce was perhaps inevitable, especially since the new head of Commerce's Bureau of Foreign and Domestic Commerce, Klein, was a specialist in Latin American economics. Eventually, a bureaucratic division resulted: "The State Department acted principally as international agent and lawyer for other bureaus and American interests with particular emphasis on political questions. Commerce was vested with major responsibility for planning and evaluating inter-American economic relations."[31] But the division between State and Commerce was rough and tension frequent.

Hughes nonetheless became spokesman on relations between the United States and Latin America. The secretary had no great expertise in Latin American affairs but gained it soon. It was symbolic that on his first day in office, March 5, 1921, he sought to mediate fighting between Panama and Costa Rica. And as he entered office the controversy between Chile and Peru over Tacna-Arica was heating up. It was clear that Latin American relations would command much of his time as secretary of state. Hughes benefited from advice from the State Department's Latin American Division, headed by Sumner Welles. Welles and his subordinates, John H. Murray, Stewart Johnson, Charles Curtis, Dana G. Munro, and William R. Manning, provided the knowledge that Hughes needed.[32]

Much Latin American policy was established well in advance of 1921. Hughes had to deal with two ideas—the Monroe Doctrine and Pan-Americanism—which had dominated relations for many years. Both ideas assumed there was something distinctive about countries in the Americas, north and south, for both stressed Americanism. Yet Pan-Americanism, as the idea evolved, meant equality and understanding. The Monroe Doctrine seemed to assume for the United States a right to control. The history of Latin American policy of the United States reveals a conflict between these ideas, for when the Monroe Doctrine was emphasized, as between 1900 and 1921, Pan-Americanism suffered. And it was difficult to stress Pan-Americanism without soft-pedaling Monroeism. At a luncheon by the director general of the Pan-American Union, Leo S. Rowe, ten days after he became secretary of state, Hughes began to explain his interpretation of the Monroe Doctrine and Pan-Americanism: "We have and will have no ulterior purposes with respect to the Republics of Latin America. We wish to help to a common prosperity, through the safeguarding of the opportunities of peace, the fostering of friendship and of mutually advantageous commercial intercourse."[33]

Hughes was convinced that the Monroe Doctrine was essential as part of the foreign policy of the United States and was a cardinal rule of self-protection. He believed that the republics of the Western Hemisphere must be kept free from encroachment upon their independence and from partition by noncontinental powers. He thought that much of the problem with the doctrine was its definition and that in the years since 1823 it had been a cover for "extravagant utterances and pretensions." Of all later extensions of the doctrine, Hughes accepted only two. The doctrine covered all non-American powers, not just European countries. The method of further colonization mattered little. Even voluntary transfer of dominion violated the doctrine. In two speeches in 1923, the doctrine's centennial year, he set out his ideas. In neither, nor anywhere else during the years 1921–1923, did Hughes renounce the right of intervention, which was so offensive to Latin Americans. He did divorce it from the Monroe Doctrine and at the same time sought to localize such action. Hughes put forth what can be termed a Caribbean Doctrine, supplementary to the Monroe Doctrine. These statements gave assurance that intervention would be limited to around the Panama Canal and only occur as a "last resort," with an explanation of "what we propose to do, and what we propose not to do." Hughes probably went as far as possible in limiting intervention. In many ways these statements anticipated the Memorandum of J. Reuben Clark on the Monroe Doctrine, published in 1930 and often cited as a policy change of the United States. All the while, Hughes was stressing Pan-Americanism: "We are all sons of the American revolutions. We have all revolted against tyranny. We have erected throughout the American continents the standards of national freedom and independence. We have thus been drawn together by a common sentiment which makes us neighbors in spirit." There were differences—language, culture, and economic development—but similarities were greater and Pan-Americanism most important.

Hughes set out to end American intervention in the Dominican Republic, Haiti, and Nicaragua, believing that intervention was more responsible than any other factor for "the impairment of the relations and mutual good-will which had at one time existed between the United States and the other American Republics." The machinery was set up, with Harding's support, and before Hughes left in 1925 American forces had pulled out of the Dominican Republic and were ready to leave Nicaragua, and it was planned for them to evacuate Haiti. The administration also removed marines sent by Wilson in 1917 to protect American railroad property in Camaguey Province in Cuba, which bettered Cuban-American relations. The Harding administration's withdrawal of troops from the Caribbean, the first step in what became known as the Good Neighbor policy, began "the thaw that deadened the memory of past interventions in the only way possible—by withdrawing troops and thus coupling convincing actions with words."[34]

The administration in 1921 obtained passage of a treaty with Colombia, similar to the Thomson-Urrutia proposal the Senate had refused to ratify in 1914. Though it did not include the "regret" clause the 1914 version contained, the treaty called for $25,000,000 for Colombia as part of American responsibility for the Panamanian revolution of 1903. Payment was viewed as a "heart balm" but proved effective as relations improved and businessmen became investors in the Colombian oil fields. Hughes worked to settle the boundaries between Costa Rica and Panama and between Peru and Chile. His help proved decisive in both disputes, as in later controversies between Colombia and Panama (1924) and between Brazil, Colombia, and Peru (1925). Hughes spent much time on the Tacna-Arica controversy between Peru and Chile, which had disturbed their relations for forty years and threatened the peace of all South America. Details of this controversy are too complex to narrate here. It suffices to say that Hughes's work in bringing the dispute to arbitration in 1922, then drafting the arbitral opinion and award in 1925, and later seeing that a settlement was reached, was of high importance for the peace of Latin America.

There was American support for two Latin American diplomatic gatherings in the Harding years—the Central American Conference of 1922–1923 and the Pan-American Conference of 1923. Hughes saw benefits from such association with the Latin American nations. The Central American Conference, which met in Washington, resulted in a treaty of amity and peace, conventions for arms limitations, a Central American Tribunal, and programs for reform, all of which promoted stability in Central America. The major accomplishment of the Pan-American Conference in Santiago, Chile, was the Treaty to Avoid or Prevent Conflicts Between the American States, known as the Gondra Treaty, which provided for commissions of inquiry to help in the "cooling off" of disputes. The Santiago conference, which Hughes was unable to attend, had its controversy, especially over American unwillingness to give up the right of intervention. But the conference nonetheless contributed to a spirit of Pan-Americanism.

The final way in which Hughes worked to better relations in the Western Hemisphere was through attention given to Latin American diplomats. Hughes frequently saw Latin American representatives at his office, dined with them, and made them feel like first-class diplomats rather than representatives of minor powers—a feeling generally present from 1900 to 1921. President Harding showed interest by journeying to New York City in April 1921 to unveil a statue of Simón Bolívar presented by Venezuela. That same day Caracas dedicated a park and avenue to George Washington as a symbol of the revolutionary heritage of both countries. And in 1922 Hughes went to Rio de Janeiro to participate in the centennial of Brazilian independence. Harding and Hughes viewed this trip as repaying a visit by Emperor Dom Pedro II to the United States centennial in Philadelphia in 1876. Hughes stressed Brazilian-American friendship, as well as Pan-Americanism, and told Brazilians: "We covet no territory; we seek no conquest; the liberty we cherish for ourselves we desire for others; and we assert no rights for ourselves that we do not accord to others."[35]

Other problems troubled Hughes: recognition, as in the case of Mexico, loans and investments, furnishing of arms, and plans for arbitration. But in dealing with these problems, as with the Monroe Doctrine and Pan-Americanism, Hughes and the Harding administration hoped to bring friendly relations between Washington and other capitals. Hughes stressed that Europe and America were separate and different and that the interests of the American countries should be peace, prosperity, and friendship. He was not able to overcome the distrust of the Latin American countries toward the United States, but he did make progress between 1921 and 1923. He harmonized the Monroe Doctrine and the Caribbean policy of the United States with the idea of Pan-Americanism and thus made a contribution to Latin American relations.

While Hughes became the leading spokesman of the Harding administration for its Latin American policy, his cabinet colleague Hoover was increasing the importance of the Commerce Department in economic relations with Latin America. Hoover's interest in Latin America was made clear by a statement he released four days after taking office, stressing the importance of United States–Latin American economic relations. Hoover hoped that the United States could work with the governments of Latin America to increase the Western Hemisphere's standard of living and thereby cement "our long established friendships."[36]

That Hoover should have been interested in Latin America was not surprising. He knew that good relations were important for commerce, and he realized that Latin America had become an ever-growing market for capital and goods. The United States had moved, from 1914 on, into a much more important place in economic activities of Latin America. With Europe, the traditional source for external loans and imports, tied up with the World War, economic dependence on the United States grew dramatically. In stocks and bonds, direct investment, and trade, United States influence increased. Investment in Colombia before the war was about $3,000,000. By 1920 it was $20,000,000, and six years later it had risen to $80,000,000. And trade with Colombia went from $61,000,000 in 1913, to $155,000,000 in 1920, and reached $219,000,000 in 1926. American goods increased from 14.7 percent of Argentinian imports in 1913 to 24.7 percent in 1925, while Britain's fell from 31 percent to 19 percent. Investment in Central America went from $40,000,000 in 1912 to $93,000,000 in 1920. Between 1912 and 1920, Brazilian exports to the United States almost doubled, from $123,000,000 in 1912 to $227,000,000. Total imports from Latin America increased from $1,200,000,000 in 1914 to $4,000,000,000 in 1920. Exports went from $1,700,000,000 in 1914 to $5,000,000,000 in 1920.

As secretary of commerce, Hoover worked to expand this economic relation. Using the Bureau of Foreign and Domestic Commerce and its head, Klein, Hoover set about to facilitate American economic opportunities in Latin America by contacts between businessmen, American government experts, and Latin leaders, leaving public displays and conferences to the State Department. As part of this effort Hoover got control of the Inter-American High Commission from the Treasury Department in late 1921. The commission had been created to bring uniformity in hemispheric commercial laws. Hoover's emphasis on Latin America was different from that of Hughes. State was interested in stability, while Commerce wanted economic contacts. While State did have some importance in economic relations with Latin America, especially in petroleum, banking, and cable companies, it satisfied itself with working out political relations with Latin America and retreated from representing American businessmen south of the border. Hoover and his department worked with Latin American countries to bring uniformity in railroad and road construction, banking and commercial laws, copyrights, patents, trademarks, and many other activities. Whether it concerned hemispheric "reconstruction and development," construction of roads, development of nitrates in Chile or coffee in Brazil, the Commerce Department during the Harding years and continuing through the Coolidge administration took over policy. Hoover's activities had the support of business and Congress as well as the White House.[37]

Hoover's policies and the ties between business and the government led to charges that Latin American policy was dominated by economics. But economics did not control policy. Strategic considerations proved more important. Only in areas where there was little likelihood of intervention did economic factors become more important in determining American foreign policy. The Harding administration was more sensitive to business than its Democratic predecessor, which explains the uneasy collaboration between Hughes's department and Hoover's expanding empire. Generally, the administration, with Hughes and Hoover leading the way, tried flexibility in applying policy. Although it would not give up United States rights in the Caribbean and it recognized the need to protect American interests, the administration worked to avoid giving undue offense to Latins. The American government "slowly learned to use the nation's power with greater subtlety—to strike a balance between pressure and influence so that it would not be necessary to assume formal control to secure policy objectives or to protect the nation's interests."[38] Generally, the Harding administration pointed the way to what later became known as the Good Neighbor policy.

6

★★★★★

FOREIGN POLICY II: ENDING THE WAR IN EUROPE AND ASIA

I

From the moment of Harding's election on November 2, 1920, one thing was certain, namely, that the United States would not join the League of Nations. Harding, of course, had tried to duck the issue during the 1920 presidential campaign. When pressed he had come out in favor of a vague association of nations but avoided the question as much as possible. Once he was elected, his views became clearer, or at least he gave voice to them. Between election and inauguration he noted publicly that the League issue was dead. As he told Henry Cabot Lodge, "the country does not want the Versailles League."[1]

Thus it was not surprising that the League issue was one of the two foreign policy questions that Harding discussed in his inaugural and in his April 12, 1921, speech to the special session of Congress he had convened. While not mentioning the League by name, he came back to the issue time and time again in the inaugural oration. His position was clear: "The recorded progress of our Republic, materially and spiritually, in itself proves the wisdom of the inherited policy of non-involvement in Old World affairs. Confident of our ability to work out our own destiny, and jealously guarding our right to do so, we seek no part in directing the destinies of the Old World. We do not mean to be entangled. We will accept no responsibility except as our own conscience and judgment, in each instance, may determine."[2] Later in the speech he said the United States could "be a party to no permanent military alliance." Nor could it enter "political commitments, nor assume any economic obligations which will subject our decisions to any other than our own authority." The closest he came to mentioning the League by name was when he said that "a world super-government is contrary to everything we cherish and can have no sanction by our Republic." He was more explicit in his April speech to Congress. "In the existing League of Nations, world-governing with its super-powers," the president declared, "this Republic will have no part." Harding wanted it known that there could "be no misinterpretation, and there will be no betrayal of the deliberate expression of the American people in the recent election; and, settled in our decision for ourselves, it is only fair to say to the world in general, and to our associates in war in particular, that the League covenant can have no sanction by us."

What was surprising about these two addresses was that Harding came back to the notion of an alternate association. The United States, he had said in the inaugural, was ready to associate with nations of the world to "participate in suggesting plans for mediation, conciliation, and arbitration." In April he emphasized that in rejecting membership in the League of Nations the United States was making "no surrender of our hope and aim for an association to promote peace in which we would most heartily join."

So Harding had given the administration its marching orders. The League was dead. As long as Secretary of State Hughes stayed clear of the League, Harding was content to let the State Department work out the relationship with the European powers. Secretary Hughes was in an awkward position as one of the signers of the "Manifesto of the Thirty-One," the pro-League Republican endorsement of candidate Harding. A vote for Harding and revision of the League's Covenant, the "Manifesto" stated, would be the quickest means to American entry. Hughes soon came into agreement with Harding's position. Years later he privately wrote that upon entering office he found the opposition to League membership "more determined than ever." He was warned that League membership would be bitterly contested in the Senate, even with reservations. "I was reluctant to accept this view," he wrote, "and I did so only when friends in the Senate who were favorable to the League—known as 'mild reservationists'—assured me that there was no hope of obtaining the Senate's approval of membership in the League on any terms."[3]

The administration made its position on the League public time after time in 1921. Ambassador George Harvey told a British audience on May 19, 1921, at a Pilgrim's Day dinner, that the United States would not be enticed into the trap of the League. His speech did little to improve British-American relations, especially when he noted that the American government had entered the war in 1917 solely to save the United States, not to rescue Europe. Hughes was embarrassed, but the sentiments reflected those of the American government, and Harvey was praised by Harding. Even such an initial supporter of League membership as President Nicholas Murray Butler of Columbia University came to favor the policy of the administration.

The League dead, the administration soon moved away from the notion of an alternate association, for the idea had a number of problems which became obvious. The anti-League Republicans were no more likely to accept membership in a Harding-sponsored association than they were to permit the United States to join Wilson's League. The irreconcilables made this point on numerous occasions, and some of them even opposed convening the Washington conference on disarmament out of fear that an association would result. Then there was the League itself, to which the major nations already belonged. In June 1921 the British indicated that they would not leave the League. The same sentiment came from the French. By mid-1922, therefore, Hughes believed that it would be useless to attempt to form an association that would "parallel the League of Nations." Hughes told fellow "Manifesto" signer A. Lawrence Lowell that "the President does not think, and I entirely agree with him, that he should refer again, at this time, to his desire for an association of nations."[4] Harding did not again refer to an alternate association. This retreat caused much distress among pro-League supporters. Hamilton Holt's liberal magazine, *The Independent*, was especially critical, reminding the secretary of his former stand on the League. But all to no avail. Hughes had become convinced that the American people would not approve participation in an association of nations, whether the League or an alternate organization.

If the United States refused to join the League and would not attempt to form an alternate association, that did not mean that the administration's problems resulting from the Senate's failure to consent to the Treaty of Versailles were over. Two difficulties remained—the United States was technically at war with the Central Powers, with American troops occupying portions of Germany;

and since the League was a reality, the United States had to decide upon relations with that body.

Harding had noted the existence of the technical state of war in his April 1921 address, stating that it should be ended as soon as possible. To attain that goal he had announced he would "approve a declaratory resolution by Congress to that effect, with the qualifications essential to protect all our rights." That was all the president wanted, noting that it would be unwise for Congress "to undertake to make a statement of future policy with respect to European affairs in such a declaration of a state of peace." The idea of ending the war by a congressional resolution was not new. In 1920 Senator Knox of Pennsylvania had introduced such a resolution and it had carried, only to be vetoed by Wilson in May. The Republicans lacked the votes to override and the resolution died, to await action from the new administration. Harding, then in the Senate, had favored the resolution and overriding. In April 1921 Knox reintroduced his resolution, and after some differences between the House and the Senate a compromise resolution passed and Harding signed it on July 2, 1921. It declared the war with Germany and the Austro-Hungarian government at an end and reserved all rights and privileges negotiated in the armistice and the Treaty of Versailles.

It was now up to Hughes, who had opposed the resolution, to secure the American rights attendant to the ending of the war. Since the Treaty of Versailles was the common document, Hughes determined that only difficulty would arise should the United States try to negotiate a separate treaty with Germany. Concerns such as disposition of the German overseas empire, reimbursement for the armies of occupation, and settlement of claims convinced Hughes that the Versailles treaty had to be the basis of any peace. He settled upon a compromise. He appended portions of the Versailles treaty to the Knox-Porter end-the-war resolution and on August 25, 1921, signed what became known as the Treaty of Berlin. He followed the same procedure with both Austria and Hungary. There were still difficulties in gaining approval in the Senate, where amendments were added specifying that the United States was not to participate in any organization created out of the Versailles treaty. But in October 1921 the Senate accepted the Berlin treaty by a vote of 66 to 20 and the other two treaties by similar margins. America was formally at peace, three years after the armistice. In August 1922 the last of the war-related negotiations with Germany was concluded, when the United States and Germany agreed to

144

commissions to settle claims of Americans against the German government.

Fifteen thousand American troops were still in the Rhineland of Germany as an army of occupation when Harding took office in 1921. During the last two years of Wilson's administration, Congress had questioned the policy that kept these troops in Germany. Congress wondered about the cost and benefits of maintaining these troops and criticized Wilson for acting without formal approval by Congress. Harding had told an audience in Omaha during his campaign in 1920 that when he took charge he would remove the troops as soon as the United States declared peace. Once in office, he changed his views, and the troops apparently were to remain indefinitely to help preserve European stability. During 1922, Congress continued to be skeptical of the arrangement. As Franco-German hostility heated up again over the Rhineland and the Ruhr valley, the Senate decided to act; and Senator James A. Reed introduced a resolution on December 27, 1922, that called for prompt withdrawal of the remaining American force, which had been decreased since March 1921. The resolution carried, 57 to 6, with 33 abstentions. When France sent its army across the Rhine on January 10, 1923, contending that Germany had defaulted on reparations, Harding decided to withdraw the American troops. American participation in the war was over.[5]

If political relations with Germany had proved difficult, the administration had an even more troublesome time determining the relationship of the United States with the League. The League Council had first met in January 1920, the Assembly convened in November of that same year with a membership of forty-two nations, and the first of many specialized League-sponsored meetings, a transit conference, met in Barcelona in March and April 1921.

For several months the State Department refused to answer any communication from the League. This policy brought criticism, and the Department turned to a form response: "the Secretary of State has taken note of this information for any purpose of relevance to the United States as a state not a member of the League of Nations."[6] This proved unsatisfactory, particularly as the League was going forward with its administrative duties. Hughes tried to communicate with member nations involved in League duties; for example, he dealt directly with Japan over mandate problems in the Pacific rather than through the League Council. The League began to take control of or establish multinational offices such as the Office Internationale d'Hygiène Publique in Paris, which became the center of the League's Health Section. The Geneva body took over the administrative work that the Netherlands had done as a result of the Opium Control Treaty of 1912. The American response was to protest such transfers and continue to try to deal with the bodies originally responsible for international cooperation. When Americans were asked to participate in the multinational bodies, Hughes did all he could to stop such involvement. He urged the American Panel of the Court of International Arbitration not to make nominations to the World Court in 1921, and he prevailed.

As the administration made clear its intention not to join the League, the secretary of state became less concerned over contacts with that organization. By 1922 the American consul at Geneva had become the conduit through which the United States government corresponded, on an unofficial basis, with League headquarters. That year American observers began to attend meetings such as the conference on Traffic in Women and the Opium Advisory Committee. The United States did not become involved in matters that might bring political entanglement, but on technical and humanitarian matters the United States began to deal with the League as it would with any association of nations. Hughes stated that the delegates to the various meetings represented the United States "just as completely as those designated by the President always have represented our government."[7] This method, Hughes believed, solved a difficult problem by avoiding the need to go before Congress requesting approval for American delegates to League bodies. Still, it was an awkward solution to the problem, for the American delegates were reluctant to speak at these gatherings and could not bind Washington to any decisions. Hughes, of course, recognized the difficulties that such a policy created. He simply believed that unofficial participation was the best the United States could do. The Hughes policy of unofficial observers for League matters was to be followed by the men who succeeded him as secretary of state.

If Hughes was reluctant to press for formal relations with the League or its agencies, he did push for American participation in the Permanent Court of International Justice, better known as the World Court. He had long supported this kind of institution. Harding had announced, in his inaugural, that the United States "would gladly join in that expressed conscience of progress, which seeks to clarify and write the laws of international relationship, and establish a world court for the disposition of such justiciable questions as nations are agreed to submit thereto." But it was not until October 30, 1922, that Hughes, in a speech in Boston, called for American entry into the World Court. "We favor," the secretary declared, "and always have favored, an international court of justice for the determination according to judicial standards of justiciable international disputes." He stated that he believed that arrangements "can be made for the participation by this Government in the election of judges of the International Court which has been set up, so that this Government may give its formal support to that court as an independent tribunal of international justice."[8]

The autumn of 1922 proved an inopportune time for membership in the World Court. The administration was occupied with the midterm elections and then with trying to recover from their disastrous results. Harding was fighting Congress over his ship subsidy bill, unsuccessfully. It was not until February 1923 that Hughes could begin to press Congress for participation in the World Court. While confined at home because of illness, he worked out a proposal to bring the United States into the Court. To counter Senate opposition to the Court's relationship with the League, he suggested four reservations: The United States should announce that membership in the Court meant no formal relationship with the League; the United States would participate in election of judges to the Court; it would contribute to expenses of the Court, subject to appropriation of funds by Congress; and statutes of the Court could be amended only with American approval. The president accepted Hughes's ideas and proposed that the Senate endorse participation.

The proposal met severe opposition in the Senate. The Foreign Relations Committee was still dominated by the irreconcilables or at least by irreconcilable sentiment. Lodge and Borah attacked the proposal. They professed agreement with the concept of international adjudication but termed the World Court a "League Court," the first step to formal participation in the League. The Foreign Relations Committee split eight to eight on the proposal, keeping it in committee. Lodge then began a procedure to tie up the plan in that committee. The Sixty-seventh Congress soon adjourned.

Hughes pushed the measure. The secretary "considered adjudication the most advanced form of third-party settlement of international disputes, surpassing conciliation or mediation in that it produces a substantive, legally binding decision." He was convinced of the soundness of the administration's proposal and set out to answer the senatorial objections. His defense of the proposal came in an address to the American Society of International Law on April 27, 1923, three days after the president had reaffirmed support for the Court in a speech to the Associated Press. To the charge that the World Court was a League Court, the secretary noted that the World Court's statute rested on a special convention separate from the League. He outlined operations of the Court, discussed methods of selecting the Court's judges and terms of service, answered charges that the Court's decisions would not be enforceable, and pointed to benefits to the United States. Hughes believed the Court would "have the most solemn sanction that it is practicable to obtain." He thought that nations agreeing to submit disputes to the tribunal would be bound to abide by its decisions: "You can really have no better sanction than this and the obligation is one which will be all the more keenly felt when the decision is not simply that of a temporary arbitral tribunal but of a permanent court supported by practically all the nations of the world."[9] Hughes continued to work, both publicly and privately, for Senate approval of Court membership. Secretary of Commerce Hoover publicly stumped for the Court. Private organizations such as the United States Chamber of Commerce, the American Bar Association, the American Legion, and the National Association of Manufacturers endorsed the proposal.

Opponents were active. Harding's former colleagues in the Senate—Lodge, Borah, Frank Brandegee, and Medill McCormick —now fought Harding's Court. So did such anti-Harding Republicans as La Follette. Dissension came into Harding's cabinet, as Attorney General Daugherty urged the president to drop the issue. Harding tried to conciliate the differences in a speech at St. Louis on June 21, 1923, on his trip to the West. He laid down two further conditions for American entry into the Court: the Court had to be separated from the League, and "perfect equality" had to dominate the Court. The speech was a poor one and resembled his orations on the League in 1920.

In the long run the proposal failed. The House did vote in favor of the World Court Protocol in 1925. The Senate proved more difficult. In early 1926 the Senate voted in favor of the Court, but with three reservations in addition to those proposed by Hughes. When the League called a conference between the United States and members of the Court to discuss American reservations, President Coolidge abandoned the proposal. It was likely that Harding, had he lived, would have done the same. The issue lasted until 1935, when the Senate again failed to agree to American participation. In this instance, as in so many others during the Harding administration, Hughes found he had company, in this case the Senate, in formulation of the foreign polcy of the United States.

With failure of the Court proposal, America's political relations with Europe and the League had become evident. Peace between the United States and Germany had allowed American troops to withdraw from the Rhine. Relations between Washington and the League of Nations, which was attempting to solve political difficulties in Europe, were tenuous, and even such an affiliation as the World Court was unattainable. Part of the reason was that while Hughes and Republican internationalists did all that they could to protect and increase financial relations with Europe, they shared the opinion of isolationists concerning political relations with Europe.[10] So did most Democrats and, for that matter, Americans. They felt that European problems had European causes and should have European solutions. With this common viewpoint, it was not surprising that the United States negotiated bilateral treaties with Germany, Austria, and Hungary, and then held the League as well as the World Court at arm's length. The policy may not have been particularly successful, or for that matter realistic, but it was the only course that had general support.

II

The second problem in foreign policy Harding had mentioned in both the inaugural and his speech to Congress in April 1921 was disarmament. In the former address Harding had noted that "we are ready to associate ourselves with the nations of the world, great and small, for conference, for counsel; to seek the expressed views of world opinion; to recommend a way to approximate disarmament and relieve the crushing burdens of military and naval establishments." The United States, the president declared, was "ready to encourage, eager to initiate, anxious to participate in any seemly program likely to lessen the probability of war," especially because the World War had so transformed the United States. While Harding announced that his administration planned to concentrate on overcoming the effects of the war and returning the country to normalcy, it was equally important to prevent future wars. Some form of disarmament was essential. Harding emphasized domestic concerns in his address to the special session of Congress which convened in April 1921, but he mentioned disarmament. Neither

Congress nor the executive could "be unmindful of the call for reduced expenditure" for national defense. While the United States would "not entirely discard our agencies for defense until there is removed the need to defend," his administration was "ready to cooperate with other nations to approximate disarmament." He was "in accord with the wish to eliminate the burdens of heavy armament. The United States ever will be in harmony with such a movement toward the higher attainments of peace."

Harding was responding to increasing sentiment to do something to prevent another arms race, as well as guarantee peace. The call for disarmament and the attack upon war on moral, idealistic, and economic grounds antedated the World War. Peace advocates had been active in the United States throughout the nineteenth century but were unsuccessful. With participation of the United States in the First Hague Peace Conference in 1899, the pressure for arms controls increased. But neither that gathering nor the Second Hague Conference of 1907 brought reductions in armaments. The tremendous expansion of the American navy in the first decade of the twentieth century, with its large expenditures, made Americans more interested than other countries in arms limitations. In 1913 Democratic Congressman Walter L. Hensley of Missouri introduced a resolution calling for a one-year moratorium on naval construction for the United States and Europe. The resolution carried, 317 to 11, but the war came before any action could be taken. During its neutrality the United States prepared for war; the 1916 Naval Act authorized the construction of 156 vessels, of which 16 were to be battleships and battle cruisers.

With the end of the war and especially with the American decision not to participate in the League, the desire for arms control grew. Harding had indicated support for reduced armaments during the campaign; but the topic had not become an important issue, and disarmament advocates were afraid it would be lost from sight. On December 14, 1920, however, all that changed. Senator Borah introduced a resolution calling for the president to come to an understanding with the other two major naval powers, Japan and Great Britain. Late 1920 was an opportune time for such a resolution. The same month Borah made his plea, the United States navy recommended a three-year program calling for the construction of 88 vessels. Britain responded with its own building program to maintain naval supremacy, and the Japanese were making plans for expansion. As the cost of a battleship had risen from $5,000,000 in 1900 to $40,000,000 by 1920, all three nations had to contemplate the enormous sums a postwar building competition would require. These plans, plus the battle over the League, threatened to make the sacrifices of fighting the war meaningless. As support for participation in the League declined, interest increased in arms limitations in cooperation with other major powers. Thus it was that Borah had introduced his resolution. Borah felt that the key to success was to control competition. Quoting the Japanese government's statement that it "could not consent even to consider a program of disarmament on account of the naval building program of the United States," he proposed that the United States, Britain, and Japan agree to a 50 percent reduction of naval building plans for five years.[11]

The reaction was swift in the United States. Newspapers supported the idea, and public figures backed it, with Generals Tasker H. Bliss and John J. Pershing speaking in favor of arms limitations. On Christmas day the Women's Peace Society assembled near the Capitol in Washington and pledged to use their newly acquired suffrage to stop war. The House Committees of Military Affairs, Naval Affairs, and Foreign Affairs held hearings, even though Congress was in a lame-duck session, with the Naval Affairs Committee calling Pershing, Bliss, Henry White, Acting Secretary of State Norman Davis, and Secretary of the Navy Josephus Daniels as witnesses. The majority of witnesses supported some kind of arms control.

Elihu Root termed Borah's resolution premature and asked Congress to wait for the new president to take office. Meanwhile, a second Borah resolution called for suspension of the naval building program for six months while Congress determined "what constitutes a modern navy." Both Borah resolutions were pushed aside, but an amendment proposed by Senator Walter E. Edge of New Jersey to add France and Italy to any limitation program was attached to the 1921 Naval Appropriation Bill. Congress adjourned before passing the bill, and the whole problem shifted to the new president.[12]

In short order, Harding's view became clear. In speeches in March and April he had stated that his administration was willing to enter international cooperation to find a solution. He had no interest in using the League but would support separate negotiations. After much maneuvering he let it be known that he could support the original Borah resolution. It was reintroduced in the new Congress and passed in July 1921 as part of the Naval Appropriations Act. The advocates of disarmament felt success within their grasp.

The naval competition was not the only problem in relations between the United States, Britain, and Japan. These three powers were dominant in East Asia, and an intense rivalry there seemed possible. By 1920 the Far Eastern balance had changed dramatically. Russian power in that area had disappeared with the revolution of 1917, not to return until the mid-1920s. Defeat by the Allies had removed Germany as a power. European concerns overshadowed France's limited interest there. Finally, three powers remained: Britain, Japan, and the United States. Compared to their worldwide interests, the Far East was not as important to the British as to the Japanese and Americans. Nonetheless, because of interests there and the alliance with Japan, which was about to come up for renewal, Britain remained involved in Far Eastern politics.

The Japanese and Americans stood out as possible antagonists in East Asia. In the years after Theodore Roosevelt left the White House, contention between Washington and Tokyo had grown. The United States began to support China as the nation of the future. First through Taft's dollar diplomacy and then through Wilson's missionary diplomacy, the United States came to realize that Japan supported the old diplomacy of imperialism while Americans (at least in their own minds) represented the new diplomacy of international cooperation. The contrast had turned the fear and respect with which the United States had viewed Tokyo to suspicion mixed with resentment. China had become the Far Eastern concern of Americans. The Shantung settlement at the Paris Peace Conference, whereby the Japanese took German rights in China, was resented in the United States; and there had been other problems with Japan, concerning immigration, trade, territorial issues, and naval rivalry.

As the Wilson administration went out of office it was apparent that some attempt had to be made to bring about a reconsideration of relations between the two countries. The administration, led by Hughes, sensed that cooperation between Tokyo and Washington was essential. Hughes believed that China had to be placed in the broader context of East Asian policy. He was willing to draw back from the Wilsonian position on foreign policy which had isolated China. Hughes lacked any strong feelings about China itself but believed that conditions of peace and economic interdependence could dominate in the 1920s only if there was order and stability in the Far East.

It was by coincidence that as the calls for a disarmament conference were increasing in the United States the British government decided that a British, American, and Japanese conclave to discuss the East Asian situation was necessary. Uneasy over possible extension of the Anglo-Japanese alliance, the British wanted to work out a tripartite agreement. Proposals came almost simultaneously, with the British requesting a Far Eastern meeting on July 5, 1921, and Hughes attempting to head off the initiative by sending invitations to Britain, Japan, France, and Italy three days later for a conference in Washington on armament limitation. The solution was to combine the two meetings, and Hughes set about to do that. Soon after his initial invitation he sought British approval to enlarge the proposed Washington conference to include Far Eastern problems and invite China. After diplomatic jockeying, the secretary got London's assent. There were difficulties yet to be overcome. Japan was interested in an arms conference but was reluctant to discuss the Far East. China wanted to know its role in the conference and presented yet another problem when Sun Yat-sen, who headed the southern China government at Canton, demanded participation. Sun said the Peking government could not negotiate for all of China. Hughes disagreed. Other nations asked to participate, and Belgium, the Netherlands, and Portugal received invitations. Soviet Russia did not; Hughes decided it was impossible to invite representatives of a country the United States did not recognize.

There were many details that Hughes had to work out. By September 1921 the State Department announced the conference's agenda: arms, including naval disarmament; Chinese territorial and administrative integrity, as well as concessions and monopolies in that country; Siberia; mandated islands of the Pacific whose status was still unsettled. At the same time, he and Harding chose the American delegates. Cognizant of Wilson's problems with the Versailles treaty, they determined to follow McKinley's precedent of naming senators to negotiate the Paris treaty ending the Spanish-American War. But Hughes and Harding decided to pass over Senator Borah, who had first proposed the disarmament conference. They chose Lodge, still chairman of the Foreign Relations Committee, and the Democratic Senate minority leader, Oscar W. Underwood of Alabama, as delegates. Root and Hughes completed the formal delegation. Hughes and Harding set up an advisory committee which included a broad grouping of members such as Secretary Hoover, Samuel L. Gompers, and General Pershing. All the time Hughes and Harding were looking past the conference to the public reaction, making sure that the Senate would approve whatever treaties resulted. In this way, they were much more skillful than Wilson had been three years earlier.

Preparations completed, the conference assembled on November 12, 1921. After a brief welcome by Harding, Hughes delivered the keynote speech to the delegates, who included Arthur Balfour, Aristide Briand, and Kato Tomasaburo, at Continental Hall, a white marble building owned by the Daughters of the American Revolution, a few blocks from the White House. Approximately a thousand people listened to Hughes, who began what seemed a conventional speech. Soon the atmosphere changed as Hughes spelled out his ideas. Admiral David Beatty of Great Britain listened with astonishment, "in the manner of a bulldog, sleeping on a sunny doorstep, who had been poked in the stomach by the impudent foot of an itinerant soap canvasser seriously lacking in any sense of the most ordinary proprieties or considerations of personal safety." Cause for Beatty's astonishment was the American plan that Hughes laid out for the reduction of capital ships in the fleets of major nations. He proposed that the United States scrap thirty vessels totaling 845,740 tons, of which fifteen were under construction. The proposal for Britain was to give up twenty-three ships, 583,375 tons, including four active battleships. Japan was asked to give up seventeen ships, 448,928 tons, and postpone construction of eight other capital ships. According to one observer, "Hughes sank in thirty-five minutes more ships than all the admirals of the world have sunk in a cycle of centuries."[13] Hughes's proposal called for a total maximum tonnage in capital ships of approximately 500,000 tons for the United States and the same for Great Britain and 300,000 tons for Japan, which became known as the 5-5-3 ratio.

Hughes and the Harding administration had worked hard on the American proposal. Only nine individuals knew of the intention to open the conference with specific proposals for disarmament, hoping to break through the pessimistic predictions that greeted the meeting. Working with representatives of the Navy Department, especially Assistant Secretary Theodore Roosevelt, Jr., and Admiral Robert E. Coontz, the chief of naval operations, Hughes had come up with the ratio proposal, shifting discussions from perceived needs to maintenance of the status quo.

154

In the end, Hughes prevailed, with the signature of the Five-Power naval treaty on February 6, 1922, the most original part of the Washington conference. The agreement provided for a ten-year moratorium on the construction of capital ships, as well as for the destruction of certain existing ships and halting of construction of others. It projected the capital ship ratio 5-5-3-1.75-1.75 Hughes had outlined in his initial speech, with France and Italy each being permitted approximately 175,000 tons of capital vessels. Hughes had to make compromises. The Japanese refused to scrap the battleship *Mutsu*, as Hughes had suggested. They were able to tie their inferior position to a pledge by the United States and Britain to maintain the status quo in fortifications and bases in the Far East. For the United States, that meant no increase in fortifications in the Philippines, Guam, and the Aleutians. Hughes thought the compromise worthwhile if it stopped the arms race. The negotiations failed to extend the ratios to auxiliary craft, when the French refused to accept a limit to the tonnage of their submarine fleet. The secretary thought the treaty a success—the beginning of negotiations that would bring peace and order among the major nations.

The other aspect of the Washington conference was a discussion of affairs in East Asia. Here Hughes attempted a broad resettlement of Japanese-American relations. The conference and its related agreements provided the opportunity for a thorough consideration of the problems between the United States and Japan. In the Four-Power Treaty the United States acknowledged Japan's wartime gains in the Pacific. In the same treaty the British, French, Japanese, and Americans agreed to respect each other's interests in East Asia and to consult in case of controversy. The treaty replaced the Anglo-Japanese alliance, an event welcomed in both Washington and London. The Nine-Power Treaty dealt with China. While Hughes supported Chinese territorial and administrative integrity and the open door, he undertook no major assault on the restrictions on Chinese sovereignty, such as extraterritorial rights and international control of China's tariff. He did seek to gain Japan's retreat from Shantung, which lay outside the work of the conference, and persuaded the Japanese and Chinese delegates to negotiate the issue. He took part in these talks, exerting pressure to bring a settlement, even holding the final meeting at his house. A treaty between Japan and China on Shantung was signed on February 4, 1922. Hughes did not gain a Japanese retreat from Manchuria. They were too entrenched. But the Japanese did make concessions and agreed to evacuate Siberia and Northern Sakhalin. Behind the

Washington arrangements, however, "there was an actual accommodation to the recent acquisitions of Japan in the Pacific and China and an attempt to secure that new status quo through international pledge."[14] The Four-Power Treaty called only for consultation by the signatories, and the Nine-Power Treaty had no enforcement provisions. The Five-Power Treaty was recognition by the United States and Britain of Japanese naval importance in the Pacific.

Hughes believed the Washington conference was a success. He felt that all the agreements—the Four-, Five- and Nine-Power treaties, the Sino-Japanese treaty on Shantung, the Japanese-American agreement settling the controversy over the Island of Yap, the Japanese promise to withdraw from Siberia, the later abrogation of the Lansing-Ishii agreement, the decision not to renew the Anglo-Japanese alliance—alleviated the tension between the United States and Japan, as well as Britain. The picture that emerged from Washington was "a procession of gigantic horse trades in which each power sought to buy maximum security at minimum expense. Concessions in one treaty were paid for in others, until the complex process to give and take had been completed."[15] Hughes hoped the nations would add self-restraint and good will to the agreements, all of which would contribute to a sense of security. He did think the conference had discovered formulas which harmonized the interests of participating nations.

Hughes's approach was a departure from the views of Wilson toward the Far East and was more realistic in dealing with Japanese-American relations, even if the powers remained unsatisfied. Two of the countries that held large stakes in East Asia before 1914—Germany and Russia—were not represented. The absence of Russia, shunned intentionally because of the revolution, was most important, for in the 1920s the Soviet government pursued its own policy and did all it could to bring expulsion of the United States, Japan, and Britain from the Asian mainland. China was slighted; it was an object in American, Japanese, and British diplomacy but not a participant in that diplomacy. Just as certainly, the United States was again asking Japan to change its role in East Asia and once more to accommodate its foreign policy to another Western model—from imperialism to international cooperation, particularly economic cooperation.

Notwithstanding these weaknesses, some of which Hughes recognized, the administration took up the cause of the treaties as soon as the conference ended on February 6, 1922. Four days later,

Harding appeared before the Senate and called for consent to the three major treaties the conference had produced, as well as the rest of the agreements, such as the treaty with Japan over Yap. Congressional participation in the delegation proved most helpful, as Lodge became the administration's spokesman in the Senate. There were opponents—Borah, Johnson, and James Reed—who charged a sellout to Japan and predicted the United States would lose control of foreign policy. The Yap treaty passed the Senate first, on March 11, 1922, by a margin of 67 to 22. The Four- and Five-Power treaties drew most of the fire, and debate became contentious. But on March 24 the Senate voted 67 to 27 to accept the Four-Power Treaty. Since the treaty was accepted by only four votes over a two-thirds majority, the twelve Democrats who were led by Underwood and voted for the treaty proved indispensable. The Five- and Nine-Power treaties were adopted with much less difficulty. The Harding administration had succeeded where Wilson could not, and the World War had come to a close in the Pacific.

The conference concluded, the administration set out to maintain its military position as well as influence in East Asia. Supported by the American Legion, the Navy League, the National Civic Federation, and other organizations, it fought further reductions in the army and navy. The army which had numbered 230,725 in 1921 had declined to 133,243 in 1923, but there was more success in preserving naval power. Navy manpower went down from 132,827 in 1921 to 94,094 in 1923. But the years of the Harding administration and those that followed saw intense activity and dramatic change in the American navy. New weapons and technology brought the navy to the fore of American defense. Air power, stimulated by Colonel William Mitchell's ideas, appeared with the experimental carrier *Langley*. Some strategists became convinced that supremacy on the seas would depend on a carrier fleet. Harding supported appropriations to convert battle cruiser hulls into carriers. The administration began to change over to the use of oil for the remaining navy cruisers, which would give more range, and to reorganize the navy, permanently stationing its most powerful unit, the Battle Fleet, in the Pacific. Of the eighteen battleships permitted by the Washington agreements, twelve (the fastest and most modern) were assigned to the Pacific. This deployment brought an improvement of the fleet base facilities, especially at Pearl Harbor.

All these changes in the navy resulted because of the administration's fear that if the United States became involved in a war it would be with Japan.[16] So while the State Department worked for peace with Japan, the navy prepared for war, and in 1924 American strategists revised their Orange Plan—battle operations for war with Japan. The Japanese government approved the Washington system, but the Japanese army and navy supreme headquarters in turn continued to regard conflict with the United States as probable and made this the basic strategic assumption.[17] Thus while civil leaders in both countries continued to stress international cooperation, planners prepared for war. In the end, at least in Japan, this separation of military policy from foreign policy had large meaning. These activities made the Five-Power Treaty lose significance, especially as the navies of the world turned away from battleships. It made future attempts at arms limitations, such as the Geneva Naval Conference of 1927, less successful than the Washington conference—indeed, nothing happened at Geneva. The Washington agreements temporarily relieved tensions between the United States, Britain, and Japan, but accomplished little more.

In the meantime, the administration worked to maintain influence in East Asia. The United States moved to reverse the policy of Wilson toward the Philippines. The Jones Act of 1916 had granted the Filipinos greater control over affairs in the islands and said it was "the purpose of the people of the United States to withdraw their sovereignty over the Philippine Islands and recognize their independence as soon as stable government can be established therein."[18] Harding had headed the Senate's Philippine Committee and opposed Wilsonian policy. He now decided to send a commission to study the situation in the Philippines and asked W. Cameron Forbes, governor general in the Taft years, and General Leonard Wood to head the commission.

The Wood-Forbes Commission, after four months of investigation, reported that the Filipinos were not prepared for independence. Underlying the report was fear that the Japanese would move in, should the Philippines be granted independence. Harding accepted the recommendations, which supported his own beliefs, and convinced Wood to become governor general, a post in which he served until his death in 1927. In this way Harding obtained an effective if overbearing administrator who concentrated on highway construction and the improvement of schools and hospitals and believed in retention. The appointment also solved a political problem. It gave Wood a position, but not one that would increase his political base. Wood saw the Philippines as the entrepôt for Far

Eastern markets, thought retention would maintain the balance in East Asia, feared Japanese advances, should the islands be set free, and believed the United States had a moral obligation to "uplift" the Filipinos. The administration accepted these arguments, viewing the Philippines as part of America's East Asian policy. But the Five-Power Treaty had forbidden construction of further fortifications in the Philippines. This became the nub of the issue. The United States did not have the capability to defend the Philippines and yet decided to remain in the islands.

The decision to remain was symbolic of all that was wrong with Far Eastern policy. Preservation of the open door in China and retention came to be the two most important parts of the Far Eastern policy of the United States. Neither was rational in view of Japanese power. Japan found itself forgotten in American diplomacy after the Washington conference. For the rest of the Harding administration and indeed until he left office in 1925, Hughes turned his attention to other areas. There were occasional efforts at good will but no concentration on resolving problems in Japanese-American relations. Hughes appears to have considered the Washington conference as a solution. It was not until 1924 that his attention came back to the Far East. The Japanese exclusion act in that year increased tensions. Hughes wrote Lodge shortly after the act became law: "It is a dangerous thing to plant a deep feeling of resentment in the Japanese people, not that we have need to apprehend, much less to fear, war, but that we shall have hereafter in the East to count upon a sense of injury and antagonism instead of friendship and cooperation. I dislike to think what the reaping will be after the sowing of this seed."[19] Combined with the Japanese public's resentment over the Washington treaties, the act led Japan to an independent course. The rest of the 1920s and the 1930s showed how independent that course was to be.

Then there was the problem with China. Support of foreign concessions and extraterritorial rights at the Washington conference earned the enmity of Chinese nationalists. As the 1920s passed, China came to consider the United States another imperialist power, and with reason. Sun Yat-sen turned to the Soviet Union for support of his revolutionary movement. This Chinese relationship with Moscow was viewed with alarm, and Chinese-American relations worsened.

The administration's policy toward East Asia proved to be a failure. The Washington conference was a first step toward cooperation in the Far East, but it was not followed up with later agreements. The United States preferred the misguided aim of keeping the Philippines and trying to maintain the open door policy. After the conference no recognition came from the United States of Tokyo's prominence in East Asia. At the same time, the Chinese were unhappy.

III

Difficulties concerning Germany, the League, disarmament, and the balance of power in East Asia were not the only problems that the World War had created for American diplomacy. Monetary issues resulting from the war proved troublesome. The administration was forced to spend a good deal of time dealing with the Allied war debts and German reparations.

That all forms of debts resulting from the war—loans, reparations, claims against governments—were related was obvious. It was equally clear that progress toward settlement would only be made by multinational negotiations. Unfortunately for the economic health of the world, "the United States insisted on handling these debts strictly on a commercial basis, and never officially recognized the connection between any of them. Operating on the assumption that international obligations had to be honored, the government chose to isolate and deal with each as a separate economic issue."[20] Concerning these financial matters, two principles remained in diplomacy from the Wilson administration through Harding, Coolidge, and Hoover: the United States opposed cancellation of the war debts, and it refused to recognize the connection between debts and reparations.

Harding had an opportunity to revise the policy of separating debts and reparations. Between 1919 and 1921 there was increasing recognition in banking, business, and agricultural circles of the relation between European economic recovery and American prosperity, as the United States moved toward economic collapse and depression in late 1920 and 1921. Some businessmen, cognizant of the effect that payment of the war debts would have on efforts to rebuild the European economy, suggested that the United States cancel part of the debts or at least defer payments over a long period, with low interest rates. While full cancellation would have contributed to European purchasing power and to currency stabilization, with resulting benefits to the American economy, "American business leaders and economic interest groups rejected it as a viable policy alternative. This was not the result of their ignorance of the impact of the war debts on the international economy, but because of their preoccupation with high domestic taxation, their concern with reparations, and their fear of a hostile public reaction."[21]

The Harding administration shared many of the sentiments of businessmen toward the $10 billion debt. At one of its first meetings, Harding's cabinet unanimously endorsed repayment. While Secretaries Mellon, Hoover, and Hughes all saw the debts from different perspectives, they worked together. Recognizing how difficult it would be to come up with a solution that could apply to all nations, Mellon gained Harding's approval for a plan to give the secretary of the treasury authority to determine interest rates and payment schedules on a country-by-country basis. While Mellon did not favor full or even partial cancellation, he determined that such flexibility would allow the United States to consider the financial condition of each nation. Congress refused to grant such power. The Senate Finance Committee and the House Ways and Means Committee came up with their own plans. Out of these actions came the Debt Funding Bill of February 9, 1922, calling for repayment of the loans within twenty-five years, setting the minimum interest rate at 4.25 percent, prohibiting the exchange of foreign bonds or obligations as payment of the debts, forbidding the cancellation of any portion of the debts, and creating the World War Foreign Debt Commission to work out details. This congressional reaction had a variety of motives. Distrust of the executive, desire to protect congressional power, and pressure by political groups concerned with increasing taxes—all contributed. The debates showed little concern, surprisingly, with the effect that the demand for payment would have on Europe's ability to trade with the United States.

The administration was unwilling to fight the congressional decision, and Harding signed the bill. He appointed Mellon, Hoover, and Hughes to the Debt Commission, along with Senator Reed Smoot and Congressman Theodore Burton. The concept of flexibility dominated. Even so, France announced it could not accept the Debt Funding Bill. Soon the administration was in a dilemma: "congressional restrictions, fiscal demands, and political expediency encouraged caution" while "diplomatic warnings, business pressures, and moral scruples compelled constructive action."[22]

The administration worked to get around provisions of the funding bill. In early 1923 the United States and Britain negotiated a schedule for the $4 billion British debt—repayment over sixty-two years with an interest rate beginning at 3 percent and increasing to

3.5 percent. Since this settlement violated the 1922 legislation, Harding submitted it to Congress, where it drew little opposition, passing the House 291 to 44 and the Senate 70 to 13. The settlement set a pattern for agreements that the Debt Commission reached with fifteen other nations. The nearly $7 billion of additional debts followed the same form, with payments over long periods with low interest rates. As in the cases of France, Italy, and Belgium, the government in effect canceled portions of the debt. The indebtedness of the Allies was reduced by approximately 43 percent. The United States made clear that the principal had to be paid in full. The administration moved from a rigid interpretation of repayment to a more flexible system that took into account ability to pay.

The United States probably went as far as the country would have permitted in reducing the debts. European countries were not satisfied, with France complaining about "Uncle Shylock." France did not even discuss repayment of the debts until 1925 and unrealistically hoped for cancellation. While American policy may have been shortsighted, the French were unfair in terming the United States a merciless creditor.[23] Perhaps the most interesting aspect of the controversy over debts during the administration was the influence of noneconomic factors. The eventual solution satisfied no one. But it did meet the minimal economic, strategic, political, and moral concerns of the American government. In the end, of course, only one nation, Finland, ever paid its debt and that debt was incurred after the war.

Reparations proved more difficult for the administration. The final reparations figure was staggering—$33 billion. The Allied Reparations Committee, created by the Versailles treaty, had decided on that amount in April 1921 and determined that Germany was to pay $375 million annually from 1921 to 1925 and $900 million thereafter. Since the Americans opposed linking debts and reparations and refused cancellation, the European nations led by France insisted on German payments. Britain in late 1921 had proposed an international conference to deal with these questions, but the United States refused, with Harding maintaining that it was impossible to consider it. The government rejected a European proposal to cancel reparations and debts at the same time.

There were many critics of reparations, with American liberal periodicals like the *New Republic* and the *Nation* agreeing with the British economist John Maynard Keynes that the reparations section of the Versailles treaty was unworkable. Within the Harding cabinet Hoover was sympathetic to this viewpoint, considering the reparations a commercial rather than political problem, but he had little support in 1921 and early 1922.

By late 1922 the situation in Europe was serious. In January 1923 French and Belgian troops occupied the Ruhr valley because of Germany's defaulting on reparation payments. Even before occupation, Secretary Hughes had determined that a change in policy was necessary, especially as Germany seemed on the verge of collapse. In an address to the American Historical Association meeting in December 1922 in New Haven, he announced a new policy. He continued to deny a link between debts and reparations. He noted that "the capacity of Germany to pay is not at all affected by any indebtedness by any of the Allies to us." He admitted that solution of European difficulties would come only when the reparation issue was solved. Recovery was possible only if Germany recovered, and he noted that permanent peace would not come to Europe until there was economic stability. To bring such a solution he proposed that the nations "invite men of the highest authority in finance in their respective countries—men of such prestige, experience and honor that their agreement upon the amount to be paid, and upon a financial plan for working out the payments would be accepted throughout the world as the most authoritative expression obtainable."[24] While he did not offer American participation, he did state that Americans would be willing to help.

The speech did not stop French seizure of German coal mines in the Ruhr. But Hughes did succeed in getting a commission to determine Germany's ability to pay. When the occupation failed to bring satisfaction to France, the Paris government proved amenable to Hughes's scheme. The meeting resulted in the Dawes plan of 1924, named after the American delegate, even though Charles G. Dawes and the two other Americans were not representatives of their government. The plan allowed Europe to back away from the political and economic tensions that had dominated that part of the world from 1914 on. As with debt settlement, Hughes's plan for reparation readjustment was an admission that the United States could not be isolated from European affairs.

The interdependence between stability in Europe and prosperity in the United States had made clear to Hughes that European events could have far-reaching effects in the United States. The United States had to substitute American dollars for the bullets of the World War. To examine the relations between the United States and Europe in 1923—contacts with the League, compromises

on the debts, assistance in working out a reparations schedule—is
to see how much the Harding administration had retreated from
its position that European problems were the concern of Europe.
Unfortunately, the administration dealt with Europe on a problem-
by-problem basis and was unwilling or unable to attempt a general
solution.

During the Harding administration and the years that followed,
the government, in cooperation with American businessmen, exerted tremendous informal influence in international economics.
Part of that influence naturally came from the major economic
changes of the war. The United States emerged as the strongest
financial power in the world. By whatever index of measure, the
United States had become dominant. One of the results was an
increased interest in international affairs by businessmen. They
recognized that the United States had become a creditor with attendant responsibilities and also sensed the economic interdependence of the nations. Businessmen began to speak about America's
responsibility. They stressed hard work and social service as the
keys to America's success. By 1920 the philosophy of corporate
liberalism was firmly entrenched among leaders of the business
community, and "they rhetorically equated their own self-interest
and economic achievements with the notion not only that they were
serving their country through their endeavors, but that what they
did was a 'glorious service to all humanity.'" This was not a new
idea, but the war and the increase in economic power had made it
more important. The businessmen had their differences on policy.
A dispute occurred over cooperation with British bankers. Some
businessmen, led by such investment banks as the Chase National,
favored cooperation, preferred short-term credit, and worked for
European recovery, which they believed would benefit the American economy. Their goals were to make New York the center of
the world and to "Americanize" Britain's finances. They believed
in gradualism. They were opposed by the National City Bank of
New York, the country's largest commercial bank. The National
City, backed by such firms as United States Steel and General
Electric, wanted to take advantage of the weakened European economic base to "Americanize" the financial system of the world
through branch banks, long-term credits, and investments. But the
goals of businessmen were generally the same, and their emergence
in the period after the war was a factor in the influence of the
United States in international economics. While businessmen had
received much sympathy from members of the Wilson administra-

tion, their views were not dominant in foreign policy from 1918 to 1921. The Wilson administration was concerned with political factors. In fact, there was little attention paid by the government or business in 1920 to the ambiguous relationship developing "between the foreign trade and investment activity conducted by private American citizens and the new position of economic and military power in which the United States found itself as a result of the war."[25] All this changed when Harding took over.

Unprecedented economic opportunities and the emergence of ideologies, especially bolshevism, hostile to Western democracy, combined with the assumption of power by officials like Secretary of Commerce Hoover, brought the corporate liberalism philosophy American businessmen had been preaching to the center of government power in Washington. More than any other official of the Harding administration, Hoover had thought about the changes brought by the war. Hoover had taken a moderate position during the debate on the League. He opposed both isolation and Wilson's League. In February 1920 he had said at Johns Hopkins University that he hoped that the League, with American participation, would use its "energies in the reduction of armament, the development of engines of reconciliation, of arbitration and codes and a court of international justice." Equally important, according to Hoover, was his hope that the League would use "its influence in the destruction of the economic barriers set up before and since the war, which stifle the recuperation and the free entry of our commerce over the world."[26] When Hoover's hope that there v 'd be American participation with guarantees disappeared, he came to the position that it was the duty of the United States to assume moral and economic leadership in the democratic world. For Hoover, there had to be cooperation between business and government to develop institutions that would bring order and stability and, in the process, American economic growth. Hoover advocated commissions of experts to gain cooperation between business and government and stressed interdependence between the American economy and developments around the globe. His views brought him to speak about the need for a world economic structure and for business principles in international relations.

One of the best examples of the philosophy Hoover advocated was his plan to control private American loans to foreign nations. The Wilson administration had decided against further government loans just before going out of office, and the Republicans decided to follow that precedent. Hoover and other officials determined to expand the limited government regulation of investments practiced by the Wilson administration, largely toward Russia and China. Hoover pressed for a long-range, government-controlled foreign loan policy. In May 1921 Harding met with Hoover, Hughes, Mellon, and business executives Thomas Lamont and Milton E. Ailes. In early June, J. P. Morgan, on behalf of his firm and other investment houses, agreed to keep the government informed of all potential foreign private loans. Loan applications would be reviewed by the Departments of State, Treasury, and Commerce and investors advised of government approval or disapproval. The government used a variety of factors—balanced budgets, excessive military expenditures, foreign monopolies, defaulting on debts owed to the United States, nonrecognition, discrimination against American products—to judge the loan applications. Hoover was at the center of this evaluation. Hoover believed loans had to be "reproductive," that is, of help to stability and growth, before they should be approved. As he wrote Hughes in April 1922, "We are morally and selfishly interested in the economic and political recovery of all the world. America is practically the final reservoir of international capital. Unless this capital is to be employed for reproductive purposes there is little hope of economic recovery."[27] With such views the administration successfully opposed the efforts of the Rumanian government to float a loan in New York in late 1922, because Rumania had not yet worked out an agreement for payment of its war debt to the United States. By 1925 Rumania had agreed on a schedule of debt payments.

Hoover's policy was not accepted by everybody in the government or in business. Hughes and the State Department tended to consider political factors more important than did Hoover and the Commerce Department. State and Treasury were less vigorous in examining economic aspects of loans than was the Commerce Department. There were severe disputes between government officials and businessmen. The governor of the Federal Reserve Bank of New York, Benjamin Strong, became the spokesman for bankers who opposed the government's suggestion that loans carry the stipulation that American goods must be purchased by the borrowing nations. American manufacturers supported the stipulation. Hoover pointed out that such provisions frequently had been attached to European loans. By the summer of 1922 the opposition of bankers to Hoover's policies had grown so severe that Harding and Mellon called for a revision of the standards. The president and secretary of the treasury agreed with Hoover that loan supervision was necessary where political and diplomatic interests were at stake (as in Russia and China). But they came to accept the position of the majority of investment bankers that most loans concerned only bankers and the borrowers.[28]

Hoover thus met defeat in his plan for close supervision of foreign loans. The opposition of the State and Treasury departments, as well as segments of the business community, proved too much. American loans thus had less supervision by the government, especially after the end of the Harding administration. Unfortunately, these loans were not part of any financial plan that involved tariff rates, debts, reparations, arms purchases, and currencies. Not until 1929, with the proposal to create a Bank of International Settlements to coordinate national financial policies, was the folly of unsound loans generally understood. By then it was too late.

If Hoover could not get control over American private loans overseas, that did not mean that cooperation between business and the administration grew less important. If anything, the close contacts formed during this dispute convinced both sides that a common policy had mutual benefits. In other matters, such as currency stabilization, import and export policies, the extension of the gold standard, and foreign monopolies, the cooperation was obvious. Additionally, the administration through Hoover and other individuals sought the views of businessmen on disarmament, commercial treaties, tariffs, settlement of debts and reparations, immigration quotas, and other topics. It was much more conscious than its predecessor of the views of businessmen. In a real sense "the diplomacy of the dollar" aptly describes international relations between 1921 and 1923.[29]

Perhaps the best example of cooperation between the administration and business occurred over expanding oil interests in the Middle East, which had made that area of strategic importance. Oil was needed for industry and also for navies and merchant marines. Two areas of contention were Mesopotamia (Iraq after 1921) and Persia (currently Iran). The British and French had moved to control oil in those areas and signed a treaty in 1920, assigning 50 percent of the interests to the Anglo-Persian Company, 25 percent to the French, and 25 percent to Royal Dutch–Shell. But difficulties developed between the British and French, and problems increased when the Americans decided to challenge the Anglo-French dominance. The Wilson administration had called for the open door in the Middle East and had protested Anglo-French attempts at monopoly but had done little else. The Harding administration decided to do more. Hoover believed in government participation in the exploitation of the oil fields in the Middle East and spent much time trying to deal with foreign problems of the oil industry. He convinced Hughes of the necessity of opening the oil industry of the Middle East to American businessmen.

The administration was not interested in a government-managed or government-owned petroleum industry, distinguishing itself from the British. But it did all it could to aid businessmen. Hoover and Hughes urged American oil companies to come together to gain a foothold in the area. Seven companies, led by Standard Oil of New Jersey, formed the so-called American group which began negotiating for a share of oil resources in Mesopotamia. The State Department continued to press the British for participation. The administration urged London to permit American and British interests to come together. The United States had not signed the treaty of Sèvres with Turkey after the World War. Nonetheless, the American group worked to get a satisfactory agreement. In 1922 the group came to an informal agreement with the Anglo-Persia group in Persia, and in 1923 with the British-controlled Turkish Petroleum Company in Mesopotamia. In each case the government had encouraged exploitation of resources by multinational companies.[30]

Interest by the United States in Middle Eastern oil took the administration into the politics of the area. The 1921–1922 war between Turkey and Greece and the massacre of Christians by the Turks brought pressure on the United States to become involved in a settlement to those difficulties. The Lausanne conference, which opened in late November 1922, proved to be a test of American interest in that section of the world. While American businessmen and humanitarian groups pressed for participation in the conference, which was attended by Great Britain and France, as well as by Greece and Turkey, Hughes decided against it. He authorized the American ambassador to Italy, Richard W. Child, the minister to Switzerland, Joseph C. Grew, and the high commissioner in Turkey, Rear Admiral Mark L. Bristol, to attend. They supported Turkey's demand for an end to foreign privileges. The Americans pressed for freedom of transit in the Dardanelles and for protection of Christians in Turkey. The Lausanne conference deadlocked, but the Turks and Allies did sign a treaty in July 1923 which guaranteed the demands the Americans had worked for, as well as the open door in Turkey and protection for Western religious and philanthropic institutions. The following month the

United States and Turkey signed a bilateral treaty granting the United States the same rights the Allies had acquired.[31]

Even though this treaty was eventually rejected by the United States Senate in 1927, events in the Middle East between 1921 and 1923 showed how far the administration was willing to go to help expand business. The oil controversy was perhaps the best example of the close working relations. There were officials and businessmen who doubted the importance of the international economy. But in general businessmen and especially government "officials assumed that the stabilization and economic rehabilitation of Europe would generate worldwide economic growth, would stimulate total world demand, would contribute to world peace and social order, and would benefit American commercial interests."[32] Because of these beliefs, businessmen and officials cooperated to guarantee American presence in the world economy as never before. Cooperation became a theme of diplomacy in the years 1921–1923 and after and in some ways was the most distinctive aspect of the foreign policy of the Harding administration.[33]

The foreign policy of the Harding administration was far from isolationist. Even so, the world of the 1920s was rapidly changing, and few Americans, least of all Harding, understood the complex relationship of the United States—the most powerful nation on earth—to that world. The result was constant pressure on the United States to participate in the benefits of the world economy while assuming no real responsibility for the social and political implications of that American economic activity.

7

$\bigstar\bigstar\bigstar\bigstar\bigstar$

THE SCANDALS

I

By the spring of 1923, Harding was a tired and confused man. In late August 1922 the Duchess had had a near fatal attack of hydronephritis, which weighed on his mind. The results of the elections depressed him, as strikes of the preceding summer had tried his patience and drained his energies. His congenial nature was pressed by contention with Congress, which was seemingly endless. He was disturbed by the failure of his ship subsidy bill. And the "best minds" were not always in agreement, so that contention reached even into the highest levels of the administration. Perhaps worse, it was apparent that he had been betrayed by some of his friends. The extent of betrayal was not yet known, but political implications, especially in view of the elections, seemed ominous.

Harding was accustomed to freedom of movement, wandering as he pleased. He came to resent the confinement of the presidency, comparing the office to a jail from which there was no escape. He allowed much of his time to be dominated by trivial aspects of his office. Late one night Nicholas Murray Butler found the president looking at a pile of unanswered correspondence in his office. Harding groaned that he had to go through the mail, but upon examining the letters Butler found that most were routine and should have been handled by secretaries. Butler protested the waste of Harding's time in answering such correspondence, to which Harding retorted: "I suppose so but I am not fit for this office and should never have been here." In May 1923 Harding telephoned Butler to come to the White House as quickly as possible because there were some problems he wanted to discuss but which could not be trusted to the wires. Butler appeared for the weekend, and the president on several occasions seemed ready to unburden himself. Ultimately he revealed nothing.

Seeking the appointment of a friend to the Court of Appeals, Senator Frank B. Brandegee arranged a meeting with Harding. To the senator's friendly query as to how he liked his job Harding responded: "Frank, it is hell! No other word can describe it."

Given this state of mental depression, Harding was haunted by the thought of a second term. Reelection would have kept him in his prison until the approach of his sixty-fourth birthday. Yet he wanted to justify his first term by winning reelection. As his popularity seemed to wane, he became more determined to seek a second term. Even so, he was embarrassed when Attorney General Daugherty prematurely announced that "the President will be a candidate for renomination." Harding was preparing for a cross-country journey and did not want it to appear to be a campaign tour. He wanted to speak as president, not a candidate, and wrote a friend, "I was a little embarrassed by General Daugherty's announcement of a candidacy, and have been seeking, in the most consistent way possible, to antidote the impression which that interview may have given that I would travel across the country as a candidate for renomination. I really want to speak as President, and am convinced that I can do so, and I look forward to good results both for me and for the better understanding of the country."[1]

Feeling weighed down by the pressures of office, he had decided it was time to reestablish contact with the people of the nation. The president loved to travel and had long planned an excursion to Alaska for a rest. He decided to turn the long journey across the country to Alaska into a "Voyage of Understanding."[2]

Shortly before departing on what turned out to be his fatal trip, the president took two steps: he sold the *Star* and made a new will. Later observers interpreted these actions as indications of a presidential sense of doom. Two Ohioans, Louis H. Brush and Roy D. Moore, purchased the *Marion Star* from the president for the inflated price of $550,000. Under terms of the sale, Harding was to remain a contributing editor for at least ten years after he left the presidency. The sale meant that he had to make a new will, which was drawn up by Daugherty and signed the day before

172

he left Washington. The will provided the Duchess with a $100,000 life estate and gave their house and possessions in Marion to her as well. His father was bequeathed a $50,000 life estate, and his brother and sisters were to receive various sums. The will granted $25,000 to the Marion Park Commission; small amounts to nieces, nephews, and his wife's grandchildren; $2,000 to the Baptist Church of Marion; and, finally, sums of $1,000 to $2,000 to old employees of the *Star*. These matters completed, Harding was ready to begin his travels.

The president stepped aboard the presidential car, *Superb*, on the afternoon of June 20, 1923, to begin the first part of the journey to Alaska. Accompanying the party were sixty-five people, including ten secret service agents, stenographers, twenty-two correspondents, five photographers, newsreel cameramen, and several telephone company employees who would go ahead to establish loudspeaker systems and arrange long-distance broadcasting of addresses. The guest list included Speaker of the House Frederick H. Gillett; Secretary of Agriculture Wallace; the new secretary of the interior, Dr. Hubert Work; and Secretary Hoover, who was to join the party on the West Coast. Also included were the Duchess, presidential doctors Charles E. Sawyer and Joel T. Boone, Mrs. Hoover, Mrs. Work, Mrs. Sawyer, Mr. and Mrs. George Christian, Jr., and Mr. and Mrs. Malcom Jennings. Notably absent was the long-time presidential crony and confidant, Daugherty.

Hoover's inclusion and Daugherty's exclusion reflected the importance of the secretary of commerce to the president. By early 1923 Hoover was clearly Harding's most trusted adviser on policy matters concerning all facets of government operations. Harding's emergence as a more confident leader of the country in 1923 appeared a result of Hoover's increasing dominance of the government. Many of Harding's new departures were traceable to the secretary of commerce. This trend would have continued had Harding lived. But with Harding's death, Hoover's influence rapidly diminished, as the new president had no use for Hoover. Coolidge was once heard to remark, "That man has offered me unsolicited advice for six years, all of it bad!"[3] Although Hoover remained in the cabinet, his progressive views were pushed into the background as the conservatives gained control of the government. Hoover was a transitional figure in the 1920s and was more in tune with the social and economic issues than either Harding or Coolidge. Hoover's conception of public versus private responsibility was limited to voluntary cooperation, and during the Great Depression he was unable to bring himself to aid individuals through federal intervention. But recent studies indicate that much more of the New Deal than had been thought is traceable to initiatives under Hoover, both as secretary of commerce and president.[4] Whatever his significance after 1923, Hoover had gained Harding's ear and thus was asked to make the trip.

President Harding's schedule included speaking stops in St. Louis, Kansas City, Hutchinson, Denver, Salt Lake City, Helena, Spokane, and Portland, before boarding the U.S.S. *Henderson* in Tacoma on July 5 for the trip to Alaska. The party planned to return to Seattle on July 27 and travel by train down the West Coast through San Francisco and Los Angeles. In San Diego, Harding was again to board ship for a leisurely trip through the Panama Canal, touching Puerto Rico and arriving back in Washington on August 26 or 27. The president was making an arduous journey during which he was "trying to learn more about the United States of America and seeking to have the people of the United States know more about their Government."[5] In this manner he hoped to restore his flagging popularity as well as defend policies of his administration.

During his trip westward Harding delivered fourteen speeches as well as numerous impromptu addresses. The speeches were a systematic presentation of normalcy as Harding then viewed it. Most were expansions of themes discussed on December 8, 1922, when Harding delivered what was to be his last state-of-the-union message.

That message had reflected the orthodoxy of his administration with its emphasis on business. The message also hinted at Harding's growing frustration and flagging spirit. "So many problems are calling for solution that a recital of all of them, in the face of the known limitations of a short session of Congress," he lamented, "would seem to lack sincerity of purpose." The burdens that selfishness had imposed on the nation were hard to assess, but the president was distressed that "everyone, speaking broadly, craves readjustment for everybody except himself, while there can be no just and permanent readjustment except when all participate."[6]

A large portion of the 1922 message was devoted to economic issues. The president was upset by the preceding summer's strikes and blamed them for slow economic recovery. "Had we escaped the coal and railway strikes, which had no excuse for their beginning and less justification for their delayed settlement, we should have done infinitely better," he postulated. Agriculture was hardest hit by the railway strike, and that fact demonstrated that "permanent and deserved agricultural good fortune depends on better and cheaper transportation." To ensure prosperity for farmer and industrialist, Harding called for a national transportation network of highways, railroads, and ocean carriers, repeating many of the points in his address to Congress in April 1921. The president desired to protect the public interest against further transportation strikes. To this end, he wanted to abolish the Railway Labor Board and replace it with a labor division in the Interstate Commerce Commission. He argued that "public interest" required the government to have power to force parties to accept the rulings of such an agency. In this manner the "security of society" would be safeguarded from future disruptions. Perhaps the president was stating his belief that it was not proper for labor to disrupt a business-oriented society.

Another portion of the 1922 message considered resident aliens. Listening to the crescendo of nativism in the country, with which he sympathized, Harding noted that "abusing the hospitality of our shores are the advocates of revolution, finding their deluded followers among those who take on the habiliments of an American without knowing an American soul." The president wanted a law to require registration of aliens so the government would have a list of people who might be involved in radical activities. The president blamed the high rate of national illiteracy on recent immigrants. He proposed a joint federal-state program to "Americanize" immigrants. Such a program would reduce revolutionaries in the country.

The remainder of the address had focused on internal improvements. The president wanted more land reclamation, irrigation, and joint federal-state reforestation, because the country was consuming forests four times more rapidly than they were being replaced. He hoped to hasten development of water power, as well as a system for distribution of water, steam, and electric power. Such a system would aid in expanding business.

Harding's message had not been a call for action. In contrast to his April 1921 address, it provided little in the way of detail. If Congress wanted to honor the president's vision, it would have to develop the programs in its own manner. The message was well received, with the *New York Times* editorializing that "the general spirit of his message is excellent." The *Times* thought it unfortunate that his remarks "cannot all be at once crystallized into the statute book."[7]

Six months later, as the president journeyed west, it was apparent that he was setting the tone for the campaign of 1924 and speaking not only for himself but the Republican party. And as his tour grew in popularity, his grip on the party seemed to tighten. In St. Louis he defended his call for joining the World Court; in Kansas City he emphasized the need for a transportation system; in Hutchinson he defended farm policies; prohibition and law enforcement were the topics in Denver; he discussed the coal problem in Cheyenne; he examined taxation and spending in Salt Lake City; Idaho Falls heard about cooperation in production and distribution of goods; business conditions were examined in Butte; he covered social justice and labor in Helena; internal improvements, reclamation of land, and water power were discussed in Spokane; Americanization of immigrants was the topic in Portland; the need for a strong merchant marine was dealt with in Tacoma. Harding's spirits were uplifted by the reception his speeches received. Before departing for Alaska he remarked, "Everywhere we have met a confident and a seemingly happy people, although as yet they may not be wholly satisfied with the conditions which require correction after the deflation incident to the war. Everywhere, however, they are hopeful and confident of the future and manifestly glad to live in this wonderful republic of ours. . . . I am very much more proud of our country than when I started westward."[8]

The president had approached his Alaska trip with a schoolboy's abandon. Even so, he was a troubled man. Hoover later related that on the trip north Harding asked what he should do if he knew of a scandal in the administration. "My natural reply was," Hoover remembered, "'Publish it, and at least get credit for integrity on your side.'" Harding ruminated that such a course might be dangerous. Hoover pressed for details and was told that Jesse Smith had been involved in irregularities in the Department of Justice. Hoover asked what Daugherty's relation was to the affair, and Harding "abruptly dried up and never raised the question again."[9]

The navy spared nothing in entertaining the presidential party on the trip to and from Alaska. The navy band and a number of first-run movies were brought aboard the 10,000-ton naval transport U.S.S. *Henderson*, and a glass-enclosed observation deck was constructed for presidential sightseeing pleasure. But even all this —buttressed by the favorable reaction to his speeches and the excitement of seeing Alaska for the first time—failed to lift Harding's spirits, which soon suffered another jar. As the *Henderson* entered

Puget Sound, returning to Seattle on the morning of July 27, it encountered heavy fog. Suddenly, it rammed into the side of the U.S.S. *Zeilin*, one of the thirteen destroyers sent out to escort the president into port. The *Zeilin* suffered major damage and was eventually beached to avoid sinking. The *Henderson* suffered only minor damages and was under way again in a half-hour. Even so, Harding remained in his bunk during the entire incident and was heard to remark, "I hope the boat sinks."

In Seattle on July 27, Harding spoke on the future of Alaska. In a speech drafted mainly by Hoover, the president asserted a surprisingly conservationist position for development of Alaska, at odds with the views of former secretary of the interior Albert Fall. But Harding was listless and had difficulty completing the speech. That evening he felt well enough to address the local press club, but he collapsed after the meal and was rushed to the train by Hoover, Work, and Sawyer. Late in the evening the president complained of cramps and indigestion. Dr. Sawyer blamed some crabmeat for the indigestion, but Dr. Boone and Secretary of the Interior Work, also a physician, suspected a cardiac malfunction. They urged Hoover to wire Dr. Ray Lyman Wilbur, president of Stanford University and former dean of the Stanford Medical School, to meet the train along with the best heart specialist from the area. All stops between Seattle and San Francisco were canceled.

Harding seemed to feel much better the next day, July 28, and Dr. Sawyer allowed the president to move about, telling the press that the president was suffering an "acute gastrointestinal attack" caused by tainted crabmeat. When the train arrived in San Francisco the following morning, Sunday, July 29, Harding was allowed to dress himself and walk to a waiting car, and was transported to a suite in the Palace Hotel. By nightfall he had suffered a relapse, and it was clear he was having cardiac difficulties complicated by bronchopneumonia. He appeared to respond to treatment and seemed to be improving in days that followed. But at 7:32 P.M., on Thursday, August 2, as the Duchess was reading out loud an article praising him (from the *Saturday Evening Post*, entitled "A Calm View of a Calm Man"), he went into convulsions. His doctors were on the scene immediately but to no avail—the president was dead.

The nation was stunned. Harding had remained a popular figure, and thousands stood by the tracks as the presidential train made its way eastward to Washington, arriving on August 7. Harding's body was taken to the East Room of the White House. The following morning the casket made the long, slow journey to the Capitol, where a brief service was held in the Rotunda. From 12:30 P.M. until 4:30 P.M., 35,000 people filed by the casket to pay their last respects, while 20,000 failed to achieve entrance. Harding's remains were returned to Marion by train for burial. Again thousands lined the tracks. The final obsequies were on August 10.[10]

Partly as a result of Dr. Sawyer's misdiagnosis, much came to be written about the death. As scandal tarnished the administration, there were rumors that something was peculiar about Harding's demise—that perhaps the president had been poisoned by his wife. But Harding's health had been visibly declining under the strains of office. Outward robustness was but the façade of a sick man. Long a golf enthusiast, Harding had been forced to curtail his game to a few holes, owing to tiredness and shortness of breath; and he had found it difficult to sleep unless propped up in bed by pillows. Even Dr. Sawyer, not trained in modern medical methods, recognized that Harding was suffering from angina pectoris and discovered that the president had extremely high blood pressure. Although the Duchess would not allow an autopsy, modern medical opinion is that Harding's death was the result of complications from an unrecognized coronary thrombosis.[11]

II

Shortly after Harding's death, it became evident that all had not been right with the administration. Corruption and malfeasance had been widespread. Before his death Harding was aware of at least some of the corruption, although he was never involved. As knowledge of his own habits and vices became public in the years that followed, his reputation suffered.

Scandal seemed without end. Harding never had a satisfactory relationship with his wife and had sought companionship elsewhere. He had a fifteen-year affair with Carrie Phillips, the wife of James Phillips, a Marion businessman and close friend. This affair ended acrimoniously in 1920, though it was not widely known until the 1960s when a researcher turned up love letters Harding had written to his mistress.[12] He had an affair with Nan Britton which may have started when she was only sixteen years old and was not ended until January 1923. The nation was scandalized in 1927 when Nan published her memoirs, alleging that Harding had fathered her child. The Carrie Phillips correspondence, discovered some forty years after Harding's death, substantiated many of Nan's claims.[13] Harding was by no means the first or last philanderer to be president, but he was the only one unfortunate enough to have one of his mistresses write memoirs.

It became public knowledge that Harding openly had consumed liquor in the White House during a time of national prohibition. Harding liked to relax by playing poker, with a highball at hand. While a senator, Harding privately had denounced prohibition but supported it for political reasons. He had little interest in the strict enforcement of prohibition, and the administration of the Volstead Act was a farce during his years in the White House. There was no systematic attempt to enforce the liquor statute, even when it became apparent that there was nationwide flouting of the law. After all, drinkers voted.

Harding became increasingly concerned about the openness with which the prohibition law was being broken and admonished the nation to obey the law, although he made no provisions for enforcement. He was troubled by the contradiction between his public statements and his private habits. At first he moved his liquor supply to his private bedroom in the White House and finally in early 1923 gave up drinking, at least temporarily. His last public statement on the subject was in Denver on his trip west. He voiced concern over the side effects of prohibition—bootlegging, local and national corruption, a higher crime rate, general disrespect for the law.[14] Despite the presidential pledge of abstinence, his personal habits badly tainted his reputation and appeared to connect him to the activities of some of the cronies he had appointed to high office.

If drinking and other habits caused harm, scandals connected with people in the administration destroyed its reputation beyond repair. Much of the scandal came about because Harding's judgment of character was poor. He allowed poker parties and light conversation to obscure the fact that some of his appointees were unscrupulous men who would not hesitate to use their offices to advance their own interests. Harding placed a premium on loyalty, and this trait made him slow to act against malefactors close to him.

A case in point was the so-called Ohio Gang, with which Jesse Smith was associated.[15] Smith was a close friend of the attorney general, living with Daugherty first in a house on H Street and then in a fashionable apartment at the Wardman Park Hotel. Smith was like a son to Daugherty and acted as housekeeper and confidant. Daugherty provided Smith with an office in the Department of Justice, although Smith did not hold any official appointment. Through association with Daugherty, Smith was a long-time associate of the president. Perhaps naïvely at first, Smith drifted into influence peddling with the help of two fellow Ohioans, Howard Mannington and Fred A. Caskey, who occupied the infamous "little green house on K Street." Using Smith's office in the Justice Department, the Ohio Gang arranged for the selling of permits to people who wanted to withdraw liquor from bonded government warehouses and worked out illegal sales of government property. Large sums were involved, with one bootlegger claiming to have paid Smith over $250,000 for immunity, while another group was paying as high as $20,000 for a permit to withdraw liquor from a bonded warehouse.

As time passed and Harding learned of irregularities within the Veterans Bureau, the president became suspicious of Smith. It was unclear how much Harding knew of Smith's acts, but he did know of them. When Daugherty placed Smith's name on the guest list for the journey to Alaska, Harding had the named removed. He ordered Daugherty to get Smith out of Washington and to keep him away. Brooding over his exile and seemingly imminent exposure, Smith on May 30, 1923, committed suicide in Daugherty's apartment. The president was shocked, though he may have been relieved. Harding's reaction to knowledge of Smith's activities had been to cover them up, getting Smith out of Washington rather than prosecuting him and his friends. Harding became criminally liable for this act alone. To have knowledge of a felony and not report it was a felony then, as it is today.

After Harding's death Attorney General Daugherty was indirectly implicated in Smith's activities. In February 1924 Senator Burton K. Wheeler demanded a full-scale investigation of the Justice Department and Daugherty's activities. Under Wheeler's supervision public hearings were initiated on March 12, 1924. Revelations from a parade of witnesses were sensational. Although the reliability of some individuals who testified was questionable, pressure was brought on Coolidge to force Daugherty's resignation. At first Coolidge hesitated because he felt it was his duty to preserve Harding's cabinet. By late March, Daugherty had become too much of a liability, and Coolidge curtly asked for his resignation.[16] Throughout the proceedings, and during his later trial, Daugherty maintained his innocence.

The most troublesome charge for Daugherty was that he had been involved, at least indirectly, in one of Jesse Smith's biggest payoffs, in collusion with the alien property custodian, Colonel Thomas W. Miller, a war hero and former congressman from Maryland with impeccable credentials. Miller was a charter member of the American Legion and held memberships in the Yale Club, the Union League, and National Press Club. He appeared uncorruptible, but through the importunities of Smith he ultimately used his position for personal enrichment. Smith arranged the illegal transfer of a German-owned firm, the American Metal Company, to an American-based firm. The American company gave the "fixers" $441,300, with $391,000 in Liberty Bonds. Fifty thousand dollars wound up in Miller's hands, with $224,000 going to Smith. Smith deposited $50,000 in the Midland National Bank in Washington Court House, Ohio, in an account entitled "Jess Smith Extra No. 3." The account was a special political account jointly drawn on by Smith and Daugherty. It was assumed by the prosecution that Daugherty had to know where such a sum originated, but the attorney general blocked all attempts to gain access to the account records.

Daugherty was soon indicted along with Miller on charges of defrauding the government. The now former attorney general maintained that he had been unaware of Smith's activities until shortly before the suicide and that the "Reds" were after him. The case against Daugherty centered on the bank account. In his trial it came out that the all-important account records had been destroyed. Daugherty refused to take the stand, implying that he was protecting the memory of Harding. Miller ultimately was convicted and given an eighteen-month jail sentence along with a $5,000 fine. The jury was uncertain about Daugherty, and charges were dropped. Miller, one of the three officials of the Harding administration to receive a jail term, served fifteen months. The former attorney general remained defiant for the remainder of his years, writing a friend: "If anybody does not like my position you can tell them to go to hell."[17]

One of Harding's worst misjudgments was the appointment of Charles R. Forbes to direct the Veterans Bureau. Harding had met Forbes while vacationing in Hawaii in 1915, and he had taken an immediate liking to the congenial and charming army colonel. To run his newly created bureau, with a budget of close to half a billion dollars, among the largest in the federal government, Forbes brought in a California lawyer, Charles F. Cramer, to act as general counsel.

Both Forbes and Cramer were soon heavily involved in defrauding the government—first through selling surplus government medical stores from the massive federal warehouses at Perryville, Maryland, at a fraction of their cost; then through kickbacks for accepting bids on new hospitals and authorizing the purchase of hospital sites at greatly inflated prices. Forbes sold goods worth millions of dollars to a Boston firm, Thompson and Kelley, for $600,000. He validated the sales by getting approval to dispose of a long list of damaged items, appending two lists of his own. At times, men were bringing newly purchased supplies in the front door of warehouses, and other men were carrying them out the back door. In return for their services Forbes and Cramer received considerable sums from the Boston firm. Concurrently, the two men were buying hospital sites at inflated prices, with sites worth $35,000 and $19,000 costing $90,000 and $105,000. They received a substantial portion of the overpayment. They worked out agreements in which they would share in profits of inflated bids to construct veterans hospitals. It is impossible to account for how much money the two men received, but the total must have been impressive. One estimate is that their activities cost taxpayers approximately $200 million.

Corrupt activities on such a scale could not be kept secret for long, and they were publicly hinted at while Harding was alive. Dr. Sawyer disliked Forbes from the beginning and warned the president about rumors of corruption. At first this had little effect. Securing proof of Forbes's activities in January 1923, Sawyer went to Daugherty, who in turn informed the president of activities in the Veterans Bureau. Harding ultimately confronted Forbes and, according to one witness, shook him while shouting "You Yellow rat! You double-crossing bastard!"

The president's first instinct was to avoid a scandal at all costs. He allowed Forbes to flee to Europe before accepting his resignation. Cramer committed suicide. Forbes eventually was prosecuted, receiving a sentence of two years in prison and a $10,000 fine.

This was the first public scandal of the administration, and the president's handling of it did him little credit. One of the most troublesome aspects of the Harding presidency was that he appeared to be far more concerned with political liabilities of a scandal than in securing justice. It was doubtful that Forbes would have been prosecuted if a Senate investigation had not occurred. Harding had refused to act. Shortly after learning of Forbes's betrayal, Harding told William Allen White during an interview: "My God, this is a hell of a job! I have no trouble with my enemies,

I can take care of my enemies all right. But my damn friends . . . my God-damn friends, White, they're the ones that keep me walking the floor nights!"[18] But walking floors at night was one thing. Justice was apparently quite another.

Teapot Dome probably was the scandal most damaging to Harding's reputation. During the Taft administration conservationists had arranged the creation of two large naval oil reserves in California, and Wilson set aside Teapot Dome in Wyoming as the third naval oil reserve. Conservationists argued that the navy had to have such reserves. Under no circumstances, with the exception of a national emergency, should these areas be opened to exploitation. This was a plan that conservationists supported, and in 1920 the navy took control of the reserves. Since the secretary of the navy, Josephus Daniels, was a known conservationist, the oil conservation movement breathed a collective sigh of relief.[19]

When Harding appointed his friend from the Senate, Fall, as secretary of the interior, he was selecting a man from the West with decidedly anticonservationist views. Although Fall favored national parks, he had long been an advocate of the idea that natural resources on public land should be made accessible to private exploitation. He was hostile to the conservationist movement. On May 31, 1921, he secured the transfer of the oil reserves from the Navy Department to Interior, by executive order, using the argument that Interior was equipped to control drainage of the federal oil reserves to adjacent private property.

Secretary of the Navy Edwin Denby believed Fall's arguments sound and therefore favored the transfer to Interior. Indeed, Denby noted his approval to Harding on May 26. His purpose was to protect the navy's oil, not to open it to private exploitation. But because he was a party to the transfer, his reputation was eventually shattered. As a result of criticism of his action, he was the first cabinet officer to tender his resignation to Coolidge, who accepted it on February 18, 1924. So Denby became the initial victim of Fall's malfeasance in office.

Fall secretly and without holding public bids leased Elk Hills in California to his long-time friend Edward L. Doheny, president of Pan-American Oil Company, and Teapot Dome to Harry Sinclair, head of the Sinclair Consolidated Oil Corporation. Sinclair's lease was to run for at least twenty years, with the government receiving a royalty of 16 percent. Sinclair was required to build storage tanks for the navy and a pipeline. The terms of Doheny's lease required a pipeline, a refinery in California, and oil storage tanks at Pearl

Harbor. Even with these expenditures, it was obvious that both companies would take enormous profits.

Conservationists began an intense examination of Fall and his department. Senator Robert La Follette sensed something wrong and began an informal investigation of the leases. La Follette was convinced Harding's executive order was not legal, and in April 1922 a resolution passed in the Senate to investigate the leases. La Follette encouraged a Democrat from Montana, Senator Thomas J. Walsh, to direct the investigation. A westerner with the same philosophy as Fall, Walsh was reluctant to press the investigation. Not until after Harding's death and knowledge of the other scandals did the investigation begin in earnest.

Fall resigned from the cabinet in March 1923. As a Senate friend of Harding he had expected to be one of his advisers. He was unhappy because Harding turned to Hoover, Hughes, and Wallace. Probably this was the reason he left the cabinet, his reputation for integrity intact—not fear of investigation of the oil leases. To succeed Fall, Harding appointed Hubert Work, a protégé of Herbert Hoover who was already postmaster general. Work turned many of Fall's policies around and pursued a moderately conservationist course at Interior for the next five years, which pleased many conservationists. Work did much more than that, as he brought modern business methods to the department and rejuvenated the Department of the Interior during a trying time.[20]

It might all have ended with appointment of a new secretary more pleasing to conservationists, except for the tenacity of the able and persistent Walsh. Beginning his hearings in the autumn of 1923, he found most of the early testimony unproductive. In two days of grilling, Walsh was unable to shake former Secretary Fall's defense of leasing policies. But late in November the senator heard rumors that Fall's financial position had visibly improved around the time of the leasing of the two reserves. Doheny and Sinclair denied giving the secretary any financial favors in exchange for the leases. Fall was frightened as the investigation crept closer and refused to testify further on account of illness. He then committed a grave error by sending a letter to the committee in which he stated that Edward B. McLean, publisher of the *Washington Post* and a friend of President Harding, had lent him $100,000 for improvements on his New Mexico ranch. Fall maintained he had never approached Doheny or Sinclair for money and considered the entire subject "more or less humiliating even to refer to."[21] McLean was in Miami due to "illness" and refused to come to

Washington. Walsh decided to go to Miami and interview the publisher. The senator was astonished when McLean broke down and admitted he had in fact not lent Fall any money. With Fall's story discredited, Walsh had the first break on the case. He was no longer dealing with rumor and allegation.

Doheny, on January 24, 1924, came forward and admitted he had "loaned" the $100,000 to the former secretary of the interior because of Fall's desire to obtain a neighboring ranch. Doheny insisted the money had nothing to do with his company's securing leases in California. In the end it was determined that Fall had received slightly more than $400,000 from the two oilmen, with the balance coming from Sinclair. Fall was convicted of taking bribes while in office and became the first cabinet-level officer to be sentenced to prison for malfeasance. He served nine months of his one-year sentence, though he never paid the $100,000 fine. Neither Doheny nor Sinclair was convicted of bribing a public official, but Sinclair served a brief sentence for jury tampering. Both men lost the leases that they had gained. Doheny, ironically, secured the mortgage on Fall's ranch at a sheriff's sale, for $168,250, the same day that Fall entered prison. Three years after Fall left prison, Doheny foreclosed the mortgage and evicted the former secretary of the interior.

Harding died unaware of his secretary's improprieties in office and the damage it would do to his own reputation. Thus there is no indication as to how Harding would have dealt with the scandal involving his friend from the Senate, though his attempts to bury the Smith and Forbes scandals give little confidence that he would have responded properly. There was a tragic quality to Fall's demise. His actions concerning the leases may have been a matter of conviction.[22] The secretary was committed to allowing private business to exploit government property on the most favorable terms. Bribery or no, Fall probably would have followed the same course. Fall died in 1944, a broken man, convinced that his policy of building oil storage tanks at Pearl Harbor for the navy in exchange for oil had been of service to the nation.

III

For the Republican party, Harding's death was timely. It allowed the party to pass off culpability. Much of the effect of the scandals on the fortunes of the party was mitigated by the fact that prominent Democrats were at least marginally associated with the scandals. William G. McAdoo, a leading Democratic contender for his party's nomination in 1924, was found to be "oily" when it was revealed that he too had been employed by Doheny. The list did not stop with McAdoo, as Doheny had employed three other former members of Wilson's cabinet in one capacity or another. The Republican party narrowly avoided another damaging revelation in 1924. After the campaign of 1920 the party found itself more than a million dollars in debt. Sinclair wanted to make a large contribution, but both he and the national chairman, Will Hays, realized it would not be wise. Somehow Walsh got wind of the offer but could not pin down details. His sources informed him that Sinclair had given Sinclair Consolidated Oil Corporation bonds to the party. In fact Sinclair had made two contributions—one for $75,000, the other a "loan" for $185,000. The latter sum was in Liberty Bonds, from the same series "loaned" to Fall. While Hays mentioned the $75,000 on the stand in 1924, he was able technically to deny Walsh's remaining charges because the senator asked the wrong questions. To disguise the Liberty Bonds, Hays sold them to wealthy Republicans for cash. When word of the contribution came out in 1928, it was too far in the past to be an issue. Hays, by then the protector of Hollywood's morals, was asked why he had kept silent four years before. "Nobody," he indignantly replied, "asked me about any Liberty Bonds."[23]

Coolidge proved himself an able politician by the manner in which he took the scandals out of the campaign of 1924. The new president appointed two special prosecutors, a Democrat and a Republican, with no strings to their appointments. Because of the prosperity that had been returning to the country in Harding's last year in office, and by transferring blame from the Republican party to the deceased Harding and associates, Coolidge was easily elected president in his own right. Coolidge, through his stern, austere conception of the presidency, rehabilitated the Republican party in an amazingly short time.[24]

With the airing of the scandals Republicans did everything in their power to dissociate themselves from Harding the man, though they maintained the policies of normalcy. It became plain that no prominent Republican was willing to participate in a dedication ceremony of the Harding memorial in Marion, scheduled for July 4, 1927. The dedication had to be postponed.

It was fitting that the only Republican with the courage to honor Harding was Hoover. Even he at first shied away from the task of dedicating the memorial to his former chief. In 1931, with his own administration in shambles, Hoover had perhaps more sympathy for the disgraced president and agreed to dedicate the memorial on June 16. Coolidge and Hughes felt compelled to attend the ceremony but said little. It was left for Hoover to speak of the former president. "Here was a man whose soul was seared by a great disillusionment," he eulogized. "Warren Harding had a dim realization that he had been betrayed by a few of the men whom he had trusted, by men whom he had believed were his devoted friends. It was later proved in the courts of the land that these men had betrayed not only the friendship and trust of their staunch and loyal friend but they had betrayed their country. That was the tragedy of the life of Warren Harding."[25] The former secretary of commerce was unable to bring himself to point to what he viewed as the accomplishments of the administration, only to Harding's personal feelings.

8

★★★★★

A PLACE IN HISTORY

Historians have not been gentle with Warren G. Harding. On almost every poll of presidential greatness, Harding ranks dead last. In 1948 Arthur M. Schlesinger, Sr., conducted a poll of fifty-five scholars to measure presidents of the United States, and Harding ranked twenty-ninth and last in greatness. Schlesinger repeated his poll in 1962, raising his sample to seventy-five experts. The result was the same for Harding, who ranked thirty-first and last. He and Ulysses S. Grant were the only failures among presidents. Other presidents were categorized as great, near great, average, below average. The years between 1948 and 1962 had not changed the ranking for Harding. As Schlesinger noted, "the verdict of total unfitness . . . was, by the overwhelming majority, reserved alone for Grant and Harding. Both were postwar Presidents who, by their moral obtuseness, promoted a low tone in official life, conducting Administrations scarred with shame and corruption." Harding ranked below Grant, according to Schlesinger, because he "could not plead Grant's political inexperience."[1]

Some six years after the Harding papers were opened and after the publication of works based on that manuscript collection, another poll appeared in 1970. An article in the *Journal of American History* related results of a poll of almost six hundred members of the Organization of American Historians, the professional organization of scholars in American history.[2] Presidents were evaluated in seven categories, but neither the expanded categories nor recent

189

historical works helped Harding. The Ohioan ranked thirty-third and last in prestige, strength of action, presidential activeness, and accomplishments of his administration, the four key categories. He ranked thirtieth in idealism, though high for practicality and flexibility.

A few historians have disagreed with this rating. Thomas A. Bailey, in a book on presidential greatness published in 1966, thought Harding had suffered at the hands of historians who admired Woodrow Wilson. He admitted that Harding had many problems but contended that the administration was "a faithful reflection of the times" and that there were many accomplishments.[3] Harding's administration, he said, was not as much of a failure as those of James Madison, John Quincy Adams, or Andrew Johnson. Bailey ranked Harding as below average but not a failure.

Harding's strongest defender among respected historians has been Robert K. Murray, who, in *The Harding Era*, disputes the polls of greatness. Summarizing both accomplishments and failures of the administration and noting Harding's personal shortcomings, Murray writes that Harding "was certainly the equal of a Franklin Pierce, an Andrew Johnson, a Benjamin Harrison, or even a Calvin Coolidge. In concrete accomplishments, his administration was superior to a sizable portion of those in the nation's history. Indeed, in establishing the political philosophy and program for an entire decade, his 882 days in office were more significant than all but a few similar short periods in the nation's experience."[4]

In a later book on government policies in the 1920s, Murray states that had Harding lived he would have been more assertive and effective.[5] He notes that Coolidge's program between 1923 and 1929 was Harding's, and that Coolidge's victory in 1924 was a vindication of the Harding policies.

While some of Murray's conclusions are disputed, his books and those of other historians have partly rehabilitated Harding. Revision of traditional accounts of certain aspects of the Harding presidency has taken place.[6] Harding sought and won his nomination in 1920; he was a shrewd politician who communicated effectively if not articulately; he was not the captive of Daugherty, or his wife, or the Senate's Old Guard; he was not involved in the scandals that shook his administration; he died of natural causes; there were some accomplishments in the administration. On these points, there seems to be general agreement.[7]

And yet the Harding administration is still viewed as a failure. Even separating the man and the administration does not help. As president, the man does not warrant high marks. He did not provide moral leadership; he did not have much understanding of forces at work in the United States after the World War; he was not willing to use the federal government to ease adjustment after the war. Many of his views—especially concerning the role of the executive branch—were reflections of opinion. He did recognize that Americans wanted relief from contentions of the war. He sought to avoid controversy, even if it meant avoiding real problems. In this he was successful. America in 1923 was more peaceful and relaxed than three years before, and this perhaps ranks as one of Harding's greatest achievements. This also meant that he did little to provide direction in a period of transition. The country ran itself, with the president content to sit back and watch.

Harding set the tone for the administration. Because of the president's views toward the executive branch, little was done between 1921 and 1923 to bring long-range, large-scale solutions to problems, with the possible exception of the creation of the Bureau of the Budget. There were accomplishments, but the majority were short-term. In foreign affairs the Washington naval conference, commonly cited as one of the successes of the administration, provided only stopgap solutions concerning both arms and the Far East. In domestic affairs the push for the eight-hour day in the steel industry was similar. It was a step, but only a small one, and it was not followed by additional steps. Many of the actions of the administration were temporizing. Harding allowed his cabinet autonomy, and the record of the administration was uneven. A Hughes or Hoover had more "successes" than a Fall or Daugherty. Even Hughes and Hoover seemed largely concerned with problems of the moment, not with the long-term causes of difficulties.

The years 1921 to 1923 comprised a critical period, with changes taking place. A good deal of the debate over the Harding administration is over what he might have done after 1923 if he had lived. By that year stopgap solutions had begun to come apart. Certainly, the president would have been involved in the political scandals revealed after 1923. One need only remember Richard M. Nixon's activities in 1973 and 1974 to be sure of that. While more action would have been required in domestic and foreign affairs, Harding would have had less time to consider alternatives. It seems evident that Harding was reluctant to clean up his administration. Indeed, Harding had already made halting efforts before his death to cover up—or at the very least, ignore—the scandals for obvious political reasons. Hoover was certainly the dominant figure in the administration by mid-1923; perhaps Hoover would have assumed a Henry Kissinger–like role as wider public knowledge of the scandals destroyed Harding's credibility as a leader. Some indication of the conduct of a continued Harding administration can be gained from looking at Hoover's career between 1923 and 1933. But that is speculation, and, although Hoover's influence was substantially reduced under Coolidge, he still had an enormous impact on the nation during the 1920s. In many ways his appointment was Harding's best achievement.

What can be said about the administration of the country between 1921 and 1923 is that Harding's presidency was transitional and that he was an ineffective leader who suffered both personal and political scandal. It is not surprising that historians rate Harding a poor president.

Warren G. Harding was elected at a time when urban-rural troubles afflicted the country. Harding was a part of the malady: he was the product of a small town, an almost rural background, and he possessed neither the education nor experience to rise above his origins. Although he had come from a rural society with its values in transition as it moved into an industrial age, Harding failed to sense what was happening to the nation. He emphasized business, but in a traditional sense, with little concern for the social and economic problems that industrialization had brought about in the United States. His was an age of transition, from war to peace, from rural to urban life, yet he governed by traditional means. He was unable to see the necessity of readjusting the government in a time of change. Indeed, "normalcy" was Harding's reaction to the changes then taking place in America, when the country might have been better served by a different approach to government.

Notes

CHAPTER 1

1. See Donald R. McCoy's excellent treatment of this period, *Coming of Age: The United States During the 1920's and 1930's* (Baltimore: Penguin Books, 1973).

2. Burl Noggle, in *Into the Twenties: The United States from Armistice to Normalcy* (Urbana: University of Illinois Press, 1974), does some interesting urban-rural comparisons in his chapter "American Society, 1920," pp. 152–178. Almost all of the statistics cited thus far, and the vast majority that appear in this chapter, are from the Bureau of the Census, *Historical Statistics of the United States: Colonial Times to 1957* (Washington, D.C.: Government Printing Office, 1960).

3. Noggle, *Into the Twenties*, p. 156.

4. There is a large controversy on what happened to progressivism in the period after 1917. The historiographic controversy is most recently summarized in Noggle's chapter "Remnants of Progressivism," in *Into the Twenties*, pp. 179–213.

5. Ibid., p. 6. Noggle notes that estimates made by John Maurice Clark in 1931 were that between 160,000 and 500,000 Americans died as a result of the war.

6. Cited in Roy Watson Curry, *Woodrow Wilson and Far Eastern Policy, 1913–1921* (New York: Bookman Associates, 1957), p. 295.

7. Noggle, *Into the Twenties*, pp. 9–13.

8. Ibid., p. 50.

9. Robert K. Murray, *The Harding Era: Warren G. Harding and His Administration* (Minneapolis: University of Minnesota Press, 1969), p. 85.

10. A good account of one of the strikes is David Brody, *Labor in Crisis: The Steel Strike of 1919* (Philadelphia: Lippincott, 1965).

11. Stanley Coben, "A Study in Nativism: The American Red Scare of 1919–1920," *Political Science Quarterly* 79 (1964): 59. Two excellent book-length treatments of the Red Scare are Stanley Coben, *A. Mitchell Palmer: Politician* (New York: Columbia University Press, 1963), and Robert K. Murray, *Red Scare: A Study in National Hysteria, 1919–1920* (Minneapolis: University of Minnesota Press, 1955).

12. Noggle, *Into the Twenties*, p. 121.

13. J. Stanley Lemons, *The Woman Citizen: Social Feminism in the 1920s* (Urbana: University of Illinois Press, 1973), p. 21. Catt's comment is cited on p. 3.

14. Noggle, *Into the Twenties*, p. 158.

15. For the struggle over the Eighteenth Amendment and its effects, see Andrew Sinclair, *Prohibition: The Era of Excess* (Boston: Little, Brown and Company, 1962). There is a good deal of dispute about the rural-urban conflict over prohibition and also on the makeup of the group who supported prohibition. For a discussion of this controversy, see Noggle, *Into the Twenties*, pp. 165–167.

16. Cited in Thomas A. Bailey, *Woodrow Wilson and the Great Betrayal* (Chicago: Quadrangle Books, 1963), p. 100. Bailey's study, which covers Wilson's efforts in the United States, is a fine study of the president's fight. Combined with his *Woodrow Wilson and the Lost Peace* (Chicago: Quadrangle Books, 1963), it presents complete coverage on the making and defeat of the treaty.

17. Murray, *The Harding Era*, p. 81. For a lengthy treatment of the president's illness, see Gene Smith, *When the Cheering Stopped: The Last Years of*

Woodrow Wilson (New York: Morrow, 1964).

18. An excellent study of American culture in this period, upon which this is based, is Roderick Nash, *The Nervous Generation: American Thought, 1917–1930* (Chicago: Rand McNally & Co., 1970), pp. 126–141.

19. Murray, *The Harding Era*, p. 91; and Noggle, *Into the Twenties*, p. 205.

20. Murray, *The Harding Era*, p. 32. Good accounts of Harding's quest for the nomination, in addition to Murray, are Randolph C. Downes, *The Rise of Warren Gamaliel Harding, 1865–1920* (Columbus: Ohio State University Press, 1970); Andrew Sinclair, *The Available Man: The Life Behind the Masks of Warren Gamaliel Harding* (New York: Macmillan Company, 1965); Francis Russell, *The Shadow of Blooming Grove: Warren G. Harding in His Times* (New York: McGraw-Hill, 1968); and Wesley M. Bagby, *The Road to Normalcy: The Presidential Campaign and Election of 1920*, Johns Hopkins University Studies in Historical and Political Science, vol. 80 (Baltimore, 1962).

21. See Donald McCoy, "Election of 1920," in Arthur M. Schlesinger,

Jr., ed., *History of American Presidential Elections, 1789–1968*, vol. 3 (New York: Chelsea House, 1971), pp. 2349–2385, which is the most balanced treatment of the election.

22. Murray, *The Harding Era*, p. 42.

23. McCoy, "Election of 1920," p. 2354.

24. Ibid., pp. 2371–2372 and 2379.

25. Ibid., p. 2373.

26. Murray, *The Harding Era*, has a good discussion of Chancellor's charges, as does Randolph C. Downes, "Negro Rights and White Backlash in the Campaign of 1920," *Ohio History* 75 (1966): 85–107.

27. See McCoy, "Election of 1920," for a discussion of Harding and the League in the election campaign, and David H. Jennings, "President Harding and International Organization," *Ohio History* 75 (1966): 149–165, for the problems the issue caused Harding between 1921 and 1923.

28. McCoy, "Election of 1920," p. 2385. For a discussion showing how 1920 was a Republican year, see Howard W. Allen and Jerome Clubb, "Progressive Reform and the Political System," *Pacific Northwest Quarterly* 65 (1974): 130–145.

CHAPTER 2

1. For the most detailed account of Harding's early life, see Randolph C. Downes, *The Rise of Warren Gamaliel Harding, 1865–1920* (Columbus: Ohio State University Press, 1970). Quote on p. 10.

2. Francis Russell, *The Shadow of Blooming Grove: Warren G. Harding in His Times* (New York: McGraw-Hill, 1968), pp. 53–55.

3. A brief chronology of Harding's career can be found in Philip R. Moran, ed., *Warren G. Harding, 1865–1923* (Dobbs Ferry, N.Y.: Oceana Publications, Inc., 1970).

4. Andrew Sinclair, *The Available Man: The Life Behind the Masks*

of Warren Gamaliel Harding (New York: Macmillan Company, 1965), pp. 64–65. For Harding's career in the Senate, see Russell, *The Shadow of Blooming Grove*, chaps. 12 and 13.

5. For the most interesting and complete version of Harding's daily activities, see Russell, *The Shadow of Blooming Grove*, pp. 443–450.

6. Sinclair, *The Available Man*, pp. 219–220; and Robert K. Murray, *The Harding Era: Warren G. Harding and His Administration* (Minneapolis: University of Minnesota Press, 1969), pp. 113–114.

7. Robert K. Murray, *The Politics of Normalcy: Governmental Theory and Practice in the Harding-Coolidge Era* (New York: W. W. Norton, 1973), pp. 23–24.
8. *New York Times*, February 22, 1921. Robert K. Murray, "President Harding and His Cabinet," *Ohio History* 75 (1966): 108–125, provides the most comprehensive treatment of the selection of Harding's cabinet; the following pages owe much to Murray.
9. See Mark Sullivan, *Our Times: The United States, 1900–1925*, vol. 6, *The Twenties* (New York: Charles Scribner's Sons, 1936), pp. 144–177. Murray discounts this episode entirely with some convincing arguments. See Murray, "President Harding and His Cabinet," p. 111.
10. Murray, "President Harding and His Cabinet," pp. 111–112 and n. 22.
11. Warren G. Harding to Henry C. Wallace, November 1, 1920, *Warren G. Harding Papers*, Ohio Historical Society, Columbus, Microfilm Edition, Roll 42.
12. Murray, "President Harding and His Cabinet," p. 113. For an extensive survey on Hoover's "good press," see Craig Lloyd, *Aggressive Introvert: Herbert Hoover and Public Relations Management, 1912–1932* (Columbus: Ohio State University Press, 1972).
13. Murray, "President Harding and His Cabinet," p. 113.
14. Harding to Harry Daugherty, February 9, 1921, *Harding Papers*, Microfilm Roll 231.
15. Bascom Timmons, *Portrait of an American: Charles G. Dawes* (New York: Henry Holt and Company, 1953), pp. 200–204.
16. Telegram, Samuel Gompers to Harding, February 7, 1921, *Harding Papers*, Microfilm Roll 81.
17. Russell, *The Shadow of Blooming Grove*, pp. 535 and 561–562; and Eugene P. Trani, "Hubert Work and the Department of the Interior, 1923–28," *Pacific Northwest Quarterly* 61 (1970): 31–40.
18. Sinclair, *The Available Man*, pp. 190–192; and Murray, *The Harding Era*, pp. 299–306.
19. Cited in Sinclair, *The Available Man*, p. 192.
20. Timmons, *Portrait of an American*, pp. 202–206.
21. Cited in Alpheus T. Mason, *The Supreme Court from Taft to Warren*, rev. ed. (Baton Rouge: Louisiana State University Press, 1968), pp. 41 and 43.
22. For excellent sketches of the three associate judges appointed by Harding, see Leon Friedman and Fred L. Israel, eds., *The Justices of the United States Supreme Court, 1789–1969: Their Lives and Major Opinions*, vol. 3 (New York: Chelsea House Publishers, 1969), pp. 2133–2218.
23. Sullivan, *The Twenties*, p. 153 n.
24. For an account of the fate of regulatory commissions under Republican rule, see John D. Hicks, *Republican Ascendancy, 1921–1933* (New York: Harper & Row, Publishers, 1960), pp. 65–66.
25. Cited in Sinclair, *The Available Man*, p. 194.
26. For an excellent account of Harding's dealings with blacks, see Richard B. Sherman, *The Republican Party and Black America from McKinley to Hoover, 1896–1933* (Charlottesville: University of Virginia Press, 1973), chap. 6. Quotation cited on page 166.
27. J. Stanley Lemons, *The Woman Citizen: Social Feminism in the 1920s* (Urbana: University of Illinois Press, 1973), pp. 74–76.

CHAPTER 3

1. For Harding's inaugural address, see *Messages and Papers of the Presidents*, vol. 18 (New York: Bureau of National Literature, Inc., n.d.), pp. 8923–8930.
2. Robert K. Murray, *The Harding*

Era: Warren G. Harding and His Administration (Minneapolis: University of Minnesota Press, 1969), pp. 124–125, provides a good account of the first days of Harding's tenure as president.

3. An analysis of the address can be found in Donald R. McCoy, *Coming of Age: The United States During the 1920's and 1930's* (Baltimore: Penguin Books, 1973). For the speech, see *Messages and Papers*, pp. 8937–8950.

4. The Republicans in the Senate are analyzed by Charles M. Cannon, "A Statistical Analysis of Senate Roll Call Vote by Party Loyalty for the Sixty-Sixth Congress and the Sixty-Seventh Congress" (M.A. thesis, Southern Illinois University, 1968).

5. For an analysis of House and Senate factions, see Robert K. Murray, *The Politics of Normalcy: Governmental Theory and Practice in the Harding-Coolidge Era* (New York: W. W. Norton, 1973), pp. 42–46.

6. Frederic L. Paxson, *Postwar Years —Normalcy, 1918–1923* (Berkeley: University of California Press, 1948), has a good discussion of these items. Quote on p. 224.

7. Quotes cited in Bascom Timmons, *Portrait of an American: Charles G. Dawes* (New York: Henry Holt and Company, 1953), pp. 206 and 209.

8. For the message to Congress, see *Messages and Papers*, pp. 8974–8984.

9. Cited in Paxson, *Postwar Years*, p. 230.

10. James H. Shideler's *Farm Crisis, 1919–1923* (Berkeley: University of California Press, 1957) contains an excellent discussion of the administration's approach to the agrarian crisis. Quotation cited on p. 157. Also, see Murray, *The Politics of Normalcy*, pp. 50–52.

11. Shideler, *Farm Crisis*, p. 159.

12. Donald L. Winters, *Henry Cantwell Wallace as Secretary of Agriculture, 1921–1924* (Urbana: University of Illinois Press, 1970), pp. 82–85. Quotation from Shideler, *Farm Crisis*, p. 162.

13. For an account of the Hoover-Wallace struggle, see Edward L. and Frederick H. Schapsmeier, "Disharmony in the Harding Cabinet: Hoover-Wallace Conflict," *Ohio History* 75 (1966): 126–136. The Schapsmeiers credit Harding with a progressive farm policy. Shideler, *Farm Crisis*, pp. 141–151, presents a somewhat different view. For the most recent view, see Winters, *Wallace*, pp. 244–246.

14. Robert K. Murray, "Herbert Hoover and the Harding Cabinet" (Paper delivered at the Hoover Presidential Library Association, West Branch, Iowa, April 1974).

15. John D. Hicks, in *Republican Ascendancy, 1921–1933* (New York: Harper & Row, Publishers, 1960), pp. 52–54, provides this view of Mellon. For a different view of the Revenue Act of 1921, see Murray, *The Politics of Normalcy*, pp. 53–58. For the Welliver quote, see Murray, *The Harding Era*, pp. 185–186.

16. John Kenneth Galbraith, *The Great Crash: 1929*, rev. ed. (Boston: Houghton Mifflin, 1972), pp. 182–183.

17. *New York Times*, September 1, 1922.

18. Hicks, *Republican Ascendancy*, p. 58.

19. For the best factual account of the shipping imbroglio, see Murray, *The Harding Era*, pp. 280–293 and 321–326. Quotes cited on pp. 283–284.

20. *New York Times*, March 1, 1922.

21. This is Murray's figure, in *The Politics of Normalcy*, p. 69. Hicks, *Republican Ascendancy*, p. 61, cites a figure of $52 million per year.

22. For Harding's addresses see *Messages and Papers*, pp. 9100–9109, and 9157–9165.

23. Cited in Murray, *The Harding Era*, p. 325.

24. For a good factual discussion of the bonus issue, see Murray, *The Politics of Normalcy*, pp. 72–76. Murray believes that Harding's veto provided firm evidence of Harding's growing strength as an executive leader.

25. Ibid., pp. 74–75.

26. Hicks, *Republican Ascendancy*, p. 52.

27. Francis Russell, in *The Shadow of Blooming Grove: Warren G. Harding in His Times* (New York: McGraw-Hill, 1968), has an interesting discussion of the midterm election. Murray, *The Harding Era*, chap. 10, prefers to skirt the fact of the disastrous Republican losses and instead focuses on the emerging "strong" executive.

28. Murray, in *The Harding Era* and in *The Politics of Normalcy*, is the chief articulator of the "new Harding" and Harding's changing view of the presidency.

CHAPTER 4

1. Robert K. Murray, *The Harding Era: Warren G. Harding and His Administration* (Minneapolis: University of Minnesota Press, 1969), pp. 413–416, provides an excellent account of the plans for reorganization, as well as the reorganizations that actually took place.

2. James H. Shideler, *Farm Crisis, 1919–1923* (Berkeley: University of California Press, 1957), pp. 134–141.

3. Murray, *The Harding Era*, pp. 177–178.

4. For accounts of the fate of some of the regulatory commissions, see G. Cullom Davis, "The Transformation of the Federal Trade Commission, 1914–1929," *Mississippi Valley Historical Review* 49 (1962): 437–455; Elmus R. Wicker, *Federal Reserve Monetary Policy, 1917–1933* (New York: Random House, 1966); and John D. Hicks, *Republican Ascendancy, 1921–1933* (New York: Harper & Row, Publishers, 1960).

5. Murray, *The Harding Era*, pp. 392–394.

6. Alpheus T. Mason, *The Supreme Court from Taft to Warren*, rev. ed. (Baton Rouge: Louisiana State University Press, 1968), chap. 2.

7. Murray, *The Harding Era*, pp. 409–411. Murray provides coverage of the administration's policies regarding transportation and communication. If anything, he does not stress enough their importance for the nation's future development.

8. For a first-rate examination of American culture during the 1920s, see Roderick Nash, *The Nervous Generation: American Thought, 1917–1930* (Chicago: Rand McNally & Co., 1970). Quote cited on p. 154.

9. For differing views on the agricultural conference, see Murray, *The Harding Era*, pp. 211–215; Frederic L. Paxson, *Postwar Years —Normalcy, 1918–1923* (Berkeley: University of California Press, 1948), pp. 267–268; and Donald L. Winters, *Henry Cantwell Wallace as Secretary of Agriculture, 1921–1924* (Urbana: University of Illinois Press, 1970), chap. 7.

10. *New York Times*, January 24, 1922.

11. Hicks, *Republican Ascendancy*, pp. 65, 193–201, provides a good discussion of McNary-Haugenism, pointing out some of the defects of the bill, as well as the administration's responses to the conference.

12. Shideler, *Farm Crisis*, pp. 161–168.

13. For the best treatment of the unemployment conference, see Robert Zieger, *Republicans and Labor, 1919–1929* (Lexington: University of Kentucky Press, 1969), pp. 90–97. Other ac-

counts can be found in Evan B. Metcalf, "Secretary Hoover and the Emergence of Macroeconomic Management," *Business History Review* 49 (1975): 71–74; Robert K. Murray, "Herbert Hoover and the Harding Cabinet" (Paper delivered at the Hoover Presidential Library Association, West Branch, Iowa, April 1974), pp. 10–14; and Carolyn Grin, "The Unemployment Conference of 1921: An Experiment in National Cooperative Planning," *Mid-America* 55 (1973): 83–107.

14. Zieger, *Republicans and Labor*. Quotes on pp. 91–92.

15. Cited in Murray, "Herbert Hoover," p. 11. It should be noted that in fact the government did on occasion lower wages, as the railway workers could attest.

16. Quotes cited in Zieger, *Republicans and Labor*, pp. 95–96.

17. Cited in Murray, "Herbert Hoover," p. 14.

18. Zieger, *Republicans and Labor*, pp. 97–108, has an excellent discussion of the drive for the eight-hour day. Quotes on pp. 104–106.

19. See Irving Bernstein, *The Lean Years: A History of the American Worker, 1920–1933* (Boston: Houghton Mifflin Company, 1960), p. 84; and Hicks, *Republican Ascendancy*, pp. 68–74. For a somewhat more sympathetic account of Harding's relationship with labor, see Murray, *The Harding Era*, chap. 8. The most balanced account is Zieger, *Republicans and Labor*, chap. 6.

20. Paul M. Angle, *Bloody Williamson: A Chapter in American Lawlessness* (New York: Alfred

A. Knopf, 1952), has the most detailed account of the violence in southern Illinois.

21. Cited in Zieger, *Republicans and Labor*, pp. 128–129.

22. Ibid., pp. 138–139.

23. Francis Russell, *The Shadow of Blooming Grove: Warren G. Harding in His Times* (New York: McGraw-Hill, 1968). Quotes on pp. 463 and 487.

24. Richard B. Sherman, *The Republican Party and Black America from McKinley to Hoover, 1896–1933* (Charlottesville: University of Virginia Press, 1973), chaps. 6 and 7, provides an excellent account of the relationship of the administration with black Americans. Quote on p. 147. For a more sympathetic treatment of Harding's views on race relations, see Randolph C. Downes, "Negro Rights and White Backlash in the Campaign of 1920," *Ohio History* 75 (1966): 85–107.

25. *Messages and Papers of the Presidents*, vol. 18 (New York: Bureau of National Literature, Inc., n.d.), p. 8946.

26. Cited in Sherman, *The Republican Party*, p. 148.

27. George Christian, Jr., to Mrs. Frank L. Applegate, April 18, 1922, *Harding Papers*, Microfilm Roll 218.

28. J. Stanley Lemons, *The Woman Citizen: Social Feminism in the 1920s* (Urbana: University of Illinois Press, 1973), has a fine account of the feminist struggle for equality during that decade. Lemons is particularly helpful on the Sheppard-Towner Act.

29. Ibid., p. 174.

CHAPTER 5

1. Cited in Betty Glad, *Charles Evans Hughes and the Illusions of Innocence: A Study in American Diplomacy* (Urbana: University of Illinois Press, 1966), p. 132.

2. David J. Danelski and Joseph S.

Tulchin, eds., *The Autobiographical Notes of Charles Evans Hughes* (Cambridge, Mass.: Harvard University Press, 1973), p. 199.

3. Cited in Glad, *Charles Evans Hughes*, pp. 134–135.

4. Danelski and Tulchin, eds., *The Autobiographical Notes*, pp. 203–204.
5. Glad, *Charles Evans Hughes*, pp. 153–162.
6. For a discussion of Hughes's ideas on recognition, as well as for exact citations to the quotes on recognition, see Eugene P. Trani, "Harding Administration and Recognition of Mexico," *Ohio History* 75 (1966): 137–148 and 190–192.
7. *New York World*, February 22, 1921.
8. Joseph Brandes, *Herbert Hoover and Economic Diplomacy: Department of Commerce Policy, 1921–1928* (Pittsburgh: University of Pittsburgh Press, 1962), p. 10.
9. For a discussion of the reasons why Wilson agreed to send troops to Russia, see Eugene P. Trani, "Woodrow Wilson and the Decision to Intervene in Russia: A Reconsideration," *Journal of Modern History* (September 1976).
10. Herbert Hoover, *The Memoirs of Herbert Hoover*, vol. 1, *Years of Adventure, 1874–1920* (New York: Macmillan Company, 1952), p. 221.
11. Cited in Eugene P. Trani, "Herbert Hoover and the Russian Revolution, 1917–1920" (Paper delivered at the Hoover Presidential Library Association, West Branch, Iowa, February 1974).
12. For the Colby Note, see *Papers Relating to the Foreign Relations of the United States, 1920*, vol. 3 (Washington, D.C.: Government Printing Office, 1936), pp. 463–465. For an analysis of the note, see Joan Hoff Wilson, *Ideology and Economics: U.S. Relations with the Soviet Union, 1918–1933* (Columbia: University of Missouri Press, 1974), pp. 14–20.
13. *Messages and Papers of the Presidents*, vol. 18 (New York: Bureau of National Literature, Inc., n.d.), p. 8928. For discussions of the possible change in policy, see Robert K. Murray, *The Harding Era: Warren G. Harding and His Administration* (Minneapolis: University of Minnesota Press, 1969), p. 348, and Randolph C. Downes, *The Rise of Warren Gamaliel Harding, 1865–1920* (Columbus: Ohio State University Press, 1970), pp. 629–630.
14. Press release cited in Benjamin M. Weissman, *Herbert Hoover and Famine Relief to Soviet Russia, 1921–1923* (Stanford, Calif.: Hoover Institution Press, 1974), p. 42. Correspondence with Hughes cited in Wilson, *Ideology and Economics*, pp. 19–28.
15. *New York Times*, March 26, 1921; and Edward M. Bennett, *Recognition of Russia: An American Foreign Policy Dilemma* (Waltham, Mass.: Ginn/Blaisdell, 1970), p. 53.
16. Wilson, *Ideology and Economics*, pp. 25 and 29.
17. Cited in Trani, "Hoover and the Russian Revolution," p. 33.
18. Ibid., p. 33. The best account of the agreement is Benjamin M. Weissman, "Herbert Hoover's 'Treaty' with Soviet Union, August 20, 1921," *Slavic Review* 28 (1969): 276–288.
19. Trani, "Hoover and the Russian Revolution," p. 34; and Weissman, *Hoover and Famine Relief*, p. 201.
20. Wilson, *Ideology and Economics*, p. 24; and Weissman, *Hoover and Famine Relief*, p. 202.
21. Bennett, *Recognition of Russia*, p. 57; Murray, *The Harding Era*, p. 353; Glad, *Charles Evans Hughes*, pp. 311–313; and Robert Browder, *The Origins of Soviet-American Diplomacy* (Princeton, N.J.: Princeton University Press, 1953), p. 18.
22. Wilson, *Ideology and Economics*, p. 32.
23. Hughes to Harding, May 3, 1923, *Harding Papers*, Microfilm Roll 181.
24. Bennett, *Recognition of Russia*, pp. 62 and 68. See also Peter G. Filene, *Americans and the Soviet Experiment, 1917–1933* (Cam-

bridge, Mass.: Harvard University Press, 1967), and John P. McKay, "Foreign Enterprise in Russian and Soviet Industry: A Long Term Perspective," *Business History Review* 48 (1974): 336–356, for more information on Soviet-American relations during the Harding era.

25. For a detailed discussion of this problem, as well as for exact citations to quotes on the Mexican recognition, see Trani, "Harding Administration and Recognition of Mexico."

26. N. Stephen Kane, "Bankers and Diplomats: The Diplomacy of the Dollar in Mexico, 1921–1924," *Business History Review* 47 (1973): 337 and 338.

27. For Obregón's propaganda campaign, see C. Dennis Ignasias, "Propaganda and Public Opinion in Harding's Foreign Affairs: The Case for Mexican Recognition," *Journalism Quarterly* 48 (1971): 41–52.

28. Cited in Murray, *The Harding Era*, p. 331.

29. Ibid., pp. 332–333.

30. For the attempt by the Wilson administration to change its Latin American policy, see Daniel M. Smith, "Bainbridge Colby and the Good Neighbor Policy, 1920–1921," *Mississippi Valley Historical Review* 50 (1963): 56–78.

31. Robert N. Seidel, *Progressive Pan Americanism: Development and United States Policy Toward South America, 1906–1931* (Ithaca, N.Y.: Cornell University Latin American Studies Program, 1973), pp. 146–147.

32. Joseph S. Tulchin, *The Aftermath*

of War: World War 1 and U.S. Policy Toward Latin America* (New York: New York University Press, 1971), p. 90.

33. Hughes's statements on the Monroe Doctrine and Pan Americanism are cited in Eugene P. Trani, "Charles Evans Hughes: The First Good Neighbor," *Northwest Ohio Quarterly* 40 (1968): 138–162.

34. Kenneth J. Grieb, "Warren G. Harding and the Dominican Republic U.S. Withdrawal, 1921–1923," *Journal of Inter-American Studies* 11 (1969): 440. See also Hans Schmidt, *The United States Occupation of Haiti, 1915–1934* (New Brunswick, N.J.: Rutgers University Press, 1971).

35. Cited in Trani, "Charles Evans Hughes," p. 148.

36. Cited in Alexander DeConde, *Herbert Hoover's Latin American Policy* (Stanford, Calif.: Stanford University Press, 1951), p. 6.

37. For extensive statistics on American-Latin American economic relations, see Tulchin, *The Aftermath of War*. Tulchin and Seidel, *Progressive Pan Americanism*, disagree over Hoover's importance in Latin American policy, with Seidel viewing Hoover's role as much more important. See also Mira Wilkens, "Multinational Oil Companies in South America in the 1920s," *Business History Review* 48 (1974): 414–446, for more information on American investments in Latin America during the Harding era.

38. Tulchin, *The Aftermath of War*, pp. 93 and 252.

CHAPTER 6

1. Harding to Henry Cabot Lodge, December 29, 1920, *Harding Papers*, Ohio Historical Society, Columbus, Microfilm Roll 81.

2. For the quotations from the inaugural address and Harding's April 1921 speech to Congress, see *Messages and Papers of the*

Presidents*, vol. 18 (New York: Bureau of National Literature, Inc., n.d.), pp. 8923–8930 and 8937–8950.

3. David J. Danelski and Joseph S. Tulchin, eds., *The Autobiographical Notes of Charles Evans Hughes* (Cambridge, Mass.: Har-

vard University Press, 1973), p. 213.

4. Cited in Betty Glad, *Charles Evans Hughes and the Illusion of Innocence: A Study in American Diplomacy* (Urbana: University of Illinois Press, 1966), p. 165.

5. The best discussion of the removal of the American troops from Germany is by Jolyon P. Girard, "Congress and Presidential Military Policy: The Occupation of Germany, 1919–1923," *Mid-America* 56 (1974): 211–220.

6. *New York Times*, September 30, 1921.

7. Cited in Glad, *Charles Evans Hughes*, p. 178.

8. *New York Times*, October 31, 1922.

9. Glad, *Charles Evans Hughes*. Quotes cited on pp. 187 and 190.

10. Ibid., p. 213.

11. Cited in John Chalmers Vinson, *The Parchment Peace: The United States Senate and the Washington Conference, 1921–1922* (Athens: University of Georgia Press, 1955), p. 51.

12. Thomas H. Buckley, *The United States and the Washington Conference, 1921–1922* (Knoxville: University of Tennessee Press, 1970), p. 13.

13. Ibid., pp. 72–73. See also Eugene P. Trani, "Four American Fiddlers and Their Far Eastern Tunes: A Survey of Japanese-American Relations, 1898–1941," in Bernard Gordon, ed., *The New Political Economy of the Pacific* (Cambridge: Ballinger, 1975), pp. 47–67, for a discussion of Hughes's goals at the Washington conference.

14. Glad, *Charles Evans Hughes*, p. 297.

15. L. Ethan Ellis, *Republican Foreign Policy, 1921–1933* (New Brunswick, N.J.: Rutgers University Press, 1968), p. 107. For an account of the Japanese at the conference, see Sadao Asada, "Japan's 'Special Interests' and the Washington Conference, 1921–22," *American Historical Review* 67 (1961): 62–70.

16. Gerald E. Wheeler, *Prelude to Pearl Harbor: The United States Navy and the Far East, 1921–1931* (Columbia: University of Missouri Press, 1963) gives the best account of the naval buildup in the post-Washington period.

17. Akira Iriye, *After Imperialism: The Search for a New Order in the Far East, 1921–1931* (Cambridge, Mass.: Harvard University Press, 1965), p. 36.

18. Cited in Gerald E. Wheeler, "Republican Philippine Policy, 1921–1933," *Pacific Historical Review* 28 (1959): 377.

19. Cited in Iriye, *After Imperialism*, p. 35. An interesting assessment of American Far Eastern policy in the 1920s is in an article by William A. Williams, "China and Japan: A Challenge and a Choice of the Nineteen Twenties," *Pacific Historical Review* 26 (1957): 259–279. For an example of the sort of "good will but little negotiation" diplomacy the administration followed toward Japan after the Washington conference, see Eugene P. Trani, "Secretary Denby Takes a Trip," *Michigan History* 51 (1967): 277–297, an account of Denby's visit to Japan in 1922.

20. Joan Hoff Wilson, *American Business & Foreign Policy, 1920–1933* (Lexington: University Press of Kentucky, 1971), p. 124.

21. Melvyn Leffler, "The Origins of Republican War Debt Policy, 1921–1923: A Case Study in the Applicability of the Open Door Interpretation," *Journal of American History* 59 (1972): 589.

22. Ibid., p. 598.

23. The best account of the French debts is Benjamin D. Rhodes, "Reassessing 'Uncle Shylock': The United States and the French War Debt, 1917–1929," *Journal of American History* 55 (1969): 787–803.

24. Cited in Robert K. Murray, *The Harding Era: Warren G. Harding*

and His Administration (Minneapolis: University of Minnesota Press, 1969), p. 366; and Glad, *Charles Evans Hughes*, pp. 220–223.

25. Wilson, *American Business & Foreign Policy*, pp. 3 and 18–19.

26. Ibid., p. 28. An excellent account of Hoover and his activities in foreign affairs is Joseph Brandes, *Herbert Hoover and Economic Diplomacy: Department of Commerce Policy, 1921–1928* (Pittsburgh: University of Pittsburgh Press, 1962).

27. Melvyn Leffler, "Herbert Hoover, the 'New Era,' and American Foreign Policy, 1921–1929" (Paper delivered at the Hoover Presidential Library Association, West Branch, Iowa, April 1974).

28. A fine account of the loan control controversy is Carl P. Parrini, *Heir to Empire: United States Economic Diplomacy, 1916–1923* (Pittsburgh: University of Pittsburgh Press, 1969).

29. See Herbert Feis's volume, *The Diplomacy of the Dollar: First*

Era, *1919–1932* (Baltimore: The Johns Hopkins Press, 1950).

30. Both Wilson, *American Business & Foreign Policy*, and Michael J. Hogan, "Informal Entente: Public Policy and Private Management in Anglo-American Petroleum Affairs, 1918–1924," *Business History Review* 48 (1974): 187–205, are good for the agreements worked out by the American and British interests.

31. John A. DeNovo, *American Interests and Policies in the Middle East, 1900–1939* (Minneapolis: University of Minnesota Press, 1963), has a good discussion of the political relations between the United States and the Middle East.

32. Melvyn Leffler, "Political Isolationism, Economic Expansion or Diplomatic Realism? American Policy Toward Western Europe, 1921–1933," *Perspectives in American History* 8 (1974): 422.

33. William A. Williams, "The Legend of Isolationism in the 1920s," *Science and Society* 18 (1954): 1–20, deals with this problem.

CHAPTER 7

1. Francis Russell, *The Shadow of Blooming Grove: Warren G. Harding in His Times* (New York: McGraw-Hill, 1968), pp. 453, 485, and 564–565.

2. Good accounts of Harding's "Voyage of Understanding" can be found in ibid., chap. 20; and Robert K. Murray, *The Harding Era: Warren G. Harding and His Administration* (Minneapolis: University of Minnesota Press, 1969), pp. 438–451.

3. Cited in Donald R. McCoy, *Calvin Coolidge: The Quiet President* (New York: Macmillan Company, 1967), p. 390. McCoy contends that Coolidge disliked Hoover personally but did not treat him nearly as badly as Wilson treated Cox or Theodore Roosevelt treated Taft.

4. Joan Hoff Wilson, in *Herbert*

Hoover: Forgotten Progressive (Boston: Little, Brown and Company, 1975), does much to rehabilitate the long-ignored progressivism of Hoover.

5. Cited in Murray, *The Harding Era*, p. 442.

6. For the text of the address, see *Messages and Papers of the Presidents*, vol. 18 (New York: Bureau of National Literature, Inc., n.d.), pp. 9174–9187.

7. *New York Times*, December 9, 1922.

8. Cited in Murray, *The Harding Era*, p. 445.

9. Hoover cited in Russell, *The Shadow of Blooming Grove*, pp. 582 and 588. For the collision near Seattle, see Robert E. Finken, "President Harding Visits Seattle," *Pacific Northwest Quarterly* 66 (1975): 105–109.

10. For good accounts of Harding's funeral train and burial, see Russell, *The Shadow of Blooming Grove*, pp. 591–603; and Murray, *The Harding Era*, pp. 451–455.

11. Although marred by superfluous opinions, such as "Like many people who are moral cowards, he had physical courage and was not given to complaining," the best account of Harding's medical problems is in Rudolph Marx, *The Health of the Presidents* (New York: Putnam's, 1960), pp. 323–336. The publication of Gaston Means's unreliable memoir, *The Strange Death of President Harding* (New York: Guild Publishing Corporation, 1930), gave wide currency to the idea that Harding had been poisoned by his wife.

12. For details on the controversy surrounding the Harding–Carrie Phillips correspondence, see Francis Russell, "The Harding Papers . . . And Some Were Saved," *American Heritage* 16 (1965): 25–31, 102–110.

13. See Nan Britton, *The President's Daughter* (New York: Elizabeth Ann Guild, Inc., 1927).

14. Andrew Sinclair, *Prohibition: The Era of Excess* (Boston: Little, Brown and Company, 1962), pp. 252–259; and Murray, *The Harding Era*, pp. 403–407.

15. For a good account of the activities of Jesse Smith, see Mark Sullivan, *Our Times: The United States, 1900–1925*, vol. 6, *The Twenties* (New York: Charles Scribner's Sons, 1936), pp. 227–238.

16. McCoy, *Calvin Coolidge*, pp. 212–217.

17. Murray, *The Harding Era*, pp. 474–482, has a good account of Daugherty's involvement. Quote on p. 482.

18. An excellent rendition of the misdeeds by Forbes and Cramer can be found in Russell, *The Shadow of Blooming Grove*, pp. 522–526 and 557–560. Quotes cited on pp. 558 and 560.

19. The best accounts of the Teapot Dome scandal are J. Leonard Bates, *The Origins of Teapot Dome: Progressives, Parties, and Petroleum, 1909–1921* (Urbana: University of Illinois Press, 1963), especially chaps. 12–14; and Burl Noggle, *Teapot Dome: Oil and Politics in the 1920s* (Baton Rouge: Louisiana State University Press, 1962). For a sympathetic view of Albert B. Fall, see David H. Stratton, "Behind Teapot Dome: Some Personal Insights," *Business History Review* 31 (1957): 385–402.

20. See Eugene P. Trani, "Hubert Work and the Department of the Interior, 1923–1928," *Pacific Northwest Quarterly* 61 (1970): 31–40.

21. Cited in Noggle, *Teapot Dome*, p. 70.

22. See Stratton, "Behind Teapot Dome."

23. Bruce Bliven, "Tempest Over Teapot," *American Heritage* 16 (1965): 20–23, 100–105.

24. For the election of 1924, see J. Leonard Bates, "The Teapot Dome Scandal and the Election of 1924," *American Historical Review* 60 (1955): 303–322.

25. Cited in Russell, *The Shadow of Blooming Grove*, p. 640.

CHAPTER 8

1. Arthur M. Schlesinger, Sr., "The U.S. Presidents," *Life* 25 (November 1, 1948): 65–67; and "Our Presidents: A Rating by 75 Historians," *New York Times Magazine*, July 29, 1962, pp. 12–13, 40–43.

2. Gary M. Maranell, "The Evaluation of Presidents: An Extension of the Schlesinger Polls," *Journal of American History* 57 (1970): 104–113.

3. Thomas A. Bailey, *Presidential Greatness: The Image and the*

Man from George Washington to the Present (New York: Appleton, Century Crofts, 1966), pp. 312–315.

4. Robert K. Murray, *The Harding Era: Warren G. Harding and His Administration* (Minneapolis: University of Minnesota Press, 1969), pp. 536–537.

5. Robert K. Murray, *The Politics of Normalcy: Governmental Theory and Practice in the Harding-Coolidge Era* (New York: W. W. Norton, 1973).

6. Eric F. Goldman, "A Sort of Rehabilitation of Warren G. Harding," *New York Times Magazine*, March 26, 1972, pp. 42–43, 80–88.

7. See Louis W. Potts, "Who Was Warren G. Harding?" *Historian* 36 (1974): 621–645, for a fine account of the writings on Harding and his administration.

Bibliographical Essay

This essay attempts to indicate the massive nature of the materials on the Harding administration. While the essay will concentrate on secondary sources, there will be mention of both primary materials and works that had much influence on the reputation Warren Harding has carried since his death. It must be emphasized that this essay is meant to be only an introduction to the materials on the administration. The interested reader should consult the items cited in this essay for additional material on the times.

PRIMARY MATERIALS

The opening to researchers of the Warren G. Harding Papers, in the Ohio Historical Society in Columbus, on April 25, 1964, was a major event in the field of American history. It meant that historians were able to gain a more complete picture of Washington between 1921 and 1923 and to come to a better understanding of Harding himself. The Harding Papers, a large collection now available on microfilm, is described in Donald E. Pitzer, "An Introduction to the Harding Papers," *Ohio History* 75 (1966): 76–84. Pitzer discusses the collection's controversial history and estimates the amount of material that was destroyed by Harding's widow. See also Kenneth W. Duckett, "The Harding Papers—How Some Were Burned. . . ," and Francis Russell, "The Harding Papers . . . And Some Were Saved," both in *American Heritage* 16 (1965): 25–31, 102–110. The latter article discusses the letters between Harding and Carrie Phillips, the wife of a Marion, Ohio, businessman, with whom Harding had an affair. Now deposited in the Library of Congress, the letters are closed to research until July 29, 2014.

The Ohio Historical Society has a number of manuscript collections of Harding's associates in Ohio politics. Among the most important are the papers of Arthur L. Garford, F. E. Scobey, and Frank B. Willis. Far more important for an understanding of the administration are the papers of Harding's associates between 1921 and 1923. They include the papers of Calvin Coolidge, Charles

Evans Hughes, William Howard Taft, James J. Davis, Edward T. Clark, Philander C. Knox, William E. Borah, George Norris, Theodore Roosevelt, Jr., and Thomas J. Walsh, all in the Library of Congress; Will H. Hays, in the Indiana State Historical Society Library in Indianapolis; Edwin Denby, in the Detroit Public Library; Hubert Work, in the Colorado State Archives in Denver; Henry Cabot Lodge, in the Massachusetts Historical Society; Albert Fall, in both the University of New Mexico and the Henry E. Huntington Library in San Marino, California; and, most importantly, Herbert Hoover, in the Hoover Presidential Library in West Branch, Iowa. The Hoover collection is vast and shows Hoover's increasing role in the administration. Additionally, the National Archives has the official government records for the years 1921 to 1923. The records of the Departments of State, Navy, Agriculture, Commerce, Labor, and Interior have been the most intensively utilized to date. Finally, there are contemporary newspapers and periodicals, such as the *Chicago Tribune, New York Times, New York Herald Tribune, Washington Post, New Republic, Nation, Independent, Saturday Evening Post,* and *Atlantic Monthly.* One should note that a convenient summary of statistical information on the Harding era is available in Bureau of the Census, *Historical Statistics of the United States: Colonial Times to 1957* (Washington, D.C.: Government Printing Office, 1960).

PUBLISHED MATERIALS

Those interested in the Harding administration are fortunate in that there are a number of essays that deal with the historiography of the 1920s in general or with the administration in particular. The most recent essay, for example, Louis W. Potts, "Who Was Warren G. Harding?" *Historian* 36 (1974): 621–645, is a fine introduction to the literature and the changing picture of the Harding presidency. Other such works are Henry F. May, "Shifting Perspectives on the 1920's," *Mississippi Valley Historical Review* 43 (1956): 405–427; John D. Hicks, "Research Opportunities in the 1920's," *Historian* 25 (1962): 1–13; Burl Noggle, "The Twenties: A New Historiographical Frontier," *Journal of American History* 52 (1966): 299–314; Randolph C. Downes, "The Harding Muckfest: Warren G. Harding—Chief Victim of the Muck-for-Muck's Sake Writers and Readers," *Northwest Ohio History* 39 (1967): 5–37; Robert K. Murray, "The Twenties," in John A. Garraty, ed., *Interpreting American History: Conversations with Historians*

(New York: Macmillan Company, 1970), vol. 2, pp. 145–168; Murray, "The Myth and the Reality," in his book, *The Harding Era: Warren G. Harding and His Administration* (Minneapolis: University of Minnesota Press, 1969), pp. 498–537; Don S. Kirschner, "Conflicts and Politics in the 1920's: Historiography and Prospects," *Mid-America* 48 (1966): 219–233; and Herbert F. Margulies, "Recent Opinion on the Decline of the Progressive Movement," *Mid-America* 45 (1963): 250–268. All of these accounts are valuable in showing how the interpretations of the Harding era have been revised.

The memoir material on the Harding administration is ample, with the following among the most important works: Herbert Hoover, *The Memoirs of Herbert Hoover: The Cabinet and the Presidency, 1920–1933* (New York: Macmillan Company, 1952); Calvin Coolidge, *The Autobiography of Calvin Coolidge* (New York: Cosmopolitan Book Corporation, 1929); Harry M. Daugherty, in collaboration with Thomas Dixon, *The Inside Story of the Harding Tragedy* (New York: Churchill Company, 1923); James J. Davis, *The Iron Puddler: My Life in the Rolling Mills and What Came of It* (Indianapolis: Bobbs-Merrill Company, 1922); David J. Danelski and Joseph S. Tulchin, eds., *The Autobiographical Notes of Charles Evans Hughes* (Cambridge, Mass.: Harvard University Press, 1973); and Will H. Hays, *The Memoirs of Will H. Hays* (Garden City, New York: Doubleday, 1955). Other valuable memoir accounts are: Nicholas Murray Butler, *Across the Busy Years*, 2 vols. (New York: Charles Scribner's Sons, 1940); William Allen White, *The Autobiography of William Allen White* (New York: Macmillan Company, 1946); James M. Cox, *Journey through My Years* (New York: Simon and Schuster, 1946); Evalyn Walsh McLean, *Father Struck It Rich* (Boston: Little, Brown and Company, 1936); William G. McAdoo, *Crowded Years: The Reminiscences of William G. McAdoo* (Boston: Houghton Mifflin Company, 1931); Edmund W. Starling, *Starling of the White House* (New York: Simon and Schuster, 1946); Irwin H. Hoover, *Forty-Two Years in the White House* (Boston: Houghton Mifflin Company, 1934); Alice Roosevelt Longworth, *Crowded Hours* (New York: Charles Scribner's Sons, 1933); George W. Norris, *Fighting Liberal: The Autobiography of George W. Norris* (New York: Collier Books, 1961); Samuel Gompers, *Seventy Years of Life and Labor: An Autobiography*, 2 vols. (New York: E.P. Dutton and Company, 1925); Lillian R. Clarke (with Frances S. Leighton), *My Thirty Years Backstairs at the White House* (New

York: Fleet Publishing Co., 1961); Henry L. Stoddard, *As I Knew Them: Presidents and Politics from Grant to Coolidge* (New York: Harper and Brothers, 1927); and Charles W. Thompson, *Presidents I've Known and Two Near Presidents* (Indianapolis: Bobbs-Merrill, 1929).

Eulogistic accounts of Harding appeared shortly after his death, such as Joe Mitchell Chapple, *Life and Times of Warren G. Harding, Our After-War President* (Boston: Chapple Publishing Company, 1924). Soon, however, the pendulum swung, and a number of hostile treatments dominated the writing on Harding and his administration, especially as more and more came to be known about the scandals. Particularly significant in the destruction of Harding's reputation were Nan Britton, *The President's Daughter* (New York: Elizabeth Ann Guild, Inc., 1927); and Gaston B. Means (as told to Mary Dixon Thacker), *The Strange Death of President Harding* (New York: Guild Publishing Corporation, 1930). The former related Britton's contention that Harding had fathered her illegitimate child, and the latter, eventually regarded as without foundation, described Harding's personal involvement in the various scandals and raised a number of questions about the nature of Harding's death in 1923. With the Britton and Means attacks, fortified by F. Scott Fitzgerald, *The Vegetable; or, From President to Postman* (New York: Charles Scribner's Sons, 1923), and Samuel Hopkins Adams, *Revelry* (New York: Boni and Liveright, 1926)—both accounts of a president surrounded by thieves —Harding's reputation fell.

Contemporary writers such as H. L. Mencken and Bruce Bliven began to attack Harding vigorously, with Mencken, even before Harding's death, concentrating on Harding's intellectual capacities and speaking style—"Gamalielese"—and Bliven exposing the "Ohio Gang." The attacks moved from journals to books with the publication of William Allen White, *Masks in a Pageant* (New York: Macmillan Company, 1928). In that work, and later in his *A Puritan in Babylon: The Story of Calvin Coolidge* (New York: Macmillan Company, 1938) and *The Autobiography of William Allen White*, the Kansas journalist criticized events in Washington between 1921 and 1923. White's initial work was followed by Frederick Lewis Allen, *Only Yesterday: An Informal History of the Nineteen-Twenties* (New York: Harper and Brothers, 1931), the book that perhaps more than any other guided students attempting to understand the 1920s. Allen's Harding was a willing victim, controlled by crooked party bosses in an America that was interested mostly in bathtub gin, the stock market, and Babe Ruth's latest exploits. While Mark Sullivan, in *Our Times: The United States, 1900–1925*, 6 vols. (New York: Charles Scribner's Sons, 1926–1935), was more sympathetic to Harding, his picture was not essentially different from Allen's. Sullivan did point to some of the accomplishments of the administration but accepted many of the views of White and Allen on the president, his administration, and the scandals. In 1939 the Harding reputation reached its lowest point with the publication of Samuel Hopkins Adams, *The Incredible Era—The Life and Times of Warren G. Harding* (Boston: Houghton Mifflin Company, 1939). Adams wrote (p. 190):

> We, the sovereign people, had chosen for leader by an unprecedented majority, at a time of decisions vital to ourselves and hardly less so to the outer world, an amiable, well-meaning third-rate Mr. Babbitt, with the equipment of a small-town, semi-educated journalist, the standards of a hand-shaking joiner and all-around good guy, the instincts and habits of a corner sport, and the traditions of a party hack; an expert on partisan mechanics, a sophomore in legislation, a tyro in economics and government, an ignoramus in world movements and trends.
> It could not work. It did not work.

Adams's work dominated the historiography of the next decade, with many of his opinions being repeated in such books as Karl Schriftgiesser, *This Was Normalcy: An Account of Party Politics During Twelve Republican Years, 1920–1932* (Boston: Little, Brown and Company, 1948).

The year 1948 also marked the beginning of the retreat from the emotional accounts on the administration. In that year Frederic L. Paxson published volume 3 of his *American Democracy and the World War, Postwar Years–Normalcy, 1918–1923* (Berkeley: University of California Press, 1948). From that point on, historians began to deal more discerningly with Harding and the 1920s. This trend increased with the opening of the Harding Papers in 1964.

With this historiography, it is possible to turn to the secondary accounts of the administration. A revived interest in the 1920s has produced a number of interesting accounts in the past thirty years. One should consult Joan Hoff Wilson, ed., *The Twenties: The Critical Issues* (Boston: Little, Brown and Company, 1972), Milton Plesur, ed., *The 1920's: Problems and Paradoxes* (Boston: Allyn and Bacon, Inc., 1969), and John Braeman et al., eds., *Changes and Continuity in Twentieth-Century America: The 1920's* (Columbus: Ohio State University Press, 1968), as each has a number of contrasting views of the decade which nicely supplement the historiographic essays cited earlier.

Valuable general treatments of the 1920s are George Soule, *Prosperity Decade, from War to Depression: 1917–1929* (New York: Rinehart and Company, 1947); William E. Leuchtenburg, *The Perils of Prosperity, 1914–1932* (Chicago: University of Chicago Press, 1958); Arthur M. Schlesinger, Jr., *The Crisis of the Old Order, 1919–1933* (Boston: Houghton Mifflin Company, 1957); Paul Carter, *The Twenties in America* (New York: Thomas Y. Crowell Company, 1969); John D. Hicks, *Republican Ascendancy, 1921–1933* (New York: Harper & Row, Publishers, 1960); and Donald R. McCoy, *Coming of Age: The United States During the 1920's and 1930's* (Baltimore: Penguin Books, 1973).

Additionally, the years since 1964 have seen a number of treatments of Harding's life and his administration, based largely on the newly opened Harding Papers. The four best are Randolph C. Downes, *The Rise of Warren Gamaliel Harding, 1865–1920* (Columbus: Ohio State University Press, 1970); Andrew Sinclair, *The Available Man: The Life Behind the Masks of Warren Gamaliel Harding* (New York: Macmillan Company, 1965); Francis Russell, *The Shadow of Blooming Grove: Warren G. Harding in His Times* (New York: McGraw-Hill, 1968); and Robert K. Murray, *The Harding Era: Warren G. Harding and His Administration*. Downes's work, the first volume of a projected three-volume biography, covers Harding's life only through the 1920 election. It is a generally sympathetic study that stresses Harding's political, rather than personal, life. In great detail, Downes recounts Harding's abilities as a political pacifier and his talents as a campaign orator. Sinclair's study is much less detailed and impressionistic, analyzing the myths—the country boy, the self-made man, the presidential state, the smoke-filled room—that he contends made Harding president. For Sinclair, Harding's "example proved that Washington had become a world city and could no longer be ruled by the man from Marion. Harding was a small man in a great place, which was daily becoming greater." Sinclair notes Harding's political abilities but nonetheless believes he was a poor president. Russell's book is the most controversial, for he stresses Harding's physical and mental health. Russell writes that Harding was a very insecure man because of the rumors of Negro blood in his family. Russell also deals at great length with Harding's sexual life. Although he was blocked from publishing extracts from the Harding–Carrie Phillips correspondence he discovered, that relationship was made central to the book, which led to criticism that the book emphasizes trivia and passes over important aspects of the history of the administration. Russell's portrait of Harding is even harsher than Sinclair's.

Murray's book is the most complete and balanced picture of events in Washington between 1921 and 1923, notwithstanding a tendency to go overboard in attempting to show Harding's role in virtually every action taken by the administration, when it is clear that on occasion Hughes or Hoover or Mellon was just informing Harding of decisions as a matter of form. He does not attempt to force his portrait of Harding into any single interpretation. He does stress, but not very convincingly, that a "new" Harding lived in the White House by the spring of 1923. This "new" Harding, according to Murray, was becoming more assertive as president and would have done much better from 1923 on. Such an argument has the normal difficulties that the "what might have happened" school of analysis always encounters. Murray has also published *The Politics of Normalcy: Government Theory and Practice in the Harding-Coolidge Era* (New York: W.W. Norton, 1973), an interpretive essay on the operating principles that came to control the government in 1921. Murray emphasizes the "new" Harding in this volume.

The Murray, Downes, Sinclair, and Russell books all deal with the question of Harding's stature as president. For works comparing Harding with other presidents, see Arthur M. Schlesinger, Sr., "Our Presidents: A Rating by 75 Historians," *New York Times Magazine*, July 29, 1962, pp. 12–13, 40–43; Thomas A. Bailey, *Presidential Greatness: The Image and the Man from George Washington to the Present* (New York: Appleton, Century Crofts, 1966); James D. Barber, *The Presidential Character: Predicting Performance in the White House* (Englewood Cliffs, N.J.: Prentice-Hall, Inc., 1972); and Gary M. Maranell, "The Evaluation of Presidents: An Extension of the Schlesinger Polls," *Journal of American History* 57 (1970): 104–113. Finally, there are articles by Eric F. Goldman, "A Sort of Rehabilitation of Warren G. Harding," *New York Times Magazine*, March 26, 1972, pp. 42–43, 80–88, and Burl Noggle, "The New Harding," *Reviews in American History* 1 (1973): 126–132, both discussions of the new books on the Harding administration.

There are many biographies of Harding's contemporaries that provide information on the administration. Among the best are:

Donald R. McCoy, *Calvin Coolidge: The Quiet President* (New York: Macmillan Company, 1967); Joan Hoff Wilson, *Herbert Hoover: Forgotten Progressive* (Boston: Little, Brown and Company, 1975); Merlo J. Pusey, *Charles Evans Hughes*, 2 vols. (New York: Macmillan Company, 1951); William T. Hutchinson, *Lowden of Illinois: The Life of Frank O. Lowden*, 2 vols. (Chicago: University of Chicago Press, 1957); Hermann Hagedorn, *Leonard Wood: A Biography*, 2 vols. (New York: Harper and Brothers, 1931); Fola and Belle C. La Follette, *Robert M. La Follette*, 2 vols. (New York: Macmillan Company, 1953); Claudius O. Johnson, *Borah of Idaho* (New York: Longmans, Green and Company, 1936); Edwin P. Hoyt, *Spectacular Rogue: Gaston B. Means* Indianapolis: Bobbs-Merrill, 1963); Russell Lord, *The Wallaces of Iowa* (Boston: Houghton Mifflin, 1947); Bascom N. Timmons, *Portrait of an American: Charles G. Dawes* (New York: Henry Holt and Company, 1953); Henry F. Pringle, *The Life and Times of William Howard Taft: A Biography* (New York: Farrar and Rinehart, 1939); John A. Garraty, *Henry Cabot Lodge: A Biography* (New York: Alfred A. Knopf, 1953); Homer E. Socolofsky, *Arthur Capper: Publisher, Politician, and Philanthropist* (Lawrence: University of Kansas Press, 1962); Philip C. Jessup, *Elihu Root*, 2 vols. (New York: Dodd, Mead and Company, 1938); and Ray Ginger, *The Bending Cross: A Biography of Eugene Victor Debs* (New Brunswick, N.J.: Rutgers University Press, 1949).

There are many specialized studies covering the era. The best single treatment of events in the period immediately before Harding took office is Burl Noggle, *Into the Twenties: The United States from Armistice to Normalcy* (Urbana: University of Illinois Press, 1974). This work examines the many problems that Wilson left to Harding in 1921. Other valuable accounts of events between the armistice and Harding's inauguration are Robert K. Murray, *Red Scare: A Study in National Hysteria, 1919–1920* (Minneapolis: University of Minnesota Press, 1955); Stanley Coben, A. *Mitchell Palmer: Politician* (New York: Columbia University Press, 1963); the same author, "A Study in Nativism: The American Red Scare of 1919–1920," *Political Science Quarterly* 79 (1964): 52–76; David Brody, *Labor in Crisis: The Steel Strike of 1919* (Philadelphia: Lippincott, 1965); William M. Tuttle, Jr., *Race Riot: Chicago in the Red Summer of 1919* (New York: Atheneum Publishers, 1970); and Gene Smith, *When the Cheering Stopped: The Last Years of Woodrow Wilson* (New York: Morrow, 1964).

The standard treatment of the 1920 election is Wesley M.

Bagby, *The Road to Normalcy: The Presidential Campaign and Election of 1920*, Johns Hopkins University Studies in Historical and Political Science, vol. 80 (Baltimore, 1962). A briefer account of the Harding-Cox race is Donald R. McCoy, "Election of 1920," in Arthur M. Schlesinger, Jr., ed., *History of American Presidential Elections, 1789–1968*, vol. 3 (New York: Chelsea House, 1971), pp. 2349–2385. See also Herbert F. Margulies, "The Election of 1920 in Wisconsin: 'The Return to Normalcy' Reappraised," *Wisconsin Magazine of History* 41 (1957): 15–22; Randolph C. Downes, "Negro Rights and White Backlash in the Campaign of 1920," *Ohio History* 75 (1966): 85–107; and James E. Wilson, "Harding's Rhetoric of Normalcy, 1920–1923," *Quarterly Journal of Speech* 48 (1962): 406–411. More general treatments of the politics of the era are Milton Viorst, *Fall From Grace: The Republican Party and the Puritan Ethic* (New York: New American Library, 1968); Malcolm Moos, *The Republicans—A History of Their Party* (New York: Random House, 1956); George H. Mayer, *The Republican Party, 1854–1964* (New York: Oxford University Press, 1964); and David Burner, *The Politics of Provincialism: The Democratic Party in Transition, 1919–1932* (New York: Alfred A. Knopf, 1968). Arthur S. Link, "What Happened to the Progressive Movement in the 1920's," *American Historical Review* 64 (1959): 833–851; Clarke A. Chambers, *Seedtime of Reform: American Social Service and Social Action, 1918–1933* (Minneapolis: University of Minnesota Press, 1963); and Paul Glad, "Progressivism and the Business Culture of the 1920's," *Journal of American History* 53 (1966): 75–89, trace progressivism during the Republican ascendancy.

A fine study of the Republican takeover of the executive branch of the government in 1921 is Laurin L. Henry, *Presidential Transitions* (Washington, D.C.: The Brookings Institution, 1960). Part three of Henry's book, entitled "The Wilson-Harding Transition of 1920–1921," is a 150-page analysis of the change in administrations. And Robert K. Murray, in "President Harding and His Cabinet," *Ohio History* 75 (1966): 108–125, describes the selection of the cabinet. The other end of the administration—Harding's death—has also occasioned literature. An account of Harding's activities on the West Coast is Robert E. Finken, "President Harding Visits Seattle," *Pacific Northwest Quarterly* 66 (1975): 105–114. In addition to Gaston Means, *The Strange Death of President Harding*, see Ray Lyman Wilbur, "The Last Illness of a Calm Man," *Saturday Evening Post*, 196 (October 13, 1923), by the physician who later served as Hoover's secretary of the interior. Two more recent accounts covering Harding's death are Rudolph Marx, *The Health of the Presidents* (New York: Putnam's 1960); and Francis W. Schruben, "An Even Stranger Death of President Harding," *Southern California Quarterly* 48 (1966).

There are many specialized accounts of events in the administration. In domestic affairs, the business ethic that dominated the administration is discussed in James W. Prothro, *The Dollar Decade: Business Ideas in the 1920's* (Baton Rouge: Louisiana State University Press, 1954). It is also covered in Joseph Brandes, *Herbert Hoover and Economic Diplomacy: Department of Commerce Policy, 1921–1928* (Pittsburgh: University of Pittsburgh Press, 1962); Craig Lloyd, *Aggressive Introvert: Herbert Hoover and Public Relations Management, 1912–1932* (Columbus: Ohio State University Press, 1972); Robert Sobel, *The Great Bull Market: Wall Street in the 1920s* (New York: Norton, 1968); John Kenneth Galbraith, *The Great Crash: 1929*, rev. ed. (Boston: Houghton Mifflin, 1972); G. Cullom Davis, "The Transformation of the Federal Trade Commission, 1914–1929," *Mississippi Valley Historical Review* 49 (1962): 437–455; Evan B. Metcalf, "Secretary Hoover and the Emergence of Macroeconomic Management," *Business History Review* 49 (1975): 60–80; Fritz M. Marx, "The Bureau of the Budget: Its Evolution and Present Role," *American Political Science Review* 39 (1945): 653–684; Frank W. Taussig, *The Tariff History of the United States* (New York: Putnam's Sons, 1931); Henry G. Hendricks, *The Federal Debt, 1919–1930: A Chapter in American Public Finance* (Washington, D.C.: Mimeoform, 1933); Darrell H. Smith and Paul V. Betters, *The United States Shipping Board: Its History, Activities and Organization* (Washington, D.C.: The Brookings Institution, 1931); John Gunther, *Taken at the Flood: The Story of Albert D. Lasker* (New York: Harper and Brothers, 1960); and Colin B. Goodykoontz, "Edward P. Costigan and the Tariff Commission, 1917–1928," *Pacific Historical Review* 16 (1947): 410–419. The Supreme Court, dominated by sympathy to business, is covered in Alpheus T. Mason, *The Supreme Court from Taft to Warren*, rev. ed. (Baton Rouge: Louisiana State University Press, 1968); Leon Friedman and Fred L. Israel, eds., *The Justices of the United States Supreme Court, 1789–1969: Their Lives and Major Opinions*, vol. 3 (New York: Chelsea House Publishers, 1969); and Joel F. Paschal, *Mr. Justice Sutherland: A Man Against the State* (Princeton, N.J.: Princeton University Press, 1951). A good analysis of the Harding-Hoover relationship, showing how they shared the same philosophy toward business, is Robert K. Murray, "Herbert Hoover and the Harding Cabinet" (Paper delivered at the Hoover Presidential Library Association, West Branch, Iowa, April 1974).

The situation of the American worker in the Harding years, as well as the relationship between the government and workers, is discussed most thoroughly in Robert Zieger, *Republicans and Labor, 1919–1929* (Lexington: University of Kentucky Press, 1969); and Irving Bernstein, *The Lean Years: A History of the American Worker, 1920–1933* (Boston: Houghton Mifflin Company, 1960). Aspects of the labor story are told in Carolyn Grin, "The Unemployment Conference of 1921: An Experiment in National Cooperative Planning," *Mid-America* 55 (1973): 83–107; Ellis W. Hawley, "Secretary Hoover and the Bituminous Coal Problem, 1921–1928," *Business History Review* 42 (1968): 247–270; and Paul M. Angle, *Bloody Williamson: A Chapter in American Lawlessness* (New York: Alfred A. Knopf, 1952), the latter an account that treats the "Herrin Massacre" of 1922.

There is a substantial literature on agrarian problems during Harding's term in office. Among the best are James H. Shideler, *Farm Crisis, 1919–1923* (Berkeley: University of California Press, 1957); and Donald L. Winters, *Henry Cantwell Wallace as Secretary of Agriculture, 1921–1924* (Urbana: University of Illinois Press, 1970). Other accounts are James H. Shideler, "Herbert Hoover and the Federal Farm Board Project, 1921–1925," *Mississippi Valley Historical Review* 42 (1956): 710–729; Edward L. and Frederick H. Schapsmeier, "Disharmony in the Harding Cabinet: Hoover-Wallace Conflict," *Ohio History* 75 (1966): 126–136; Theodore Saloutos and John D. Hicks, *Agricultural Discontent in the Middle West, 1900–1939* (Madison: University of Wisconsin Press, 1951); and Gilbert C. Fite, *George N. Peek and the Fight for Farm Parity* (Norman: University of Oklahoma Press, 1954).

This does not end the material on domestic affairs during the Harding administration. Conservation is covered in Preston J. Hubbard, *Origins of the TVA: The Muscle Shoals Controversy, 1920–1932* (Nashville: Vanderbilt University Press, 1961); Judson King, *The Conservation Fight: From Theodore Roosevelt to the Tennessee Valley Authority* (Washington: Public Affairs Press, 1959); Donald C. Swain, *Federal Conservation Policy, 1921–1933* (Berkeley: University of California Press, 1963); and Eugene P. Trani, "Hubert Work and the Department of the Interior, 1923–1928," *Pacific Northwest Quarterly* 61 (1970): 31–40. The Teapot Dome scandal, which grew at least in part out of a battle over conservation, is the subject of a vast literature. Among the best accounts are Burl Noggle, *Teapot Dome: Oil and Politics in the 1920's* (Baton Rouge: Louisiana State University Press, 1962); J. Leonard Bates, *The Origins of Teapot Dome: Progressives, Parties, and Petroleum, 1909–1921* (Urbana: University of Illinois Press, 1963); the same author, "The Teapot Dome Scandal and the Election of 1924," *American Historical Review* 60 (1955): 303–322; and several articles by David H. Stratton on Fall and Teapot Dome: "New Mexican Machiavellian?" *Montana: the Magazine of Western History* 7 (1957): 2–14; "Behind Teapot Dome: Some Personal Insights," *Business History Review* 31 (1957): 385–402; and "Splattered with Oil: William G. McAdoo and the 1924 Democratic Presidential Nomination," *Southwestern Social Science Quarterly* 44 (1963–1964): 62–75. Less reliable works on Teapot Dome include Marcus E. Ravage, *The Story of Teapot Dome* (New York: Republic Publishing Company, 1924); M. R. Werner and John Starr, *Teapot Dome* (New York: Viking Press, 1959); and Morris R. Werner, *Privileged Characters* (New York: R. M. McBride and Company, 1935). The latter covers all the Harding scandals.

The battle over prohibition and its history are treated in Andrew Sinclair, *Prohibition: The Era of Excess* (Boston: Little, Brown and Company, 1962); Charles Merz, *The Dry Decade* (New York: Doubleday, Doran, 1931); Herbert Asbury, *The Great Illusion: An Informal History of Prohibition* (New York: Doubleday and Company, 1950); and Richard Kottman, "Volstead Violated: Prohibition as a Factor in Canadian-American Relations," *Canadian Historical Review* 43 (1962): 106–126. Fundamentalism, out of which much of the support for prohibition came, is dealt with in Norman F. Furniss, *The Fundamentalist Controversy, 1918–1931* (New Haven, Conn.: Yale University Press, 1954); and Robert M. Miller, *American Protestantism and Social Issues, 1919–1939* (Chapel Hill: University of North Carolina Press, 1958). Aspects of the urban-rural conflict in the 1920s are covered in Don S. Kirschner, *City and Country: Rural Responses to Urbanization of the 1920s* (Westport, Conn.: Greenwood Publishing Corporation, 1970); David M. Chalmers, *Hooded Americanism: The First Century of the Ku Klux Klan, 1865–1965* (Garden City, N.Y.: Doubleday, 1965); Kenneth T. Jackson, *The Ku Klux Klan in the City, 1915–1930* (New York: Oxford University Press, 1967); William Preston, Jr., *Aliens and Dissenters: Federal Suppression of Radicalism, 1903–1933* (Cambridge, Mass.: Harvard University

Press, 1963); John Higham, *Strangers in the Land: Patterns of American Nativism, 1860–1925* (New Brunswick, N.J.: Rutgers University Press, 1955); and Blake McKelvey, *The Emergence of Metropolitan America, 1915–1966* (New Brunswick, N.J.: Rutgers University Press, 1968).

In addition to the Downes article cited earlier, black Americans are covered in Richard B. Sherman, *The Republican Party and Black America from McKinley to Hoover, 1896–1933* (Charlottesville: University of Virginia Press, 1973). Other accounts, covering black leadership in the 1920s, are E. David Cronon, *Black Moses: The Story of Marcus Garvey and the Universal Negro Improvement Association* (Madison: University of Wisconsin Press, 1969); Francis L. Broderick, *W. E. B. DuBois: Negro Leader in Times of Crisis* (Stanford, California: Stanford University Press, 1959); and Elliott M. Rudwick, *W. E. B. DuBois: A Study in Minority Group Leadership* (Philadelphia: University of Pennsylvania Press, 1960). Women are the subject of J. Stanley Lemons, *The Woman Citizen: Social Feminism in the 1920s* (Urbana: University of Illinois Press, 1973); and William L. O'Neill, *Everyone Was Brave: The Rise and Fall of Feminism in America* (Chicago: Quadrangle Books, 1969). Finally, there is a vast literature on American culture during the 1920s. The best summary is Roderick Nash, *The Nervous Generation: American Thought, 1917–1930* (Chicago: Rand McNally & Co., 1970), especially helpful in understanding popular culture.

Turning to foreign policy of the 1920s, the literature is also enormous. General accounts are Selig Adler, *The Uncertain Giant, 1921–1941: American Foreign Policy Between the Wars* (New York: Macmillan Company, 1965); L. Ethan Ellis, *Republican Foreign Policy, 1921–1933* (New Brunswick, N.J.: Rutgers University Press, 1968); and Arnold A. Offner, *The Origins of the Second World War: American Foreign Policy and World Politics, 1917–1941* (New York: Praeger Publishers, 1975). Other works covering the diplomacy of the administration are Betty Glad, *Charles Evans Hughes and the Illusions of Innocence: A Study in American Diplomacy* (Urbana: University of Illinois Press, 1966); Dexter Perkins, *Charles Evans Hughes and American Democratic Statesmanship* (Boston: Little, Brown, 1956); Robert J. Maddox, *William E. Borah and American Foreign Policy* (Baton Rouge: Louisiana State University Press, 1969); and William A. Williams's provocative article, "The Legend of Isolationism in the 1920's," *Science and Society* 18 (1954): 1–20.

Relations between the United States and Latin America are treated in Joseph S. Tulchin, *The Aftermath of War: World War I and U.S. Policy Toward Latin America* (New York: New York University Press, 1971); Robert N. Seidel, *Progressive Pan Americanism: Development and United States Policy Toward South America, 1906–1931* (Ithaca, N.Y.: Cornell University Latin American Studies Program, 1973); Alexander DeConde, *Herbert Hoover's Latin American Policy* (Stanford, California: Stanford University Press, 1951); Samuel Flagg Bemis, *The Latin American Policy of the United States* (New York: Harcourt, Brace and Company, 1943); Dana C. Munro, *The United States and the Caribbean Republics, 1921–1933* (Princeton, N.J.: Princeton University Press, 1974); William A. Williams, "Latin America: Laboratory of American Foreign Policy in the Nineteen-Twenties," *Inter-American Economic Affairs* 11 (1957): 3–30; and Eugene P. Trani, "Charles Evans Hughes: The First Good Neighbor," *Northwest Ohio Quarterly* 40 (1968): 138–162. More specialized studies are D. A. Graber, *Crisis Diplomacy: A History of U.S. Intervention Policies and Practices* (Washington, D.C.: Public Affairs Press, 1959); Sumner Welles, *Naboth's Vineyard: The Dominican Republic, 1844–1924*, 2 vols. (New York: Payson and Clarke, 1928); Kenneth J. Grieb, "Warren G. Harding and the Dominican Republic U.S. Withdrawal, 1921–1923," *Journal of Inter-American Studies* 11 (1969): 425–440; Robert F. Smith, *The United States and Cuba: Business and Diplomacy, 1917–1960* (New York: Bookman Associates, 1960); Hans Schmidt, *The United States Occupation of Haiti, 1915–1934* (New Brunswick, N.J.: Rutgers University Press, 1971); Mira Wilkens, "Multinational Oil in South America in the 1920s," *Business History Review* 48 (1974): 414–446; and four articles on Harding's Mexican policy: Eugene P. Trani, "Harding Administration and Recognition of Mexico," *Ohio History* 75 (1966): 137–148; two articles by N. Stephen Kane, "Bankers and Diplomats: The Diplomacy of the Dollar in Mexico, 1921–1924," *Business History Review* 47 (1973): 335–352, and "American Businessmen and Foreign Policy: The Recognition of Mexico, 1920–1923," *Political Science Quarterly* 90 (1975): 293–313; and C. Dennis Ignasias, "Propaganda and Public Opinion in Harding's Foreign Affairs: The Case for Mexican Recognition," *Journalism Quarterly* 48 (1971): 41–52.

The question of the newly created Soviet state is covered in Robert Browder, *The Origins of Soviet-American Diplomacy* (Princeton, N.J.: Princeton University Press, 1953); Edward M.

Bennett, *Recognition of Russia: An American Foreign Policy Dilemma* (Waltham, Mass.: Ginn/Blaisdell, 1970); Peter G. Filene, *Americans and the Soviet Experiment, 1917–1933* (Cambridge, Mass.: Harvard University Press, 1967); Joan Hoff Wilson, *Ideology and Economics: U.S. Relations with the Soviet Union, 1918–1933* (Columbia: University of Missouri Press, 1974); and Benjamin M. Weissman, *Herbert Hoover and Famine Relief to Soviet Russia, 1921–1923* (Stanford, California: Hoover Institution Press, 1974). More specialized treatments of relations with Soviet Russia are Eugene P. Trani, "Herbert Hoover and the Russian Revolution, 1917–1920" (Paper delivered at the Hoover Presidential Library Association, West Branch, Iowa, February 1974); Benjamin M. Weissman, "Herbert Hoover's 'Treaty' with Soviet Union, August 20, 1921," *Slavic Review* 28 (1969): 276–288; and John P. McKay, "Foreign Enterprise in Russian and Soviet Industry: A Long Term Perspective," *Business History Review* 48 (1974): 336–356.

There are many accounts on the Washington Naval Conference, events in the Far East, the press for disarmament, and the state of the American armed services during the Harding years. The conference itself is treated in Thomas H. Buckley, *The United States and the Washington Conference, 1921–1922* (Knoxville: University of Tennessee Press, 1970); John Chalmers Vinson, *The Parchment Peace: The United States Senate and the Washington Conference, 1921–1922* (Athens: University of Georgia Press, 1955); Sadao Asada, "Japan's 'Special Interests' and the Washington Conference, 1921–22," *American Historical Review* 67 (1961): 62–70; Akira Iriye, *After Imperialism: The Search for a New Order in the Far East, 1921–1931* (Cambridge, Mass.: Harvard University Press, 1965), a first-rate general account; and C. Leonard Hoag, *Preface to Preparedness: The Washington Disarmament Conference and Public Opinion* (Washington, D.C.: American Council on Public Affairs, 1941). The Far East is also covered in Richard D. Burns and Edward Bennett, eds., *Diplomats in Crisis: United States-Chinese-Japanese Relations, 1919–1941* (Santa Barbara, California: ABC-Clio, 1974); Russell H. Fifield, "Secretary Hughes and the Shantung Question," *Pacific Historical Review* 23 (1954): 373–385; J. Bartlet Brebner, "Canada, the Anglo-Japanese Alliance and the Washington Conference," *Political Science Quarterly* 50 (1935): 45–58; Eugene P. Trani, "Four American Fiddlers and Their Far Eastern Tunes: A Survey of Japanese-American Relations, 1898–1941," in Bernard Gordon, ed., *The New Political Economy of the Pacific* (Cambridge: Ballinger, 1975); the same author, "Secretary Denby Takes a Trip," *Michigan History* 51 (1967): 277–297; Gerald E. Wheeler, "Republican Philippine Policy, 1921–1933," *Pacific Historical Review* 28 (1959): 377–390; and William A. Williams, "China and Japan: A Challenge and A Choice of the Nineteen Twenties," *Pacific Historical Review* 26 (1957): 259–279. Disarmament is discussed in John Chalmers Vinson, *William E. Borah and the Outlawry of War* (Athens: University of Georgia Press, 1957); while the navy is dealt with in Gerald E. Wheeler, *Prelude to Pearl Harbor; The United States Navy and the Far East, 1921–1931* (Columbia: University of Missouri Press, 1963); Harold and Margaret Sprout, *Toward a New Order of Sea Power: American Naval Policy and the World Scene, 1918–1922* (Princeton, N.J.: Princeton University Press, 1943); Ernest Andrade, Jr., "The United States Navy and the Washington Conference," *Historian* 30 (1969): 345–363; and Stephen Roskill, *Naval Policy Between the Wars*, vol. 1, *The Period of Anglo-American Antagonism, 1919–1929* (London: Collins, 1968). Two accounts cover the controversy over air power: Lester H. Brune, "Foreign Policy and the Air Power Dispute, 1919–1932," *Historian* 23 (1961): 449–464; and Alfred F. Hurley, *Billy Mitchell: Crusader for Air Power* (New York: F. Watts, 1964).

General treatments of American relations with Europe and the League of Nations include Melvyn Leffler, "Political Isolationism, Economic Expansion or Diplomatic Realism? American Policy Toward Western Europe, 1921–1933," *Perspectives in American History* 8 (1974): 413–461; Denna F. Fleming, *The United States and World Organization, 1920–1933* (New York: Columbia University Press, 1938); the same author, *The United States and the World Court* (New York: Doubleday, Doran and Company, 1945); David H. Jennings, "President Harding and International Organization," *Ohio History* 75 (1966): 149–165; H. A. Allen, *Great Britain and the United States: A History of Anglo-American Relations, 1783–1952* (New York: St. Martin's Press, 1955); and Kurt and Sarah Wimer, "The Harding Administration, the League of Nations, and the Separate Peace Treaty," *Review of Politics* 29 (1967): 13–24. Specialized accounts on Europe and the League are Jolyon P. Girard, "Congress and Presidential Military Policy: The Occupation of Germany, 1919–1923," *Mid-America* 56 (1974): 211–220; Benjamin D. Rhodes, "Reassessing 'Uncle Shylock': The United States and the French War Debt, 1917–1929," *Journal of American History* 55 (1969): 787–803; Melvyn Leffler, "The Origins of Republican War Debt Policy, 1921–1923: A Case Study in the Applicability of the Open Door Interpretation," *Journal of American History* 59 (1972): 585–601; Michael J. Hogan, "Informal Entente: Public Policy and Private Management in Anglo-American Petroleum Affairs, 1918–1924," *Business History Review* 48 (1974): 187–205; and William A. Williams, "A Note on American Foreign Policy in Europe in the Nineteen Twenties," *Science and Society* 22 (1958): 1–20.

Finally, in addition to Joseph Brandes, *Herbert Hoover and Economic Diplomacy*, there are a number of accounts on the importance of economic considerations in American foreign policy in the 1920s. Among the best are Joan Hoff Wilson, *American Business & Foreign Policy, 1920–1933* (Lexington: University Press of Kentucky, 1971); Herbert Feis, *The Diplomacy of the Dollar: First Era, 1919–1932* (Baltimore: The Johns Hopkins Press, 1950); Carl P. Parrini, *Heir to Empire: United States Economic Policy, 1916–1923* (Pittsburgh: University of Pittsburgh Press, 1969); Melvyn Leffler, "Herbert Hoover, The 'New Era', and American Foreign Policy, 1921–1929" (Paper delivered at the Hoover Presidential Library Association, West Branch, Iowa, April 1974); and John A. DeNovo, *American Interests and Policies in the Middle East, 1900–1939* (Minneapolis: University of Minnesota Press, 1963).

Index

World Court, 146–147; supports
conference on disarmament, 151–
152; hopes for second term, 172;
last will and testament of, 172–173;
annual message of 1922, 174–175;
Alaskan tour of, 176–177; last
speeches of, 176; last illness of,
177; death of, 177–178, 203*n11*;
funeral of, 177–178; love affair with
Nan Britton, 178–179; love affair
with Carrie Phillips, 178–179;
drinking habits, 179; poor judge of
character, 179; reaction to scandals,
180, 182–183, 185; dedication of
memorial to, 186–187; lack of effectiveness as president, 190–192
Harrison, Benjamin, 190
Harvey, George: on League of Nations, 143; mentioned, 23, 111
Haugen, Gilbert N., 91. *See also* Mc-
Nary-Haugenism
Hay, John, 114
Hays, Will: as Chairman of Repub-
lican National Committee, 23; se-
lected postmaster general, 42; as
postmaster general, 43–44; selected
president of Motion Picture Pro-
ducers Association, 43; opposes
spoils system, 46; concealment of
irregular campaign contributions,
186
Health: statistics on, 4–5
Helena, Montana, 176
Hemingway, Ernest, 89
Hensley, Walter L., 150
Hepburn Act, 9
Hero Worship, 20
Herrick, Myron T., 111
Herrin, Illinois: murder of strike
breakers in, 98
Herter, Christian, 70
Highway Act of 1921, 87–88
Hill, David Jayne, 114
Hines, Gen. Frank T.: appointed
head of Veterans Bureau, 66. *See
also* Veterans Bureau
Holt, Hamilton, 143
Hoover, Herbert: selected as secretary of commerce, 39–40; supports
ship subsidies, 76; differences with
Wallace, 69–70, 85; expands Department of Commerce, 84–85; en-
courages trade association, 84;
wants to regulate radio, 88; calls
national conference on commercial
aviation, 88; opposes conference on
agriculture, 90; opposes lower railroad rates, 91; on unemployment,
92–94 *passim*; importance in Harding's administration, 94, 173–174,
191–192; on twelve-hour day in
steel industry, 94–96; on coal strike,
97–98 *passim*; involvement in railroad strike, 99–100; on economic
foreign policy, 115; involvement in
foreign policy, 115–116; gains control of policy toward U.S.S.R., 116–
127 *passim*; predicts Russian Revolution, 117; reaction to Bolsheviks,
117; believes government of
U.S.S.R. will collapse, 118; fears
spread of Bolshevism, 118; advises
Wilson on U.S.S.R., 118–119; heads
American Relief Administration,
119, 122–123; announces policy toward U.S.S.R., 120; on trade with
U.S.S.R., 125; interest in Latin
America, 137–139; gains control of
Inter-American High Commission,
138; favors corporate liberalism,
165; works to control foreign loans
of U.S. banks, 165–167; interest in
middle eastern oil, 168; Coolidge
distaste for, 173, 202*n3*; dedicates
Harding Memorial, 186–187; mentioned, 21, 68, 70, 154, 160, 161,
173, 176, 177, 184
Hoover, Mrs. Herbert, 173
Horatio Alger, 89
Houghton, Alanson B., 111
Huerta, Victoriano, 114, 127
Hughes, Charles E.: as candidate for
president in 1916, 21; selected as
secretary of state, 39, 109; relationship with Harding, 110; background of, 110–111; work habits as
secretary of state, 111; appointments in State Department, 111–
112; belief in a professional foreign
service, 112; relations with the
press, 112–113; views on foreign
policy, 113; recognition policy of,
113–114; woos Congress, 115;
works well with Hoover, 115; loses
control of policy toward U.S.S.R. to
Hoover, 116–127 *passim*; letter to
Samuel Gompers on U.S.S.R., 121;
on trade with Russia, 125; on recognition of Mexico, 128–130; pressures banks to refuse loans to Mex-